Divine Calling

Divine Callings

Understanding the Call to
Ministry in Black Pentecostalism

Richard N. Pitt

NEW YORK UNIVERSITY PRESS
New York and London

NEW YORK UNIVERSITY PRESS
New York and London
www.nyupress.org

References to Internet websites (URLs) were accurate at the time of writing.
Neither the author nor New York University Press is responsible for URLs
that may have expired or changed since the manuscript was prepared.
All biblical quotations have been taken from the New King James Version (NKJV).

Library of Congress Cataloging-in-Publication Data
Pitt, Richard N.
Divine callings : understanding the call to ministry in Black
Pentecostalism / Richard N. Pitt.
p. cm.
Includes bibliographical references (p.   ) and index.
ISBN 978-0-8147-6823-5 (cloth : alk. paper)
ISBN 978-0-8147-6824-2 (pbk. : alk. paper)
ISBN 978-0-8147-6825-9 (ebook)
ISBN 978-0-8147-6876-1 (ebook)
1. Church of God in Christ—Clergy—Appointment, call, and election.
2. African American clergy. 3. Vocation, Ecclesiastical. I. Title.
BX7056.Z5P58   2011
262'.14973—dc23   2011033400

New York University Press books are printed on acid-free paper,
and their binding materials are chosen for strength and durability.
We strive to use environmentally responsible suppliers and materials
to the greatest extent possible in publishing our books.

Manufactured in the United States of America

c   10 9 8 7 6 5 4 3 2 1
p   10 9 8 7 6 5 4 3 2 1

For Richard and Patt,
with Love and Appreciation

Contents

Acknowledgments   ix

PART I. INTRODUCTION

Introduction   3

1 The Church of God in Christ: 17
   Pentecostal History, Doctrine, and Polity

PART II. BECOMING THE CALLED

2 "Heard a Voice from Heaven Say":   41
   Calling Narratives among Black Pentecostals

3 "All the World's a Stage":   72
   How Congregations Create the Called

PART III. BEING THE CALLED

4 "A Stutter And A Stick":   107
   The (Non-) Value of Educational Credentialing

5 "Don't Quit Your Day Job": Redefining Religious Work   149

6 "Chew the Meat and Spit Out the Bones":   182
   Negotiating Women's Clerical Identity

PART IV. CONCLUSION

7 Legitimating New Understandings of Ministry and the Clergy   213

   Appendix   229

   Notes   235

   References   247

   Index   259

   About the Author   265

Acknowledgments

First I want to thank my amazing family, particularly my parents—Richard Sr. and Patt—who have so lovingly exhorted and affirmed me for four decades. I am who I am—and this book is what it is—because of their guidance and support. Thanks for making me do my homework. I guess it did pay off. Thanks also to my siblings, Kelli and Duane, for reminding me to not take myself (and when necessary, my interviewees) so seriously.

Special thanks go to the men and women whose words make up a third of this text. While they remain anonymous to you, each of them has left an indelible mark on my understanding of the convictions that undergird the work done in religious communities all over this country. I also thank the unnamed pastors, bishops, and other COGIC officials who so freely offered me a backstage pass to this immense organization and its people. I especially thank them for the permission they gave me to be honest about what I saw and heard, particularly in those moments when I felt like I was exposing some uncomfortable truths.

I would also like to thank Lynn Smith-Lovin, Richard Arum, Mark Chaves, and others at the University of Arizona for teaching me how to do sociological research carefully, thoughtfully, and effectively. I'm especially thankful that I was able to continue to be mentored by Lynn and Mark during my time at Duke; they were wonderful sounding boards.

There are many people at Vanderbilt University who deserve thanks. Ethnographic research is expensive, and there is no way I could have even begun this project without the university's considerable financial investment in my research. In particular, I'd like to thank Dennis Hall, Carolyn Dever, and Katharine Donato for overseeing the processes that enabled me to take a year-long leave to finish the manuscript. Certainly, all of my colleagues in the sociology department have inspired me, encouraged me, and (sometimes) challenged me in ways that shaped my research and this book, but one colleague deserves special mention. Steven Tepper has been a great resource throughout the writing of this book: raising questions, offering solutions, and just providing encouragement when that was all the situation called for. For that, he has my gratitude.

I am extremely grateful to Ken Spenner, Eduardo Bonilla-Silva, Ed Tiryakian, Andy Perrin, Saylor Breckenridge, and other colleagues at Duke University, the University of North Carolina, and Wake Forest University for making my time in North Carolina comfortable and productive. Special thanks also go to graduate students David Eagle and Charles Seguin for being so generous in sharing their time and intellectual energies with me.

Other friends and colleagues provided both support and constructive criticism as I struggled through the research and writing phases of this project. Thanks to Mark, Wil, and Sean whose friendships made some really rough weeks in the field bearable. I am particularly indebted to my Amen Corner—Martin Hughes, Perry Broadnax, Rachel Starks, Richard Tillman, and Josh Packard—who agreed to have their email accounts cluttered with my daily musings and drafts. Not only did they help keep me on task, but their responses to those drafts were constant reminders that I had something to say. Thanks also to Keri Day and Keon Gerow. My conversations with these two COGIC scholar-preachers were turning points for this book. In the same way, conversations—both brief and lengthy—with sociologists Christine Williams, Nancy Ammerman, Shayne Lee, Gerardo Marti, and John Bartkowski were helpful in pulling apart some of the intellectual knots a project of this size can produce.

Ironically, doing research in the social sciences can be a lonely experience. This is especially the case in the long process of writing a book. I was blessed to have a number of friends also writing books at the same time. The camaraderie (and sometimes, commiseration) they provided was invaluable. So, thank you to Laura Carpenter, Whitney Harris, Jennifer Lena, Terrence McDonnell, Rebecca Sager, Christine Sheikh, Carrie Smith, and Heather Talley for affirming my "book-person" identity so consistently. I look forward to sharing shelf space with you all.

Speaking of shared shelf space, I want to thank *two* book editors. First, I am deeply appreciative of my thoughtful and creative editor at NYU, Jennifer Hammer. I can't imagine having a better Sherpa through the mountainous terrain of the publishing industry. She and her team have been wonderful to work with, and this book you hold in your hand is a testament to their professionalism and talent. I also want to extend my thanks to one of the most patient and genuine professionals I've encountered in academia: Peter Mickulas at Rutgers. His exuberant support of my work was meaningful in ways it is difficult to convey. He has my genuine thanks.

Finally, I should probably thank Mark Zuckerberg, the founder of Facebook for creating a platform where hundreds of friends and associates could follow my progress on the book, lifting up my hands during difficult parts of the process and celebrating those moments when the twin giants of "writer's block" and "doubt" were defeated. To all of you who helped, heartfelt thanks!

PART I

Introduction

Introduction

And He himself gave some to be apostles, some prophets, some evangelists, and some pastors and teachers, for the equipping of the saints for the work of ministry, for the edifying of the body of Christ.

Ephesians 4:11–12 (NKJV)

Be ready for whatever happens because it's going to be a long journey, it's going to be a tough journey, and it's not going to be easy.

Jeff, Licensed Minister

Consider three professionals:

First, Adam. At thirty, Adam's youthful indiscretions caught up with him and he was incarcerated. While in prison, Adam acquired something of a layman's sense of the law by reading books in the prison library. He was able to gain enough rudimentary knowledge to serve as a kind of "jailhouse lawyer," informally helping other inmates understand basic legal matters related to their sentences. It was there that he began to feel something of a call. As he describes it, "I felt a lot of pleasure in that. Not self-gratification. Purpose." Upon his release, Adam spent his weekends volunteering at a growing neighborhood law firm. It was there that his decision to practice law matured. He approached the head of the firm with his intentions, arguing that he felt a strong pull to serve men like him: men who had made bad decisions but who deserved a second chance. Adam pursued a part-time apprenticeship in the law firm. Within a year, the head of the firm was delegating significant responsibilities to him. Three years later, Adam was named as chief operating officer at the law firm. The firm's senior partner presents cases in court, but Adam is trusted with day-to-day mentoring and management of the firm's lawyers. He holds a key role in the firm, yet everything he learned about law, he learned there; he's never been to law school. Adam has only a high school diploma.

Unlike Adam, Seth received a considerable amount of formal education. As a young man he had never considered himself a particularly good student. In fact, he joked about the fears he had bringing his report card home to his well-educated parents, a high school principal and an English professor at a nearby historically black college. Upon his graduation from high school he attended the local university to pursue a degree in accounting. After some setbacks in his educational career, in his junior year he took some courses in literature and creative writing at the suggestion of his father. He was surprised at both his interest in and, even more surprisingly, his aptitude for the material. In his words, "things clicked for me there. I probably never realized how much I liked it because, I don't know, because that's what my parents did." After receiving his accounting degree, Seth pursued a doctorate in English but ran into a difficult labor market. Unable to find a professorial position, he sought employment elsewhere. Three years after receiving his PhD, Seth is satisfied with managing a household electronics store, only occasionally guest-lecturing in his father's English classes.

Eve was also well educated. Unlike the two men, she has always known what she wanted to do. Even as a young girl, her interest in medicine was clear to anyone who knew her well. No one was surprised when she ignored her father's assertions that "women don't make good doctors" and became a pre-med major in college. Upon graduating, she pursued a master's degree in public health while working part-time as a medical transcriptionist. While she considered staying in the public health field, she felt that God had something different in store for her: "I began to hear a voice in my spirit. The voice said, clearly and simply, 'heal.'" She enrolled in one of the top medical schools in the country, earning accolades from her professors for her strong work in their classes and her obvious talents with patients. She passed her exams with flying colors, scoring higher than any of the men in her cohort. Today, Eve is caring for patients as a licensed nurse-practitioner because of a long-standing belief in her religious community that only men can be physicians.

The stories of these legal, educational, and medical professionals may puzzle us because we expect professionals to have significant levels of professional training, to actively seek and gain employment in their chosen field, and to be able to be credentialed regardless of ascribed characteristics like gender. These three accounts are meant to offer insight into the unusual status of many members of a different profession: the clergy.[1] In fact, Adam, Seth, and Eve are three clergy members in the African American Pentecostal denomination, the Church of God in Christ (COGIC). Their true stories reveal a problematic set of facts for any scholar seeking to understand this vocational identity.

Adam felt a call to ministry while assisting with prison Bible studies. He is now ordained and serves as an associate minister in the COGIC. He holds this position in spite of the fact that he has never been to seminary or taken even one college course. He learned to operate in ministry under the tutelage of his church's senior pastor. The well-educated son of a pastor, Seth received his call to ministry in college. Seminary-trained, ordained, and licensed as a church elder, he cannot find employment as a pastor or even as an associate pastor in the denomination. Instead, he works full time as a social worker, hoping a clerical opportunity will present itself. Eve has felt a call to ministry from childhood, maintaining that interest through her years in college as first a religious studies and then divinity school student. She serves as an unordained lay-minister in the denomination, which bars women from ordained leadership. She is surprisingly content with her status, indicating no interest in a higher formal position.

Even without seminary training (Adam), clerical employment (Seth), or ordination (Eve), these three ministers describe themselves as "the elect," as "the called," and as "clergy." One of the black boxes plaguing religious, occupational, and identity scholarship has been the idea of a "divine calling," which distinguishes clergy, both at the vocational level and at the identity level, from other professionals. It has become an accepted premise that people often feel a particular pull (or push?) into ministry that is different from the forces that lead people into other professions. As the theologian William Myers points out in his study of the call to ministry among some African American clergy, "This may be one of the important differences in how churches view the call as a vocation when compared to other secular vocations. Whereas one may choose—for economic or other reasons—other secular vocations, one is chosen for the ministry."[2] But how do these men and women know they're chosen? And once chosen, how do they maintain a sense of themselves as "the chosen" in the absence of the most conventional markers of the clerical identity: religious training, employment, and credentials?

This book draws on a series of more than one hundred in-depth interviews with Pentecostal African American ministers to examine how these men and women defend their identities as clergy in light of the educational deficiencies, constrained labor market, and gender discrimination that threatens both the legitimacy and the pursuit of those identities. I argue that defending unconventional expressions of an identity—in this case, the clergy—requires two activities. First, the claimant must stake a convincing claim to at least one recognizable marker of the identity. For clergy, that marker is the "call to ministry," a phenomenon explained in great detail in this book. Second, the claimant must exploit the gaps inadvertently left in institutionalized understandings of these identities. In spite of layers of organizational meaning and mandate, enough ambiguity exists to grant these men and women the space to find their own understandings of what clergy *need*, what clergy *do*, and who clergy *are*.

We'll see that ministers use the following strategies to negotiate the aforementioned structural handicaps: claiming a different source for clerical knowledge, embracing a different look and location for clerical work, and choosing to recognize a different standard for clerical legitimacy. These strategies not only produce opportunities to meaningfully inhabit the identity of a cleric, but they also produce new understandings of the forms that identity might take.

Understanding the Clergy: Why It Matters

Both scholarly and popular interest in the clergy has always been high, but lately we have seen a surge in curiosity about the clergy prompted in great part by clerical malfeasance,[3] and clerical involvement in secular and political arenas.[4] A clergy shortage in Catholicism and major mainstream Protestant denominations has served as a catalyst for another trend in scholarly examinations of the clergy. Recent books have taken readers inside churches to show how organizations that license and employ religious professionals are beginning to rethink who these professionals might be. Most book-length treatments on the question of calling reflect scholarly interest in the question of the *congregational* call to ministry, probing institutions to determine who can be called, what claimants are called to do, and how that call is to be certified. Most of this interest has centered on the ordination of women[5] and the Roman Catholic Church's formal recognition of unordained "lay-ministers."[6]

This book emphasizes the agency of religious professionals themselves in reconceptualizing clericalism in terms of these same dynamics of "who," "what," and "how." This emphasis allows us to extend established scholarly approaches to understanding the clergy and the clerical identity by forcing us to reconsider (1) some methodological, definitional, and theoretical dilemmas posed by narrow preconceptions about who the clergy are, (2) what matters along the way to that identity, and (3) what we can expect to see from those who claim it. With these reconsiderations in mind, there are three questions that serve as a framework for this book. Who are the called? What is a calling? How is the called-identity defended in the absence of professional knowledge, professional employment, or professional credentials?

Who the Called Are: A Methodological Problem

Of the four characteristics—altruism, authority, autonomy, and abstract expertise—that social scientists use to separate professions from other occupations, none has survived empirical scrutiny better than the last of these: professionals' almost monopolistic control of abstract knowledge.[7] Many occupations require proficiency in a set of skills or procedures as a condition of entry into their trade. Both professionals and other workers in the fields of law, medicine, and divinity share this characteristic. Lawyers and paralegals must be able to draft contracts, physicians and nurses can systematically obtain medical histories, and priests and deacons serve as administrators of congregations. But what separates the professionals from what might best be described as "paraprofessionals" is the claim that the professionals have mastered a body of esoteric knowledge, knowledge to which neither clients nor paraprofessionals are privy. While medicine and law have settled on an expectation that this competence in esoteric bodies of knowledge can be gained only in formal institutions of learning, there has been and continues to be considerable disagreement about the source of this special competence for clergy. Yet, when scholars seek samples of those who are in pursuit of clerical credentials, they almost always approach what seems to be a logical source for data: seminaries and Bible colleges. This approach enables us to only partially account for the role training might play in the strength of one's sense that one is equipped to "do ministry."

Second, while research on religious professionals has been a staple of occupations research since the 1930s, relatively few studies have explored the subjective meaning of religious work for those who, while licensed/ordained, don't practice their craft in pastoral offices. This book disrupts that meme by focusing on ministers who, for a host of reasons, are not serving in a pastoral or priestly office. It also explains how the "called" frame their clerical aspirations when institutional and personal characteristics hinder their access to professional positions. As licensed and ordained ministers, my respondents see themselves as much a part of the clerical "profession" as any church pastor or other presbyter. That said, very few of them currently hold or are likely to ever hold full-time pastoral appointments. Nevertheless, they maintain a vocational identity even as they express it in what a scholarly observer might perceive as avocational behavior. Adding these voices to the literature affords us a better understanding of the way in which clerical identity might inhabit a different space from other professional identities, as something other than just a vocational or occupational title.

Finally, previous research on what I term "new clericalism" suffers from a too-narrow focus on the issue of ordaining and placing women in full-time clerical positions. While ultimately feminist in its origins, this line of inquiry privileges paid labor as work in a way that countermands a feminist theory of labor, one that seeks to include unpaid labor and labor *not* located exclusively in the public sphere as part of our understanding of work. Much of this emphasis is based on the essentialist assumption that all male clergy either work or seek work as paid professionals and, therefore, so must all women who are drawn to religious labor. This book overcomes the problematic tendency of much feminist scholarship on the clergy to assume a priori that discrimination in terms of ordination processes denies women in some denominations access to both the work and the status of clergy. With rich empirical data on the thoughts and experiences of women who are called to, operating in, but not formally ordained for, ministry, we find empirical support for claims that meaningful variation exists in how women make sense of, justify, and value other approaches to religious labor.

What a Calling Is: A Definitional Problem

In his classic definition of the call to ministry, the theologian H. Richard Niebuhr speaks of the call as a "secret." Niebuhr, best known for his serenity prayer, describes the call as "that inner persuasion or experience whereby a person feels himself directly summoned or invited by God to take up the work of the ministry."[8] This call is not the general call to discipleship that all Christians might claim or the ecclesiastical (or congregational) call that serves to confirm, rather than initiate, one's belief that they are to engage in the work of the ministry.[9] The "secret call" is a crisis moment where the response is unrelated to the promise of either future benefits (e.g., eternal life) or current ones (e.g., a paycheck). Instead, the response should be one of obedience and a spirit of duty to God—the source of the charge. Is this an accurate picture of a call? What are people called to do? What form do these callings take?

How one finds entry into ministry as a vocation and what one understands that vocation to be is as much a sociological question as a theological one. In the stories that people tell about how they came to be "chosen" for this particular vocation—a story that few people outside of a religious context ever feel compelled to share—can be found a description of and an accounting for the social action and social identity that is born from this experience. A phenomenological perspective suggests that religious communities are embedded in the common everyday society, but that they have their own meanings, which are not shared by other people and other circumstances. This idea of a calling to a kind of labor (i.e., ministry) may be both defined by and limited to this social microcosm.

Most Protestant denominations affirm the idea that there must be a specific encounter with God that leads people to devote their lives to ministry. This moment, the "call to ministry," is essential to many ministers' beliefs that they are legitimate vessels for God's work. Unlike ordination processes, which are explicitly social in nature, call-experiences are almost always described as a personal journey where the only other participant is God. Most studies of Protestant clergy recognize that the call-to-ministry is an important part of the credentialing process, but they tend to gloss over it, focusing instead on the more easily analyzed institutional processes. Yet this moment is the foundation for everything that follows it. The call-experience is more than a catalyst for the pursuit of a professional credential; it is an essential plank in the argument for legitimacy, especially when other more verifiable evidence is in short supply. Therefore, comprehending the call-experience is a critical component of understanding its impact on both the decision to pursue and the decision to embrace a ministerial identity.

How a Called Identity Is Derived and Defended: A Theoretical Problem

As a graduate student, I taught undergraduate courses. In order to make a point about the power of expectations and symbols, I would occasionally come to the first day of class dressed in jeans and a T-shirt and sit near the back of the sixty-student classroom, notebook open, and wait for students to file in. We'd sit there for the customary ten-minute window that students have been primed to wait, and then I'd watch as the first few students looked around and started making their way to the exits. Only then did I announce myself as the instructor for the class. A useful conversation would then ensue about what students expected a professor to look like and how they expected a professor to behave: professors arrive on time, can be found in the front of the class, and they wear "professor-appropriate" clothing. When I conducted this exercise in my sociology of gender class, some students would suggest that they expected the professors to be female. Regardless of the class, one or two students would shyly point out their expectation that the professor would be white. They didn't recognize me as "professor" because I didn't meet their expectations.

Social scientists believe the social world operates on what the sociologist Erving Goffman refers to as "systems of enabling conventions."[10] We understand each other and, ultimately, ourselves based on the "normative consensus" that forms around idealized performances of roles and identities. While most of my students might have differing opinions on whether a professor wears a tweed jacket or just a shirt and tie, not nearly as many would expect one to wear a T-shirt and jeans, and practically none would expect a clown suit with a cowboy hat. It may be true that students might find me more likeable and approachable in jeans, but it is formal or professional dress that they expect and reward with perceptions of credibility, intelligence, and competence.[11]

Even without the empirical evidence of the role that appearance plays in shaping people's evaluations of our vocational identity, professors know to dress in accordance with certain conventions. Though other structural markers of my "professor-ness" are available to students—I'm in the front of the room, the syllabus has "Dr. Pitt" written at the top of it—I know that I enhance my performance of the professor role simply by putting on a tie and a tweed jacket. I don't just know the conventions; I rely on them in an attempt to successfully impress upon my students that I am who I claim to be.

In recognition of this tendency, Goffman says we put on a "front." That is, in these performances, we bring to bear a number of concrete/abstract props (or "expressions") in the service of defining ourselves for observers.[12] The best fronts conform to convention, thereby standardizing our performance so that the audience has something to hang their expectations on. Goffman's use of the term "performance" in his description of our "presentation of self in everyday life" gives the impression that these fronts are part of an attempt to mislead. While an argument can be made that this is not the case, it is important to consider the fact that some actors might, in fact, use their performances to mislead, particularly if the benefits of that deception may increase their status or access to other advantages. This possibility is especially relevant in the case of the clergy.

Much of the clerical identity is tied up in its credibility. The nearly universal Protestant requirement that ministerial aspirants claim a supernatural calling is an important component of establishing intention. Ultimately, the authority of the clerical identity doesn't reside in the practice of it; its authority comes just from being named to it by God. In lieu of applying some supernatural gift of discernment (that few credentialing bodies claim to have), a conventional calling story helps to verify the integrity and honesty of one's pursuit of clerical credentials.

This book is not focused on divining the veracity of ministers' claims to the ministerial identity. Goffman offers some advice for why taking that approach might ultimately be a fruitless exercise: "Whether an honest performer wishes to convey the truth or whether a dishonest performer wishes to convey a falsehood, both must take care to enliven their performances with appropriate expressions, exclude from their performances expressions that might discredit the impression being fostered, and take care lest the audience impute unintended meanings."[13] Whether trying to deceive or not, clerical aspirants likely recognize the conventions surrounding the clerical identity and, as any smart performer should be, are careful to use those conventions to maintain a credible performance. But what happens when those conventions aren't available?

While I did observe some of my respondents' performances as ministers, this book focuses primarily on their responses to a number of questions about their understanding of themselves as clergy. These conversations about their clerical identities, while much more comprehensive, reproduced the interviews many had had with their pastors at the beginning of their formal pursuit of the identity. At the outset of each interview, the ministers were informed of my own upbringing in their denomination. My asking them to tell me about their calling, as a presumed cultural insider, put me in the place of friendly interrogator in the same way that their pastor's request might have done years before. The open-ended nature of that first part of my investigation gave my respondents the opportunity to wrap themselves in the conventions of the clerical identity. This engagement gave me an opportunity to learn what conventions they deem relevant in the experience—or at least a description of the experience—of a call to the ministry.

These interviews were not only a chance for the respondents to describe themselves as clergy but also an opportunity to defend their belief that they indeed have this identity. In legitimating their status as clergy, they had to prove that they were who they claimed to be. This defense was complicated by the absence of conventional explanations. Goffman posits that "to be a given kind of person . . . is not merely to possess the required attributes, but also to sustain the standards of conduct and appearance that one's social grouping attaches thereto."[14]

Providing details of their possession of the required attribute—a calling—is certainly part of their defense. But in addition to those expressed in the narratives, there exist other sets of conventions about clerical conduct and "appearance" that we, as a society, also attach to our expectations of the clerical identity. As discussed, three of those conventions are seminary or other substantial religious training, paid employment as a religious professional, and the attainment of the credential (ordination) that separates clergy from congregants. In all but a few cases, these ministers could not use these conventions as part of the "clerical front" they were trying to depict. My asking them about this inconsistency, as a social scientist, put me in the place of hostile interrogator, a role few of my respondents had encountered formally, though many have had to deal with such challenges in informal conversations with friends, family members, and peers both in and out of the denomination. Their answers help us to better understand an issue not commonly engaged in our understanding of clerical, and other, identities: in the absence of conventional evidence, how do people make a credible case for their identity? We will see that the flexibility present in practically every aspect of this denomination's practice and principles allows these men and women ample room to stretch the boundaries of their own, and ultimately the denomination's, definition of "conventional clergy."

Sample and Methodology

The analysis in this book is based on my observation of and in-depth interviews with 115 ministers and ministry aspirants in the Church of God in Christ (COGIC), the largest Pentecostal denomination in North America. Its six million parishioners also make COGIC the largest of the Black Christian denominations. With its paradoxically presbyterian, episcopal, *and* congregational form of polity, COGIC has a distinctive structure for entry into ministry. Each ecclesiastical jurisdiction has considerable representation of men and women at all the stages in this ministerial "career ladder." This combination makes it an ideal source for examining the differences in people's responses to ministerial callings.

My respondents included people at all stages of the "call to ministry." This includes men holding the offices available to them (Aspiring Ministers, Licensed Ministers, Elders, Pastors, and Bishops) and women holding the offices available to them (Aspiring Missionaries, Deaconesses, Missionaries, Evangelists, and Chaplains). The sample was drawn from four ecclesiastical jurisdictions, one in the Northeast and three in the Southeast, which are the organizing bodies of this religious tradition.[15] The sample varies on a number of characteristics including age, gender, marital status, education, and of course, stage in their pursuit of licensing.

Because the call is a very personal and self-reflective experience, the interviews initially took on the form of testimony as the respondents shared their experiences without my direction. In order to capture the subjectivity and individuality of the informant's self-understanding of his or her call, each minister was asked the same initial question, "Would you tell me about your call," and was then given an opportunity to tell his or her story without interruption. This approach, drawn both from anthropological and social psychological methodology, enabled me to get a sense of calling from the "native's point of view." The words "ministry," "vocation," "calling," and "called" may have very different meanings based on both a person's ascribed characteristics and on their affiliations. Intersubjective meanings become shared within a subpopulation and can be coded in the narratives expressed by members of that subpopulation. We can then focus on that narrative as the place where self-concept is constructed, justified, and maintained. The second part of each interview took the form of a more structured interview with questions intended to discover how the respondents express their call and where they believe legitimization of the call lies. My data analysis consisted of carefully reading interviews, exploring and coding responses, and allowing themes, issues, and answers to emerge during the process.

Studying God

In a 1994 essay in the *New York Times Magazine*, the Catholic priest and sociologist Andrew Greeley wrote that "religion is experience, image, and story before it is anything else and after it is everything else." In these words, Greeley exposes readers to sociology's growing sense that religion's strength lies fundamentally within individuals' experiences with something unexplainable, the images and symbols that give meaning to those experiences, and the stories we use to preserve them.

As important as religious experience is to many people's lives—after all, more than 80 percent of Americans believe God answers prayers[16]—social scientists' training provides us neither the tools nor the appetite for serious attempts at understanding how explicitly supernatural phenomena operate. While I occasionally joke that some of the unexplained variance in sociological phenomena might be reduced if we could throw "God" into the regression equation, as a sociologist I am inclined to believe that human behavior is informed by some other socially structured behavioral trigger. These forces can be observed, and as a result it is religious behavior, not religious experience, that tends to draw our attention.

That said, whatever weight one attaches to the need for researchers to be able to *observe* supernatural phenomena, we cannot ignore these "breaches [of] the reality of ordinary life," as the sociologist Peter Berger refers to them.[17] For many, their religious experiences are part and parcel of their ordinary life. The sociologists Nancy Ammerman, Tim Nelson, Omar McRoberts, and others posit that religious people's real or imagined interactions with the sacred—be they *mysterium tremendum* or *mysterium fascinans*—have real implications for their social attitudes, behaviors, and outcomes.[18] This research supports these assertions.

My informants' descriptions of conversations with God were treated no differently from their descriptions of conversations with their pastors *about* those conversations with God. Sitting through more than 150 hours of conversation, I respected each minister's experience as truth, taking Rodney Stark's advice that a basic framework for research like this "sociology of the Gods" must be a recognition that for my ministers, like members of many religious traditions, God is a person with whom they can, should, and do interact.[19]

As an analyst of these conversations, I approach each case as if the religious experience happened as described, bringing what tools sociology and psychology offer to uncover how culture, context, and community might inform or affirm those experiences. I endeavored to maintain a position of phenomenological epoché, that is, an analytic stance that "brackets" or suspends any of the biases I might bring to this project as a representative of either my scientific or religious community.[20] Therefore, this book is not a scientific attempt to either prove or disprove the existence of God. Similarly, I don't seek to divine—through scientific method or any other technique—whether God calls people to ministry generally, or if God called any of my respondents specifically. That said, it was clear to me that if God is operating in the lives of these men and women, He's apparently wise enough to use the cultural tools of symbol, image, and story endemic to these religious communities to capture their attention.

Plan of the Book

The chapters that follow are arranged in four sections. The first chapter provides a foundational background. Chapters 2 and 3 offer descriptions and analysis of the birth of a called clerical identity. Chapters 4 through 6 examine how my respondents negotiated and maintained this identity given the structural obstacles that threaten both its legitimacy and its practice. The final part concludes with some reflections on the intersection of personal and congregational calls, and the need for social scientists to begin to reconsider our definition and understanding of the clergy.

Specifically, chapter 1 provides an introduction to the Church of God in Christ, offering brief glimpses of its one-hundred-year history, from its humble beginnings in a borrowed cotton gin to its current position as the largest Pentecostal denomination in North America. Drawing primarily on secondary sources, the chapter provides some context to the stories explored in the rest of the book and depicts what is distinctive about this denomination as both a Black and a Pentecostal denomination, highlighting both its differences and similarities with its peers.

Chapter 2 lays out the findings of previous research on the call to religious labor. While there is a long legacy of scholarship examining religious labor, the focus has been on the impact of secularization, de-professionalization, and stress on the lives of professional clergy. While some of that research will be brought to bear in this book, the emphasis here is on the sequence of events that led to these former layperson's decisions to become ministers. After laying out this background, the chapter turns to a systematic description of the accounts of my informants' calls to the ministry.

Drawing on both participant observation and interviews, chapter 3 offers a glimpse into the role originating congregations play in enhancing the very strong beliefs ministers have that they have been called to religious labor. It examines processes that, when examined through a social psychological lens, explain why even clearly noncompetent candidates continue to pursue the credential. In particular, it shows how religious communities' reluctance to directly reject ministers' sense that they are called inadvertently strengthens aspirants' commitments to the called identity.

Chapter 4 focuses on the ways in which these ministers legitimate their sense of themselves as clergy in spite of a nearly complete absence of what we have come to believe is an essential feature of religious credentialing: Bible school, divinity school, or seminary training. This chapter examines my respondents' assertion that their special competence as ministers comes not from any particular training (which they often deride), but instead through what they call "the anointing." The chapter describes how ministers explain this anointing, detailing the complex ways they say the anointing operates within them as a resource, rendering their lack of seminary training irrelevant. It also demonstrates how many of these ministers denigrate educational credentialing as an illegitimate means of certifying one's calling, thereby claiming less easily challenged evidence of their position as religious laborers.

Most men and women are unlikely to find full-time paid positions in their local COGIC churches. Chapter 5 explains why this is the case and how this situation handicaps opportunities to serve in the kinds of positions, even as unpaid laborers, where their peers in other denominations might be found. It shows how they construct a new framework for understanding religious labor in order to legitimate their continued secular employment. It argues that the rhetorics these ministers deploy in talking about their secular work and their calls to ministry help them overcome the structural constraints that might otherwise hinder a coherent sense of themselves as religious laborers.

Chapter 6 seeks to give voice to a set of ministers who have until now been absent from the samples informing our understanding of the clerical identity. Church of God in Christ women are missing from most studies of clergy because that institution continues to bar women from ordained ministry. This chapter examines the complex relationship between the church's rules against women's leadership and the various means by which female ministers continue to pursue their call to religious leadership positions. They, even more than men, find ways to exploit the zones of ambiguity present in institutional mandates intended to constrain their opportunities.

Taken as a whole, this book offers a better understanding of a phenomenon that is so ordinary that we've come to take it for granted, and yet so extraordinary that even theologians struggle with ways to measure or find meaning in it. Ultimately, I hope you will come away from this text with a clearer sense of how, in the innovative hands of these religious actors, the Brobdingnagian forces of discrimination and social structure interact with the personal complexities of faith and identity to promote new meanings and new opportunities for religious labor.

The Church of God in Christ

Pentecostal History, Doctrine, and Polity

For you, brethren, became imitators of the churches of God which are in Judea in Christ Jesus.

1 Thessalonians 2:14a

When I opened my mouth to say Glory, a flame touched my tongue which ran down to me. My language changed and no word could I speak in my own tongue. Oh! I was filled with the Glory of the Lord. My soul was then satisfied.

Charles H. Mason, founder, COGIC

More than 80 percent of all Black church attendees are members of one of eight Black denominations. Three are Methodist (African Methodist Episcopal, African Methodist Episcopal Zion, Christian Methodist Episcopal), four are Baptist (National Baptist USA, National Baptist Convention of America, National Missionary Baptist, and Progressive National Baptist), and the last is the pentecostal Church of God in Christ. The remaining Black Christians can be found split evenly between smaller Black denominations (e.g., Pentecostal Assemblies of the World, Full Gospel Baptist Church Fellowship), predominantly White Protestant denominations (e.g., United Methodist, American Baptist), and Roman Catholicism.[1]

Referred to enthusiastically as one of the "fastest growing Christian bodies on the planet" by the Chicago sociologist Omar McRoberts, the Church of God in Christ represents one of the fastest-growing segments of the religious family: the Pentecostals.[2] The church has been studied before, but like Pentecostalism itself, has been mostly overlooked by social scientists.[3] Much of what we do know about the denomination has been written by religious historians who have sought to raise the profile of Black leaders of the Pentecostal movement.[4] Understanding the history, doctrinal perspectives, organizational structure, and credentialing opportunities of the denomination is key to understanding the institutional framework that both liberates and constrains individuals' sense of what it means to be called.

Denominational History

The Church of God in Christ (COGIC) began as part of the Holiness movement, which had its origins in Methodism's "entire sanctification" and "holiness" teachings. These teachings, promulgated by John Wesley's reforms of the late 1860s, propose that one does not have to wait until death to be cleansed from sin. Instead, after salvation the believer is capable of being "made" holy instantaneously here on earth.[5] As is common for new religious movements or sects, the Holiness movement came as a back-to-basics response to the secular turn that American Protestantism was taking. Just as the Industrial Revolution transformed the secular economic landscape, it also changed the churches. Urban congregations were becoming middle-class congregations. Churches were getting larger, more bureaucratic, and more rational. Religious leaders were being trained in seminaries, steadily moving away from the spiritual as they learned more about philosophical and scientific explanations for natural phenomena.[6] The line between "the world" and "the church" was blurring and the Holiness movement, a movement started mainly by the poor and working class, grew in response to it.

In order to stand against the encroaching secularization, Holiness preachers condemned materialism and its accompanying ills. Instead, they urged followers to obey a stricter interpretation of biblical values and standards of holiness. If sanctification made one holy, the proof of receiving that grace was one's public displays of holiness. This formula is similar to Max Weber's description of Calvinism's impact on capitalism. He argues that God's chosen could be determined by their worldly success. Therefore, if one wanted to evince "chosenness," one had to work hard (at his "calling") in order to be successful.[7] In the same way, to prove their sanctification, the sanctified would eschew materialism and adhere to a host of prohibitions and taboos: they had to enact holiness to prove they were holy.

This belief had many detractors, mainly because it seemed to conflict with the apostle Paul's statement that "if we say that we have no sin, we deceive ourselves, and the truth is not in us" (1 Jn. 1:8). This reality—that people who claimed to be sanctified still sinned—led to some modification of the doctrine and the addition of the idea of sanctification being accompanied by a "baptism of the Holy Ghost." In that baptism, the power of sin to separate a person from God was broken and sanctified believers were no longer compelled to sin. Sin was thereby suppressed, not eradicated. In addition, believers now baptized in the Holy Ghost were thought to have access to supernatural powers similar to those possessed by the New Testament apostles. These powers made them more capable ministers. These changes made the idea of sanctification more palatable to those in non-Wesleyan churches, especially those evangelical denominations that valued Christian service as an important part of their understanding of their religious identity.

These messages weren't just transforming White congregations. As independent Black churches were emerging, their pastors began to accept the doctrine of Holiness and sanctification as well. As evangelical churches, they sent out itinerant preachers—both male and female—to convert new believers. In 1893, an autobiography about one of these Black preachers was written. This autobiography, *The Story of the Lord's Dealing With Mrs. Amanda Smith, The Coloured Evangelist,* got in the hands of a young Arkansas minister, Charles Harrison Mason, and changed his life.[8]

Initially, Mason was a minister at the Mount Olive Missionary Baptist church where his stepbrother served as pastor. He read Smith's autobiography, and moved by the message of this Black Holiness evangelist, experienced "entire sanctification" and began to preach about holiness. These sermons led the Missionary Baptist church community to expel him as a heretic. That led him to start an independent congregation that stressed both "entire sanctification" and the outpouring of the Holy Ghost as its defining doctrines. This church, originally housed in a Mississippi cotton gin, was one of a number of new churches led by pastors who had been expelled by their Baptist churches for preaching about sanctification. Along with his colleagues Charles Price Jones, James Jeter, and Walter Pleasant, Mason began to run revivals as the nondenominational Christ's Association of MS of Baptized Believers. Eventually they became known as the "Churches of God in Christ," a movement that had more than fifty congregations located, primarily, in Arkansas and Mississippi.[9]

In 1907, the Azusa Street revival taking place in California caught the eye of members of the quickly growing organization. This revival was taking place under the leadership of William J. Seymour, a Black Baptist preacher and former Louisiana slave. Trained by the Holiness heavyweight Charles Fox Parham, Seymour taught that one had to be baptized in the Holy Ghost with the evidence of speaking in tongues. This new doctrine and the unusual evidence of it caused Seymour's small Bible studies and prayer meetings to grow quite quickly, drawing adherents from all races and economic backgrounds. The Azusa revivals were rare for their time because of the degree to which race, gender, and even lay-status were nearly meaningless. They were also ecumenical in nature as everyone from Baptists to Quakers attended the meetings.

Mason and Jeter were selected to attend the Azusa Street meetings on COGIC's behalf. It was at Azusa that Mason received the gift of tongues, an experience that the Holiness pastor was anxious to have. As a believer in the importance of bearing supernatural gifts as evidence that one had been fully "filled with the Spirit," Mason's inability to heal the sick or cast out demons had been causing him some concern. He went to California a skeptic, wondering if what was occurring at the Los Angeles revivals was similar to the Pentecost experience detailed in the biblical story in Acts 2–4. Both his skepticism and his concerns were resolved at the Azusa Street meeting where he received what he declared was a baptism of the Holy Ghost evidenced by the speaking of tongues. Upon his return to Memphis, Mason began to teach this new doctrine that required three spiritual moments: salvation, sanctification, and (now) speaking in tongues.

Just as the doctrine of sanctification caused a rift between Mason and the Baptists, his passion for this new doctrine drove a wedge between him and the Churches of God in Christ association. At their August convention, Jones objected to two key aspects of Mason's message: that a third crisis was required beyond sanctification, and that the tongues they spoke were not recognizable foreign languages. This disagreement led to Mason being expelled from COGIC; the organization split in half with Jones's supporters eventually forming (in 1911) the Church of Christ Holiness and Mason retaining the name "The Church of God in Christ." Mason was declared the sect's general overseer and bishop, which gave him plenipotentiary levels of authority over the new denomination.

Under Mason's leadership, the denomination grew by leaps and bounds. Mason appointed bishops to oversee and develop new churches in Tennessee, Arkansas, Mississippi, Texas, Missouri, and California. As Blacks migrated during World War I and II, Mason sent evangelists and their families to northern and western cities to establish churches in urban centers like New York, Detroit, Chicago, and New York. From its early origins of ten small southern churches, it has blossomed into what is now a mostly urban denomination with hundreds of congregations in the United States and sixty other countries. As other denominations plant churches in suburbs, most COGIC churches remain planted within cities' boundaries.

Mason himself stayed in Memphis, building the Mason Temple Church. While some scholars suggest that COGIC's Wesleyan roots leads it to avoid sociopolitical engagements, Mason allowed the American Federation of

State, County, and Municipal Employees (AFSCME) to use the church as its headquarters in the 1968 sanitation strike. In fact, Dr. Martin Luther King preached his "I've Been to the Mountaintop" sermon from the Mason Temple pulpit less than twenty-four hours before he was assassinated. Mason himself had died seven years earlier after serving for sixty-four years—the longest of any church leader—as the head of the church. After him, COGIC has had only six other senior bishops: Bishop O. T. Jones (1961–68), Bishop J. O. Patterson (1968–89), Bishop L. H. Ford (1990--95), Bishop C. D. Owens (1995–2000), Bishop G. E. Patterson (2000–07), and now Bishop C. E. Blake (2007–present).

According to a 1996 article in *Christianity Today*, the church gained 600 congregations and an average of 200,000 members every year between 1982 and 1992.[10] At 48 percent growth during those ten years, it was (and likely remains) the fastest-growing denomination in the country. In that same time frame, it grew faster than the Church of Jesus Christ of Latter-Day Saints (22 percent), the Assemblies of God (22 percent), the Roman Catholic Church (14 percent), and the Southern Baptist Convention (9 percent). Now COGIC has nearly 6.5 million members worshipping in more than 12,000 churches located primarily in North America, but existing on every inhabitable continent. While still predominately and disproportionately lower class, COGIC is becoming more and more working and middle class, particularly as well-heeled Blacks begin to migrate from their northern urban churches to southern ones. From the 1930s to 1950s, the church "appeared in sociological studies as the 'sanctified people' in storefront churches whose ecstatic worship, speaking in tongues, and lower-class background were either scorned or ridiculed."[11] This is no longer the case as COGIC has clearly evolved from a lower-class, sectarian movement to a middle-income, denominational one.

The center of neo-Pentecostalism in the Black church, COGIC's influence can be seen in multiple arenas. The church's long-standing mission to maintain an urban presence makes the denomination one of the most visible religious organizations in cities such as Chicago, Dallas, Detroit, Los Angeles, Memphis, and Philadelphia. Megachurches in those cities, including Presiding Bishop Charles Blake's 20,000-member congregation, are helping to shape their local communities with multimillion-dollar community development corporations. The denomination's Urban Initiative, with its emphases on crime, economic development, education, family, and financial literacy, is only the latest in a series of enterprises aimed at balancing the church's concerns for their communities' spiritual and material well-being. Leaders of congregations, such as Philadelphia's Bishop E. C. Morris and Detroit's

Bishop P. A. Brooks promote economic, social, and racial equality as leaders of ecumenical organizations in their cities.

Informed by an ongoing engagement with liberation and womanist theologians, some of whom—Drs. Robert Franklin, Eric Greaux, Adrienne Guilford, Antipas Harris, Michelle Jacques-Early, Leonard Lovett, and Billie Roberts-Spann—are themselves members of the denomination, the church is slowly moving beyond a theological parochialism that threatens to marginalize it. While at its core, COGIC remains as theologically conservative as some of its well-known predominantly White fundamentalist and evangelical peers, its primary identification with the Black church and the urban communities it serves sometimes puts it at odds with the priorities of those peers. While the bulk of the twentieth-century's civil rights leadership came out of the Baptist and Methodist traditions, the prominence of the denomination and its own leadership is fast making it one of the leading voices on issues that might be viewed as politically progressive if not liberal.[12]

COGIC Doctrine

In order to understand the denomination better, it is useful to know the key components of the Church of God in Christ's doctrine. The church lists those components as a formal statement of faith, accordingly:[13]

1. We believe the Bible to be the inspired and only infallible written Word of God.
2. We believe that there is only One God, eternally existent in three persons: God the Father, God the Son, and God the Holy Spirit.
3. We believe in the blessed Hope, which is the rapture of the Church of God, which is in Christ, at His return.
4. We believe that the only means of being cleansed from sin is through repentance and faith in the precious Blood of Jesus Christ.
5. We believe that regeneration by the Holy Spirit is absolutely essential for personal salvation.
6. We believe that the redemptive work of Christ on the Cross provides healing for the human body in answer to believing prayer.
7. We believe that the Baptism of the Holy Spirit, according to Acts 2:4, is given to believers who ask for Him.
8. We believe in the sanctifying power of the Holy Spirit, by whose indwelling the Christian is enabled to live a holy and separated life in the present world.

As you can see, in some ways, the Church of God in Christ is no different from other Protestant denominations. Their statement of faith highlights a belief in the Bible as the inspired Word of God; the relationship of God the Father, Son, and Holy Ghost; the blood of Jesus as the price for redemption; and the second coming of Jesus as an impending reality. Further investigation of the statement reveals subtle ways COGIC differs from some other denominations. Some of those differences include their belief in a Triune God, in a strict interpretation of the Bible, that Christ will return both visibly and bodily to the planet, and that immersion (not sprinkling) is the appropriate technique for baptizing converts. These differences are shared with branches of some of the largest religious communities in contemporary Protestantism. But it is the last four statements in their list that tend to set COGIC apart from most Protestant denominations. These statements reflect COGIC's orientation as both a Holiness and a Pentecostal denomination. It is these dynamics that are, ultimately, most relevant in understanding the worldview of COGIC lay-members and, by extension, its aspiring and credentialed clergy.

Most Protestants, and particularly evangelical sects (which COGIC can be counted as), believe in conversion as the first stage, or "crisis experience," that must take place in the life of a new believer. They believe that we are all born into the world as spiritually dead, separated from communion with God as a result of an essentially inherited capacity for wrongdoing. In that state, we are all considered "dead in trespasses and sin" (Eph. 2:1) and must be "born again." This is accomplished by recognizing that one is in this state, making a decision to change their mind/direction as relates to the past sinful identity (repentance), and then seeking justification by believing in Jesus as a conciliatory sacrifice for their misdeeds. The Church of God in Christ joins other evangelical denominations as synergists, believing that the regeneration made available through the Holy Ghost must be accepted in order to be activated.

The Holiness doctrine of sanctification adds a second stage, or "crisis experience." The church defines sanctification as "that gracious and continuous operation of the Holy Ghost, by which He delivers the justified sinner from the pollution of sin, renews his whole nature in the image of God, and enables him to perform good works."[14] Because the third stage, baptism of the Holy Ghost, cannot happen without sanctification, this sanctification has to be instantaneous. Otherwise, few believers would be capable of being filled with the Holy Ghost; the sacred Holy Ghost cannot cohabitate within a profane human vessel.

So instantaneous or "entire" sanctification, defined more narrowly as "separation for sacred purpose," was tied directly to the conversion experience. Therefore, while COGIC considers salvation a three-stage process, in practice the first and second stages are too extrinsically linked to truly be considered separate stages. That said, COGIC doctrine does leave space for progressive sanctification in its description of it as a "continuous operation of the Holy Ghost." Whether instantaneous or progressive, the doctrine of sanctification requires the appearance of sanctification and behavioral cleanliness. While COGIC's belief in sanctification explicitly argues that holiness cannot be worked toward, in practice the denomination emphasizes appropriate and "holy" behavior as something believers should attempt to exhibit.

As an evangelical denomination, COGIC takes very seriously the biblical command mentioned as one of the last statements of Jesus to his disciples: "Go therefore and make disciples of all the nations, baptizing them in the name of the Father and of the Son and of the Holy Spirit, teaching them to observe all things that I have commanded you" (Matt. 28:19–20a). This is the gospel commission to spread the message of salvation/conversion explained earlier. While conversion is a change in standing and sanctification is a change in nature, a final stage is required in order to not only live a moral life but to be empowered to complete the commands laid out in the commission. This third stage, and the one that makes Pentecostalism and the Church of God in Christ distinctive, is the Baptism of the Holy Ghost.

A key component of COGIC doctrine is the belief that the events of the day of Pentecost were not limited to antiquity but could be repeated with every believer as an experience separate from, but as necessary as, conversion and sanctification (Acts 2–4). The Baptism of the Holy Ghost is considered a major credential for ministry. Prior to this moment, the disciples were powerless to truly engage in ministry in any meaningful way. As a result, the COGIC argues that the Baptism of the Holy Ghost is necessary for one to be able to do ministry. The church leaders describe it this way: "The Holy Ghost is a gift bestowed upon the believer for the purpose of equipping and empowering the believer, making him a more effective witness for service in the world. He teaches and guides one in all truth."[15] They go on to say "Since the charismatic demonstrations were necessary to help the early church to be successful in implementing the command of Christ, we, therefore, believe that a Holy Ghost experience is mandatory for all men today."[16]

This experience—referred to as "infilling"—with the Spirit of God must be requested. One "tarries" for the experience and a successful infilling is marked by glossolalia. The Church of God in Christ views glossolalia, or speaking in tongues, as the initial evidence of God's Spirit (the Holy Ghost) taking residence in believers. Tongues, which may be foreign or "angelic," are always presumed to be unknown to the speaker. Other Black Pentecostal denominations (for example, the Church of Christ Holiness) reject this doctrine, which ultimately led to the schism between Jones and Mason in 1907. While the church believes that speaking in tongues is a consequence of being filled with the Holy Ghost, they do not believe that beyond the specific moment of the Baptism of the Holy Ghost, there must be subsequent expressions of glossolalia. In fact, they argue that the supernatural gift of tongues, which is presumably something different than the tongues spoken at the Baptism, may be made available to certain Christians but not others. The gift of tongues, unlike the required "sign" of tongues, is like other gifts doled out by the Holy Ghost upon those who are filled or baptized with it.

These gifts, including tongues, are part of the continuing work of the Holy Ghost. The ongoing role of the Holy Ghost in both sanctifying and empowering believers focuses Pentecostals' attention much more on pneumatological and supernatural phenomena. Pentecostals unapologetically operate under the conviction that the Holy Ghost—the invisible, intangible, and scientifically difficult to verify contemporary incarnation of God— can and does possess them.[17] While possessed, a Spirit-baptized believer is assumed capable of exhibiting any number of supernatural abilities, from the aforementioned ability to speak in unlearned languages to being able to heal people of crippling illnesses. In addition to these abilities, the energetic worship style of Pentecostals is often attributed to this Spirit-possession. The sociologist George Lundskow, who describes Pentecostalism as a "spectacle"[18] religion says, "Pentecostals energetically, even ecstatically, participate in the service, with enthusiastic and boisterous singing and dancing. Possession by the Holy Ghost always takes precedence over any official itinerary. A person so possessed . . . may manifest other behavior as well, such as writhing on the ground and experiencing various manner of convulsions."[19]

While scholars give Charles Parham the credit for initiating the conceptual foundations for supernatural displays (e.g., tongues, healing) as evidence of Holy Ghost Baptism, most point to the Black revivalist William Seymour's Azusa Street Revival as the first widespread display of this evidence.[20] Many point to Seymour's race as playing a considerable role in these more ecstatic worship experiences, experiences that seem to reflect the kind of traditions (e.g., spirit possession, sacred dance, direct links between the natural and supernatural) known to be characteristic of African religious ritual. These traces of African worship, practiced by both Black and White attendees of Azusa, actually led to Parham's rebukes of Seymour's ministry as voodoo and his complaints about Whites "imitating the unintelligent, crude negroisms of the Southland, and laying it on the Holy Spirit."[21] Parham's criticism of Pentecostalism as being governed by hypnotic, spiritualistic, and mesmeric influences, unseemly behaviors he felt the Holy Ghost would never engage in, were considered to be grounded more in racism than any theological response to the new doctrine.

As one of Charles Mason's priorities was "preventing the loss of slave religion's vitality," it is understandable that he would be drawn to what he experienced at Azusa.[22] It was that experience, of a seemingly supernatural move of God culminating in his own "possession" by the Holy Ghost, that led him to adopt the Pentecostal perspective that guides the Church of God in Christ today. While many middle-class Blacks rejected both Pentecostalism and COGIC for fear that they would be too closely associated with America's history of slavery, the appeal of the "mystical wonder of God" on display in COGIC revivals and services was, and remains, a draw for the working-class Blacks that make up the bulk of its membership.[23]

Organizational Structure

All organized churches and denominations have a governance structure that usually follows one of four models of ecclesiastical polity: episcopal, presbyterian, charismatic-leader, and congregational. They can be described based on the levels of control over the local church residing in the hands of either internal or external actors. In the episcopal model, the denomination is governed by a series of bishops who maintain power in a hierarchical structure. In presbyterian churches, members of the denomination are governed by a series of elders' councils or "presbyters." These councils are hierarchical as well, with the highest level, the General Assembly, being composed of representatives of the regional presbyters.

Charismatic or founder-led churches are governed by the leader who started the church. He or she may have full authority over the conduct of the church, including both administrative and doctrinal decisions. Any internal hierarchy exists to manage administrative functions; major decisions reside, ultimately, in the hands of the leader. Finally, congregational churches tend not to have any external authority and are, instead, governed by members of the local church. Some of those members may have elected leadership roles, but major decisions are usually voted on by the congregation itself. Both charismatic and congregational churches may gather with similar churches in religious assemblages, but those institutions generally have little control over the function of individual congregations.

Of the major Black churches, the African Methodist Episcopal (AME) churches represent an episcopal polity on one end and the National Baptist Convention represents a congregationalist polity at the other. While the Church of God in Christ is, ostensibly, episcopal in its polity, it actually has an unusual mixture of all four models of polity. Its episcopal bishopric, presbyterian general assembly, congregational autonomy, and charismatic-founder led churches make it somewhat unique among church bodies. This combination also makes it useful for a study of denomination-level, jurisdictional-level, and church-level authority over ministers' callings. While COGIC has a civil organizational structure that includes a president, vice presidents, secretaries, and treasurers, its primary governing structure is an ecclesiastical one. This structure is composed of a General Assembly, a General Board, Jurisdictional Assemblies, departments, and local churches.

At the denomination's founding, it had an explicitly episcopal structure where one leader, Senior Bishop Mason, exerted considerable control over the denomination's governance and doctrine. This changed in 1968 when the denomination's constitution was changed to abolish both the office of Senior Bishop and the Executive Board of Bishops, replacing them with a Presiding Bishop who oversees—but still, ultimately, answers to—the General Assembly and the General Board. The General Assembly is a large voting body (sometimes upwards of 50,000 people) that meets twice a year during a National Convocation in April and an International Convocation in November. It serves as the doctrinal and legislative authority of the church.[24]

The General Board comprises twelve bishops elected by the larger General Assembly. They act as the executive arm of the church. They are led by a Presiding Bishop, also elected by the General Assembly, who is usually a member of the General Board. The Presiding Bishop is considered the Chief Apostle of the denomination, operates as the Chief Executive Officer of COGIC, Inc., and has the authority to appoint all bishops, department heads, and national officers. Again, COGIC has had seven Presiding Bishops, culminating in the current leadership of Bishop Charles Blake, Pastor of the West Angeles Church of God in Christ located in Los Angeles, California.

In addition to serving as members of the General Board, these twelve bishops also oversee regional collections of local churches called "jurisdictions." They serve alongside nearly two hundred other men as "Jurisdictional Bishops." There are more than two hundred COGIC jurisdictions in the country, with some states having as many as sixteen. Jurisdictional Bishops are selected by the Presiding Bishop from the corps of ordained Elders (all men), usually with the recommendation of the pastors in that jurisdiction. New jurisdictions are born out of administrative need, usually to accommodate churches planted in other countries or burgeoning church growth in a United States geographic area. Jurisdictional Bishops are responsible for the churches in their prescribed region. Like the Presiding Bishop, they oversee an assemblage referred to as the Jurisdictional Assembly whose composition mirrors that of the General Assembly. The authority to ordain COGIC Elders resides in their hands, and they administer local convocations similar to the larger body's national and international ones. Collectively, these Jurisdictional Bishops sit on a body called the Board of Bishops and also serve as members of the General Assembly.[25]

Another important role in each jurisdiction is the Jurisdictional Supervisor of Women's Work. Nearly from its creation, women wielded considerable power—some granted, some taken—in the denomination. Mason's 1911 appointment of Lizzie Robinson to the position as "overseer of the women's work," essentially made her the bishop over women in the church. She had considerable authority over every aspect of women's ministry in the COGIC, including the ministerial track for women that serves as the parallel to that of men in the denomination. At the international level, women are organized in the church's large and formidable International Women's Department, led by a female General Supervisor appointed by the Presiding Bishop. Serving under and reporting to her are the Jurisdictional Supervisors of Women's Work. These women, also called "Mothers," serve alongside the Jurisdictional Bishop and have the authority to license, but not ordain, female ministers in their jurisdiction.[26] While women's positions nationally and regionally seem to parallel those of the men, they remain subordinate to them. Both the National Supervisor's and the Jurisdictional Supervisors' authority to appoint or license is constrained; the Presiding Bishop or Jurisdictional Bishops have veto power over these appointments. The Jurisdictional Supervisors also sit as delegates to the General Assembly.

In order to manage their regions, most Jurisdictional Bishops appoint District Superintendents. These men oversee subdivisions of jurisdictions, consisting of about ten to fifteen pastorates. They may hold annual district meetings (similar to jurisdictional or national convocations) but do not have any of the licensing/ordination authorities held by jurisdictional leaders. As with most positions in the church, District Superintendents have a female counterpart; she is referred to as a District Missionary. Two district mission-aries from each jurisdiction are sent as delegates to the General Assembly.

The final level of ecclesial responsibility in the Church of God in Christ is the local pastorate. While not fully autonomous like congregational churches, local COGIC pastors have a great deal of autonomy. While COGIC started as a church-planting denomination, the denomination now grows more organ-ically as ordained ministers take it upon themselves to either start a church or assume leadership of a dead/dying congregation. As a denomination that is just barely one hundred years old, most of the churches founded since 1907 are still led by their founding pastors or that founder's designated succes-sor. Unlike other episcopal denominations, COGIC pastors tend to serve for life, and church property is held in the founding pastors' name. While it is the Jurisdictional Bishop's formal responsibility to appoint pastors to local churches, families tend to control church succession lines. As a result, this role is practically never played.

The Pastor, as the chief executive officer of his church, has ultimate authority to appoint and remove all officers (e.g., deacons, auxiliary leaders) as well as to license male and female ministers to serve in his local congre-gation. They also recommend ministers to their Jurisdictional Bishops and Supervisors for terminal licenses. While they lose some authority over men and women they recommend for these licenses, they still wield full con-trol over any ministry that takes place in the congregations they lead. Pas-tors serve as members of their Jurisdictional Assemblies, as delegates to the General Assembly, and sit on a General Council of Pastors and Elders. The last of these, the Pastors' Council, is also open to associate ministers who are ordained but not leading congregations.

Just as women serve in parallel positions at every other stage of COGIC pol-ity, there is a local church position reserved for the most experienced, often elderly, women in the church. These women, referred to as Church Mothers, often serve as the leaders of the women in any congregation and wield con-siderable power as spiritual leaders alongside, but subordinate to, the church's pastor.[27] The most senior of these Church Mothers often oversees the train-ing, licensing, and ministerial assignments of the church's female ministers. In many congregations, the head Church Mother is the spouse of the founding pastor. In those cases when a pastor dies, leaving the church in the hands of his spouse, the Church Mother may lead, but cannot officially pastor, that church.[28] As a result, no women can sit on the Pastors' Council and can only serve as vot-ing delegates to the General Assembly if they also serve as their jurisdiction's District Missionaries or Jurisdictional Supervisors of Women's Work.

Credentialing

At various points in the COGIC's history, its constitution, mission, and statements of faith have been produced in a manual for the consumption of interested lay-members, lay-leaders, and clergy. That document, *The Official Manual of the Church of God in Christ*, was reformulated and expanded in 1973. The manual includes the history of the church, its constitution, doctrinal statements (on both religious and secular issues), and prescriptions for ministerial practice. Nearly twenty pages of the document are dedicated to explaining "The Christian Ministry." This section describes the credentialing processes used by the church to license and ordain aspirants to ministerial office. In addition to theological insights on the so-called "five-fold ministerial orders"—apostles, prophets, evangelists, pastors, and teachers—the document offers details about the four distinctly COGIC clerical credentials: Licensed Ministers, ordained Elders, Deaconess-Missionaries, and Evangelist-Missionaries.

It starts with a section "The Call to the Ministry," which details how a congregation is to proceed with one's calling. Note the gender specificity here: "When a lay member or deacon of the local church expresses to the pastor *his* desire to preach the gospel, the pastor shall then counsel with *him* regarding his sincerity, soundness or authenticity of *his* calling, and the requirements of the ministry. If the pastor is convinced that the person possesses the necessary qualities to be a minister, the pastor shall then prepare *him* for qualifying."[29]

Two aspects of this description of entry into the career ladder of COGIC clergy are important. First, the use of the words "him" and "his" are intentional. Only men can express callings to preach and become licensed—and eventually ordained—preachers. Women in ministry do what any observer would refer to as preaching, but the act is recognized in COGIC only as teaching or, even, just speaking. While many consider this double standard a function of male leaders' sexism, this tradition was championed and enforced by early female church leaders. For example, Mother Lizzie Robinson stated categorically that "Jesus never called a woman's name. He never called a woman to preach."[30]

Second, the call is specific: that is, to "preach the gospel." This emphasis on preaching is continued in the description of the local preachers. For example, it states that "he should be able to convince others that God called him to preach" and "his license to preach must be renewed each year unless he has been ordained." That act of "preaching" is so critical to this role that "no member [of the church] is authorized to preach, representing the Church of God in Christ, without a license." Surprisingly, given its prominence as the key act of ministry, the manual never explicitly defines what preaching is or how it differs from teaching. It does define teaching as holding "a discourse with others in order to instruct them or to deliver a didactic discourse." This implies that the essential difference between preaching and teaching is that preaching is *proclaiming* the gospel message and teaching is *explaining* the gospel message. Ordained leaders—especially pastors—are expected to do both.

There is some incongruence here. While it seems that preaching is a task reserved for ordained ministers (along with administering the sacraments), unordained licensed preachers count preaching as one of their duties. This shows that the prohibition against women preaching is not merely a function of their serving in unordained leadership positions. By describing the call to ministry in terms of both gender and task, the manual makes explicit the illegitimacy of the call to preaching ministries that many of the female ministers claim to have. How these distinctions are understood by women and, more importantly, how they impact women's religious work is as complicated as any phenomena this book uncovers.

There are four main ministerial credentials that one can earn in the Church of God in Christ: two are earned by men and two are earned by women. The first credential a man might receive is that of the Licensed Minister.[31] Once he professes a call to ministry, his pastor may label him an Aspiring Minister until such time as he determines that the aspirant is ready to begin the credentialing process. To qualify for a ministerial license, he "should be personally convinced of his call to the ministry . . . be able to convince others that God called him to preach, possess a holy conversation, sound understanding of the things of God, and have a good report of those within and without. He must be willing to 'study to show himself approved unto God, a workman that need not be ashamed rightly dividing the world [*sic*] of Truth.' He should be one that has served faithfully in attendance, tithing and offering and obedience to his pastor."[32]

If, after a year, he has shown that he possesses an acceptable level of commitment, competence, and character, his local pastor may grant him a minister's license. Licensed Ministers are licensed to preach, but are still officially only lay-members. This license is an intermediate license that only allows the Licensed Minister to preach either within his local church or in prisons or hospitals as a representative of that congregation. He must seek permission of his pastor to preach outside of these boundaries. While not officially considered clergy, both this license and the tasks assigned to them (e.g., conducting worship services) mark them as religious leaders. This license must be renewed annually until he is ordained as an Elder.

The path to Eldership includes both a recommendation from his Pastor to his jurisdiction's ordination committee and a recommendation of that committee to his Jurisdictional Bishop. The recommendation of the ordination committee usually follows a battery of written and oral examinations. If the Jurisdictional Bishop approves, the Licensed Minister will become an ordained Elder. The manual describes this moment, becoming an Elder, as more than imparting a new status upon these men. Pointing to New Testament examples of the laying on of hands (part of the ritual of ordination), it describes ordination as "the communication of a spiritual gift or its invocation."[33] In essence, ordination endows these ministers with particular supernatural abilities. Elders receive a permanent license that grants them further rights to administer the church's ordinances, to bless homes and sacred buildings, and to legally perform the rites of marriage and burial. Upon receipt of this license, often received within three years of announcing the call to ministry, ordained Elders can pastor churches and, ultimately, be appointed as Bishops. Many Elders serve as associate ministers in local churches, most often doing so under the pastor who ordained them.

Women, as explained earlier, cannot be ordained but have a similar career ladder as male clergy. While the COGIC manual never actually refers to them as "called to the ministry," a woman who seeks a ministerial credential must meet the same requirements of male aspirants, including claiming a call to ministry. Upon claiming that call, either to her pastor or to his female designate (usually the Church Mother), she becomes an Aspiring Missionary. Like the Aspiring Minister, the Aspiring Missionary is observed for a year—more likely by the Church Mother than the pastor—to determine her fitness for the ministerial license. If she meets the requirements, she will usually receive a Deaconess-Missionary (hereafter referred to as Deaconess) license. Some churches have another liminal stage for women called, simply, "Missionary," in which women serve for one to two years before being granted the Deaconess license.

Both the Deaconess and the Missionary licenses are local licenses, constraining these women's ministries to their local church. They partake in many of the same tasks that the Licensed Ministers do, except they "teach" or "speak" even when doing so from a pulpit. After two or four years serving as Deaconesses, women who choose to move beyond the Deaconess license seek the final credential available to them: the Evangelist-Missionary (hereafter referred to as Evangelist) license. The requirements for this license are similar, and in many jurisdictions identical, to the requirements men need to be ordained. They must pass a series of examinations, be recommended by ordination committees, and finally are granted the Evangelists' license by the Jurisdictional Supervisor of Women. Most lay-delegates to the General Assembly are either Deaconesses or Evangelists and, therefore, almost always women.

Evangelists can found new churches but must turn those churches over to ordained Elders to lead. That said, a woman can also be given charge over a local congregation in exceptional circumstances. Unlike true congregational churches, in which the church property is owned by the congregation, most COGIC churches are kinship churches in which the church itself is owned by the family who founded it. As a result, the church can be passed directly from father to son or, if he chooses to, from husband to wife. In the latter case, his wife serves as pastor of the congregation but does not have the Elder or Pastor label. Instead, she is formally considered to be the congregation's Shepherdess Sans Portfolio, with the rarely realized understanding that she will turn the pastorate over to the denomination's chosen successor to her husband. Of course, these women have all of the necessary capabilities of any head of a congregation, including administering the sacraments and marrying and burying members of her congregation.

While not explicitly recognized as Elders, some women are allowed to administer the sacraments and may, in fact, be ordained by their jurisdictional leaders. These women, Chaplains, merit a special and limited ordination primarily because of their employment as either healthcare, corrections, or military chaplains. In 1974, under the leadership of COGIC's third Presiding Bishop, J. O. Patterson, the Commission on Military and Institutional Chaplains (CMIC) was formed. This ministry's mission is to "to extend the mission of The Church Of God In Christ with compassion to military personnel, prisoners, hospital patients, their families and other secular institution."[34] As the position of military, hospital, or university chaplain is as much a professional role as it is a religious one, a number of women who were graduating from seminaries began seeking out these professional opportunities. The CMIC enables these women to serve in these positions with the required ecclesiastical endorsement of their religious community. All COGIC Chaplains are required to have five years of ministerial experience and both a bachelor's and master's degree. They are also required to have one to four units of clinical pastoral training. These requirements make female Chaplains more qualified to pastor churches than many of the ordained Elders and Pastors they serve under when not serving in their professional capacity.[35]

The Assemblies of God

While the Church of God in Christ is the largest Pentecostal body in the United States, more scholarly attention has been paid to the Assemblies of God (AOG), a denomination with half as many U.S. adherents and more than twice as many international ones. As the little we know about Pentecostal ministry comes from surveys or historical analyses of Assemblies of God ministers, it is important to understand the relationship between the Church of God in Christ and this assemblage of Pentecostal churches.

The Azusa movement, which prompted the creation of the Church of God in Christ, was widely perceived as radical. This reputation was not just a function of its unusual claims of supernatural occurrences, like speaking in tongues and healings. It was also revolutionary for its time—only ten years after the *Plessy v. Ferguson* ruling—because of its attractiveness to men and women of all races, nationalities, and classes. This interracial, nonsexist mixing did not only occur in the pews. The movement was organized by a twelve-member team of elders who were Black and White, male and female. While Azusa's Apostolic Faith Gospel Mission was responsible for sending missionaries of all races throughout the world, it was the Church of God in Christ that played a major role in the formation of an interracial Pentecostal movement here in the United States.[36]

In 1909 the church gained the legal name, "The Church of God in Christ, Incorporated." In addition to protecting COGIC's leaders from certain legal challenges, this incorporated status also made Charles Mason the only Pentecostal cleric capable of ordaining other clergy. Without these ministerial credentials, Pentecostal ministers would not have important legal authorities (e.g., to perform weddings) or other civil perks that came with ordination, such as riding at a reduced cost on public transportation. As a result of Mason's unique authority, many White Pentecostal ministers were ordained by Mason, carried COGIC credentials, and pastored interracial COGIC congregations. In fact, there were as many White COGIC churches as there were Black ones.[37] While other denominations were making distinctions between their Black and White members, "Mason and COGIC surpassed the rhetoric of racial equality and the practice of racially mixed worship by erecting an interracial denominational structure and creating an interracial leadership."[38]

All of that changed in 1914 when a collection of White COGIC leaders met in Hot Springs, Arkansas, and formed the Assemblies of God. Reportedly, the meeting was called to address some new doctrinal controversies, particularly William Durham's arguments against sanctification as a "second crisis," but no Black ministers other than Mason were invited to attend this meeting. It was largely suspected that White ministers were finding it problematic that their credentials were being issued by Mason. In fact, some were already asking to retain the COGIC seal but to have their own local leaders sign their licenses.[39] At its formation, the Assemblies of God rejected denominationalism, considering themselves an assemblage of like-minded churches. They had neither a constitution nor a doctrinal statement for a number of years as they worked through a series of doctrinal issues. Arguments about sanctification, the role of tongues as evidence of Spirit baptism, the importance of religious training, and the ordination of women plagued the denomination for much of its first decade.[40]

The racial environment that, clearly, led to the church's creation in 1914 continued to affect the relationship between the now exclusively Black and exclusively White Pentecostal sects. Thirty years later, these divisions were exacerbated when eight White Pentecostal denominations met in Des Moines, Iowa, to form the Pentecostal Fellowship of North America (PFNA). The largest of these was the Assemblies of God; no Black denominations were invited. Ironically, while churches, denominations, and now large-scale organizations like PFNA were segregated, Blacks and Whites were still coming together at Azusa-like revivals being led by White Pentecostal evangelists like Oral Roberts, Rex Humbard, and the now-notorious James Bakker and Jimmy Swaggart, both of whom were Assemblies of God ministers. In 1994, members of the PFNA traveled to Memphis, an event dubbed "The Memphis Miracle," where they apologized for excluding the Church of God in Christ from the organization. At that meeting, they created the cross-racial Pentecostal and Charismatic Churches of North America (PCCNA). The first chairman of that organization was the COGIC Bishop of Brooklyn, Ithiel Clemmons.

The Assemblies of God/Church of God in Christ split did not just create Black and White versions of the same denomination: the two sects are different in several important ways. While COGIC retains an episcopal structure, with bishops overseeing regional jurisdictions, the AOG has continued to reject denominationalism and endeavors to take on very little central authority. Its churches are congregational, with elected leaders who do not serve for life. In fact, many AOG ministers serve part-time as the fellowship's self-sufficient congregations are fully responsible for their financial arrangements. While churches are autonomous and self-governing, the church has a clear structure of districts (similar to COGIC jurisdictions), policymaking boards and councils, and even a superintendent who serves as the chief executive officer for the fellowship of churches. This structure makes AOG a blend of congregational and presbyterian polity where churches are affiliated with the Assembly's "General Council."[41]

Recommendations for ministerial credentials are made at the district level, but the credentials themselves are issued by a General Council Credential Committee. The General Council is similar to COGIC's General Assembly; it meets biennially and is (when in session) the legislative authority of the fellowship. Evidence of a "divine call" and active engagement in ministry are base requirements of credentialing. The fellowship offers three credentials: a provisional certificate, a license, and ordination. These credentials are similar to the Aspiring Minister, Licensed Minister, and Ordained Elder credentials in the Church of God in Christ, but there are fundamental differences. All three credentials are transferable across the fellowship's churches (i.e., the first two are not local licenses only) and possessors of any of these credentials are authorized to perform the ordinances and ceremonies of the church.[42] While there are a number of Bible colleges, institutes, and one seminary associated with the Assemblies of God, no degrees or diplomas are required for licensing or ordination.

While some administrative duties (e.g., voting on the General Council) were originally reserved for men, most of the important ministerial duties of clergy have always been available to women. As early as 1918, women served as pastors, assistant ministers, both home and foreign ministers, and evangelists. In those and other roles, women were free to perform any of the ordinances of the church as an ordinand. That ended, briefly, in 1931 when the AOG General Council was asked to address the question of women's roles and decided women would only be ordained as evangelists. As such, they were denied the "priestly" abilities to perform sacerdotal acts. In fact the words "bury the dead, administer ordinances of the church, and perform the rites of marriage" were actually stripped from women's credentials at both the General and District levels.[43] This change was undone four years later by another resolution. Today, women can qualify for any grade of credential, have full rights to administer church ordinances, and can serve in all levels of church ministry and leadership.

COGIC's Institutional Identity Crisis

Like most large institutions, the Church of God in Christ is a complex organism. The second youngest of the eight major Black denominations, it has successfully straddled multiple boundaries in ways that have made it an extremely attractive option for Black parishioners in the United States and hundreds of non-Black parishioners around the world. Much of the credit is due to how seriously it takes its responsibility, as a primarily urban and Black church, to be *in the world* while never abandoning its strongly held theological mandate to not be *of the world*. A strategic blending of orthodoxy and orthopraxis, of conservative theology and liberal politics, of hierarchical and autonomous polities make the denomination unique among its peers.

That said, it is not so unique as to be easily disregarded as an anomaly in our attempts to understand the behavior of either religious communities or religious individuals. In fundamental ways, this immense organization looks identical to other mainline Protestant denominations, historically Black and predominantly White alike. The COGIC statement of faith is nearly identical to that used in other denominations. The themes and styles in its music and liturgy represent both a reflection of and the evolution of non-Pentecostal worship. Again, it hasn't always been a "Black-denomination" and shares an active engagement of the supernatural with the Assemblies of God and other Pentecostal denominations. Certainly the relationships between call and practice are, in part, attributable to the racial and theological dynamics governing the Church of God in Christ. However, the experiences and phenomena described in the chapters that follow are certainly found in any number of Black or White, Pentecostal or non-Pentecostal, evangelical or mainstream congregations.

In many ways, COGIC's complexities leave the church struggling with the same kind of identity negotiation processes that are uncovered in conversations with its clergy. The issues I raised with COGIC clergy are being wrestled with by COGIC leadership. Does the church have the authority to affirm or denounce one's belief in a call to the ministry? Does the competition for parishioners, particularly the well-educated professional types who can support an expanded (and expensive) vision, require a matching slate of well-educated, professional clergy? Can the denomination's desire to evangelize the world as a *global* entity be accomplished with a mostly volunteer army of clergy whose secular responsibilities constrain even their labor in *local* congregations? Finally, how long can they withstand the encroaching demands of hundreds of well-qualified women to have their say in local pastorates, the regional bishopric, and beyond?

These institutional challenges provide a backdrop for the identity work that the men and women who serve within this church must engage in. The claims that ministers make about their clerical identity are shaped by the culture and context of this complex organization. Certainly, the church has conventional expectations for its clergy. They would like them to be knowledgeable about scripture, doctrine, and religious principles. They also take great care to describe their rationale for continuing the conventional-traditional separation of spheres for men and women in ministry. Nevertheless, the complicated social contexts that exist around and within this organization make strict adherence to these expectations difficult. The institutional ambiguities that these difficulties yield create opportunities for clerical aspirants to overcome potential barriers to both ministerial practice and ministerial progress.

Becoming the Called

"Heard a Voice from Heaven Say"

Calling Narratives among Black Pentecostals

Eli perceived that the Lord had called the boy. Therefore Eli said to Samuel, "Go, lie down; and it shall be, if He call you, that you must say, 'Speak, Lord, for Your servant hears.'" So Samuel went and lay down in his place. Now the Lord came and stood and called as at other times, "Samuel! Samuel!" And Samuel answered, "Speak, for Your servant hears."

1 Samuel 3:8–10

When someone says they're called to the ministry, the Lord has a specific task for them and a leadership position, preferably for the upbringing and edifying of the saints. It means He brings them to the forefront.

Kenya, Missionary

When Church of God in Christ ministers describe what it means to be called to the ministry, they talk about it as an inescapable imperative. This sense of requirement is different from any sense of commitment they may feel just serving as members of a church or even in other leadership positions. As Jimmy explained:

I was already very committed to my work as a deacon. When [my pastor] called me to be a deacon, I felt like I was serving him. Sometimes I would slack off because I knew that if I wasn't available, the other brothers would pitch in. But when God called me to preach? Slacking went out the window because you get a higher level of accountability. God picked me specifically for a job no one can do but me.

Jimmy, like many ministers, was already active in some kind of church work before receiving a call to ministry. Some were simply contributing members of church ministries, and others were already leaders. In either case, involvement in church work was often a result of some human imploring them to join or take a leadership position. This would commonly happen through friend or family networks where, for example, a singer would be recruited by friends who sang in the choir. Leadership positions may then be earned through nomination processes, similar to elections for leadership in any other voluntary association. While parishioners are encouraged to seek divine direction on how they should connect to congregations, many find themselves doing church work through fairly routine introductions to it.

The "call to ministry" is quite different. While human social networks may play a role in confirming one's belief that she is called, the major player in the calling narrative is always God. Regardless of whether the call comes through a series of experiences or one key encounter, God alone is credited with directing them into ministry. This "vertical call," between the earthly aspirant and a heavenly God, is described as a social experience. Some of those experiences are much more social than others. But even when experiences come as "an emptiness in my spirit" rather than a voice or a God-given vision, accounts inevitably include some clarifying moment confirming this as an encounter with God.

In terms of impact on one's sense that they are called to the ministry, there are fundamental differences between these encounters with God and the interactions with credentialing boards that follow. The process of credentialing, described in chapter 3 as a "horizontal call," is intended to affirm the calling narrative. Churches affirm an aspirant's belief that he or she did not choose ministry, but that it was chosen for them. This affirmation is, by definition, a social experience. Yet, the idea that someone or something else chose the aspirant's path suggests a more "vertical call" involving a human chosen and a divine chooser.

The sociologist Emile Durkheim said "the believer who has communed with his god is not simply a man who sees new truths that the unbeliever knows not; he is a man who is stronger."[1] The stories in this chapter speak to ministers' beliefs that they had real encounters with God, encounters that initiated their transition from lay-members and lay-leaders to something fundamentally different. Accounts of this "communion with their god" suggest that some of these encounters may be seen as conversational and interactive as any other social interaction. Sociological accounts of religious experience are full of descriptions of, presumably, one-way, bottom-to-top "conversations" religious adherents claim to have with God through prayer and meditation; adherents pray to God and maybe God responds. This is certainly not the case in these narratives. These top-to-bottom vertical social interactions are thought to be initiated by God (the caller) through various means; the respondent, in this case, is the callee.

The Call and Professions

In order for an aspiring minister to be licensed in many Christian denominations, they have to convince a credentialing body that they have received a vertical call. While some denominations may have tried to downplay the idea that this call should be some kind of explicitly supernatural experience, the requirement that an aspirant articulate some sensation of being specifically set apart for religious service is fundamental to licensing. Ordination committees would consider "choosing to do ministry" an unacceptable choice. While it is acceptable to choose to join a church auxiliary, one must have had something external to them serve as a catalyst to pursue the ministries legitimated by clerical credentials.

The idea of a calling is not unique to the clergy. In fact, early definitions of professions and vocations—which include medicine, teaching, and the law—have included the idea that one must be "called to the field." Even the Latin roots of the words "profession" and "vocation" suggest religious origins. The *professio* was a sacred oath taken by monastic clergy in response to a call to ministry. The word "vocation" comes from *vocare*, which means "to call." Compared to "occupation" (*occupatio*), whose Latin root translates as "a means of passing one's time," one can see how having a profession is fundamentally much more important that merely having an occupation. This is similar to the distinctions some might make of a "career" and a "job": one is a lifelong pursuit while the other may just be a temporary employment situation.

Ultimately, Max Weber and other sociologists argued that vocations and professions were the secular means whereby we play out spiritual callings. Weber criticized the idea that one could play out the demands of a divine call by stealing away in monasteries. Instead, he argued, "the only way of living acceptably to God was not to surpass worldly morality in monastic asceticism, but through the fulfillment of the obligations imposed upon the individual by his position in the world. That was his calling."[2] Even as he made the call a secular task, Weber still retained the sense that the obligation was not to self, or even to religious community, but to God. The sociologist Richard Christopherson, in his study of the relationship between "calling" and "career" amplified this reasoning, describing a calling as a "task set by God with a sense of obligation to work for purposes other than one's own."[3] This sense that physicians, teachers, jurists, and clergy were primarily responsible to a higher power was instrumental in increasing not only the status afforded them by their clientele but also the considerable amount of trust they received.

Another sociologist, Robert Bellah, defines jobs and careers as work that, at its essence, benefits the worker either financially or in social standing and prestige.[4] A calling, on the other hand, is not to be judged or measured by what one reaps from it. Instead, a calling is best measured by the benefits others gain from how actively "the called" pursues it. Being called to a vocation signifies a rejection of financial motivations for working. This ethic of service suggests that callees do not work for compensation. Instead, they are satisfied with being barely compensated for the work they do. The distinction is important, particularly in the lives of these ministers, because many of them will never receive a paycheck or anything else physical in exchange for their service. In fact, many of them describe the "decision" to accept the call as irrational because of the costs incurred by doing so.

As the remuneration received by professionals in the medical and legal fields began to rise, the trust and status they received was tied less to their altruism than to their mastery of esoteric medical and legal knowledge. Referring to oneself as being "called into medicine" slowly went out of fashion as physicians' professional prestige was retained without such acknowledgements. In defining "calling" as something different from "career" and "job," Bellah argues that those professions that have historically been categorized as callings are becoming more career-like. While he doesn't speak directly to any changes in the clergy, the decreasing benefits accrued by clerical aspirants places those called to ministry squarely within the boundaries of his definition: "It's harder and harder to understand the idea of calling as society has become more complex and utilitarian and expressive individualism more dominant."[5]

As it is, only the social-service professions (including teaching) have managed to retain the use of the word "call" to describe their motivations for doing this kind of work. Understanding oneself this way, as having a "call" to it, appears to have empirically testable outcomes. For example, the education scholar Robert Serow offers evidence that teachers who claim a call to teach display significantly more enthusiasm, commitment to teaching, and willingness to accept extra duties.[6]

Some scholars suspect that the choice to go into the ministry is likely a result of the same kinds of factors that lead people to enter other professions.

David Moberg argues that religious values lead Roman Catholics to enter the clergy while Jews and Protestants are motivated by "humanistic values."[7] Family influences, like being a child of a minister or having relatives in religious or social work, also play a role. Methodist theological students listed four factors: early religious training, participation in church youth activities, influence of a pastor, and higher than average marks in school. Moberg writes that "personal ambition and striving for status are sometimes underlying motivations making men feel a call to the ministry."[8]

That said, in their comparisons of the call to ministry for congregation-centered (e.g., Southern Baptists), institution-centered (e.g., Episcopalians, United Methodists), and Spirit-centered (e.g., Assemblies of God, COGIC) denominations, the historian Barbara Zikmund and her colleagues state that clergy in Spirit-centered denominations are more likely than clergy in the others to claim a specific moment "when they realized that God was calling them to the [ordained] ministry."[9] They state that "clergy in the Spirit-centered denominations are quite unlikely to become clergy in their denominations unless they can recall a particular moment when they became convinced that God wanted them to devote their lives to ministry—ordained and otherwise."[10] Clergy in denominations like COGIC are more likely than the others to cite the "importance of their conviction that God wishes them to be ordained and their belief that through ordained ministry they can serve God better."[11]

Conventional Calls vs. Blitzkrieg Calls

Before we turn to more detailed descriptions of the calling moments described by these clergy, it is important to discuss calling narratives more broadly. When I encounter new people and we engage in the usual conversations about our geographical origins and jobs, I often ask how they chose that occupation. The stories are as varied as you would imagine. From childhood dreams of pursuing a career to plans diverted by bad grades in pre-med courses, everyone has a story they can tell about the path into their current line of work. Even these ministers, most of whom have full-time jobs in secular occupations, were able to explain how they became bus drivers and hair dressers, teachers and bank managers. People's descriptions of their career decisions usually took two forms: the more common long and winding road, and the more occasional sudden revelation. Similarly, the clergy have descriptions of the events that led them to pursue a "career" as ministers. These stories take two forms as well.

First are the seemingly ordinary calls, calls to the ministry that look very much like the long and winding road that leads others into their professions. People follow inclinations that they have had since their youth; they grow into ministry. Others are nurtured along. Like the descendants of Aaron, the biblical priest, they follow in family footsteps, pursuing ministerial credentials because it is a family tradition. Still others are drawn into the ministry at later points in their lives. Some are converted to Christianity and find such value in the way that conversion changed the trajectory of their own lives that they seek out ways to share that life-changing message with others. These and other means of transformation from lay-member to aspiring clergy exist across denominational and temporal boundaries. While our attentions are often drawn to the dramatic stories—Moses hearing a voice from a burning bush, St. Augustine hearing a voice commanding him to read his Bible—most of the aspirants who sit in seminaries across the country describe far less extraordinary pathways into the ministry. That is not is not to say that they do not credit God with leading them into ministry or consider this decision a major turning point in their lives. They certainly do credit God, but this process of discernment is less clear. They are more likely to have found what the philosopher Carol Ochs refers to as "the holy in the ordinary."[12]

We are especially likely to find these more conventional experiences in the more mainline religious traditions, what Zikmund calls institution-centered and congregation-centered denominations. She and her colleagues determined that the majority of clergy in these denominations could not point to an explicit moment where God led them to pursue credentialing (i.e., become clergy) in order to render service to their religious community.[13] While God played a role, they were much less clear about what God was asking them to do.

They have their models throughout the biblical record, even in the stories of Jesus' call of his own disciples. While the story of Jesus' call of Andrew and Peter depicted in the Gospel of Mark might lead readers to believe these two fishermen were suddenly stricken by a passion to follow Jesus merely at the command "follow me,"[14] the expanded version of this history in the Gospel of John shows a different story.[15] These men were already serving as disciples of Jesus' cousin John the Baptist. They were primed for at least a year to consider Jesus' command and agreed to follow him only after John had been jailed. Critics of more dynamic calls point to this story as well as the fairly ordinary means whereby Isaac became a patriarch, Daniel became a prophet, and Timothy (a "preacher's kid") became the first bishop of the church at

Ephesus. They argue that God speaks slowly through scripture, prayer, circumstances and open doors, circumstances of our own interests and abilities, our gifts, and through inner impressions.[16]

The radio personality, author, and pastor Woodrow Kroll actively implores churches to be more attentive to those who have these conventional calls. He is even more direct in his advice for people who are waiting for a more dynamic revelation that they should pursue lifetime ministry as a career:

> Certainly nothing is wrong with one being a plumber . . . or a postal employee. For what are you waiting? Throw down that plunger . . . and pick up the powerful and living Word of God. Listen to His gentle prodding, hear His still, small voice; examine your gifts; and assume that He wants you in lifetime ministry. When you step out in faith, He will confirm His call. You'll know.[17]

The alternative to these more conventional encounters is what Kroll dubs "blitzkrieg calls," named after the tactic German pilots used in World War II. These "lightning war" attacks were sudden, surprising, and thought to shock their enemies as if they were struck by lightning. The biblical model most often given when Black preachers are asked about their own call is that of Paul's call on the road to Damascus: "Suddenly a light shone around [Paul] from heaven. Then he fell to the ground, and heard a voice saying to him, 'Saul, Saul, why are you persecuting Me?'" (Acts 9:3–4). This sudden call, while more dynamic than some, is a good example of a blitzkrieg call in both its suddenness and its impact.

Unlike the more conventional calls, which may go unheeded until after multiple confirming experiences, blitzkrieg calls seem designed to shove rather than draw callees into submission. While these calls do not always come in the same fantastic way that Paul experienced, these "clarion calls"[18] or "flashes of insight"[19] are clearly recognized as powerful catalysts for those men and women who experience them. For them, there is no mistaking them for anything other than an encounter with the divine aimed at redirecting their lives.

While these are the stories we hear about most often in the Bible, we are still surprised when someone experiences them in a contemporary context. In fact, John Calvin, in championing the role of the preacher, suggested that God may not operate this way any longer, stating that "He dwells not among us by a visible presence, so to make an audible declaration of his will to us."[20] He goes on to say that "it is true that He might do this either by himself, without any means or instruments, or even by angels; but there are many reasons why He prefers making use of men."[21] Kroll, too, is dismissive of these blitzkrieg calls, stating that "if budding preachers and missionaries are looking for burning bushes, fire flashes from heaven, or angelic announcements, they can forget it. God doesn't normally work that way. He works quietly—convicting, convincing, and confirming that He has a work for us to do."[22] Kroll worries that people mistakenly expect the call to ministry to come in a dramatic way and, as a result, miss the call when it does come.

In spite of some scholars' beliefs that God does not operate in this manner, examples of blitzkrieg calling experiences can be found throughout biblical and historical records. Citing the pastoral psychologist Robert Wicks, the journalist Larry Witham reports that many Protestant ministers do report having an "experience" that prompted them to enter the clergy: "Rarely is it something slow."[23] Blitzkrieg calls are especially prevalent in both Black and Pentecostal accounts. In fact, extraordinary calls were so common in Black religious communities that the famous author and orator Booker T. Washington claims:

> In the earlier days of freedom almost every coloured man who learned to read would receive "a call to preach" within a few days after he began reading. Usually the "call" came when the individual was sitting in church. *Without warning*, the one called would fall upon the floor as if struck by a bullet, and would lie there for hours, speechless and motionless.[24]

While Washington's story is likely intended to ridicule the idea, his description of the calling moment is not that far from the way some in my sample described their personal calling experiences.

Sometimes those experiences can be just as eerie as the one Washington describes. For example, Mona describes two experiences she had in church that made clear to her that God intended her to be more than just a Sunday school teacher:

> We began to speak in tongues, and the Holy Ghost interpreted those tongues saying, "I have anointed you to teach My Word." He said that, "My Word will cut, cut, and cut," but the Lord also said, "But My Word will heal, heal, heal." And another Sunday at a different church, the Holy Ghost began to move on one of the ladies. She got up from the piano and came

over and said exactly the same words that the Holy Ghost had spoken, "I have anointed you to teach My Word. My Word will cut, cut, cut," and this woman took my hand and just began to move my hand up and down, saying, "My Word will cut, cut, cut." Then the Lord used her to take my hand to bring it back and forth, sideways, to let me know, "but My Word will heal, heal, heal." I knew that I had heard from the Lord, and I knew the change, the complete change that had come in my life.

As implausible as this story might seem, Mona described it with as much excitement in the interview as she might have experienced the day it happened. Other blitzkrieg stories were presented with the same commitment and air of veracity. Mona certainly could have told me a more conventional story. After all, she was already a popular Sunday school teacher when God called her into the credentialed ministry. But there may be a benefit to these more spectacular calls. Having a dramatic story, within certain culturally defined boundaries, may inoculate a callee from accusations of illegitimacy in ways a conventional tale may not.

Certainly, anyone with the requisite set of skills—teaching, writing, speaking, leadership—can look and feel like a minister. This is especially possible if aspirants also have the character and commitment to church work that ordination committees deem important for successful ministry. There is no reason a person with those traits should not be able to say "I enjoy this kind of work" or "I see the money people with my skills make in this field" and then be drafted into the ministry. Neither statement would surprise or be problematic for other professions' gatekeepers. In the case of COGIC clergy, a calling narrative—that is, a story of an interaction between God and man—is a requirement. The COGIC manual says this explicitly: "[an Aspiring Minister] should be able to convince others that God called him to preach."[25] It isn't enough to say you chose ministry; one must prove, in this story, that ministry chose them.

Receiving the "Call to Ministry"

Whether they experienced it conventionally or in a sudden, blitzkrieg fashion, none of the ministers found it difficult to respond to the simple request: "Tell me about your call." Their accounts of this influential moment were varied, ranging from drifting into ministry when the environment around them changed to being dragged into ministry when they felt changed themselves.

Drifting into Ministry

One of the patterns that was immediately discernible in my conversations was that very few ministers were strangers to ministry in some form. In nearly every case, at the moment they received their call, most of them were already involved in some ministry: either as a leader or, more commonly, as a member. This level of church involvement is not abnormal in Black congregations. In Stephen Rasor and Christine Chapman's study of Black congregations, 74 percent of the lay-members they surveyed reported holding at least one leadership position in their congregation.[26] This was nearly double the average reported in Woolever and Bruce's survey of mostly White congregations.[27] These leadership positions took any number of forms, from heading key governing boards and committees to serving as officers (e.g., president, social chairperson) in church choirs and usher boards. Black churches have more opportunities for people to get involved than the national average. In fact, one of the COGIC churches that some of these ministers attended offered nearly one hundred different auxiliaries and ministries one could join.

Some aspirants could not pinpoint a moment when they felt God calling them into ministry. Instead, they describe a process whereby their lay ministry morphed into clerical ministry mainly because of their church's reorganization of how that ministry functioned. Because the COGIC license does not distinguish between those whose focus is primarily on service-oriented ministries and those whose focus is on preaching, some service-oriented ministries become inundated with people who claim a specific call to those ministries. As a result, it becomes an expectation that anyone participating in those ministries, whether they receive a distinct call or not, would pursue and be granted a clerical license. This was especially the case if that person were leading one of these ministries. Essentially, the responsibilities became "clericalized."

Debra's case is instructive. She had been raised in the church and was accustomed to being taken with her mother, a "Mother" of the church, to assist her in her duties. One of those duties required her to visit convalescent members of the church, reading the Bible to them, taking them meals, and assisting them with household cleaning. Even at a young age, Debra enjoyed these opportunities to serve members of the church in this way, but she never considered it "ministry." She continued serving in this capacity, eventually being put in a leadership position as the church reassigned those responsibilities to a church auxiliary dedicated to meeting those needs. As other women claiming a call to ministry—and this ministry in particular—began joining the ministry, Debra's lay-leader status was considered inappropriate. She was approached by the Church Mother and encouraged to pursue licensing as a Deaconess, the first stage in women's path to clergy. Seeing this as a formality, Debra first became a Deaconess and ultimately an Evangelist in the church. At the time of the interview, her primary ministry continued to be service to seniors and convalescent members even though, as an Evangelist, she is now capable of running revivals and other less service-oriented tasks.

Those ministers who described this slow march into ministry were often older and always female. This is likely the case because of shifts that took place in the roles and responsibilities assumed by women as opportunities for church leadership expanded beyond the roles of the Church Mother. As the Deaconess and Evangelist roles began to become more prominent and take on more responsibilities, women who were already serving the church in service-oriented lay-ministries were drawn into the clergy as those ministries became licensed clerical ministries. For example, women who were visiting hospitals and prisons were eventually required to carry a clerical license in order to maintain their access. For them, the environment changed; they didn't.

Urges

From an outsiders' perspective, the catalyst for "drifting" ministers' moves into ministry was changes in how ministry was organized. The ministers still attributed their "call" to God. Amelia, who found herself in a cohort of women required to pursue licensing in order to continue participating in her church's street-evangelism ministry, appealed to the idea of "ordered steps." This framing, drawn from a passage in Psalms (37:23), allows for a vertical call in which God directed people into ministry by shaping the environment around them, even if they never felt a key moment where he seemed to actively direct their movements. This is a different perspective than that expressed by people who describe their sense that God was actively shaping their passions. Those ministers spoke about feeling a sense that they were to do something more profound in ministry than they already were.

This understanding that they were to do ministry, as clergy, sometimes came as a result of experimentation. For Chris, he felt that he had to do something, but clarity about that task came over time:

I didn't know the youth ministry was going to be my calling. It took a few years for that to develop in my life. As years went by I started finding myself gravitating more to the youth ministry. But then I started seeking God and saying, "Lord is this where you want me" and He would affirm that by "yes this is where I want you to be." He didn't say it so much as I felt that was all my heart desired to do.

In some ways, Chris sits at the intersection of those who drifted into clerical ministry and those who felt a specific urge to become a minister. Like the "drifters," those ministers who felt urged into the clergy were already involved in ministry at some level. Unlike the drifters, many of them were involved in lay-ministries unrelated to the clerical roles they ultimately found themselves pursuing.

Natalie, who had been a choir member, started to feel a growing interest in what she refers to as "outreach ministry" (i.e., street ministry, foreign missions). Experiencing success in these ministries as a layperson led her to the belief that she was called to become a missionary, work that does not require a clerical credential but is considered a clerical office in the Church of God in Christ. This sense that one should pursue ministry was described in many ways. Some described feeling an almost physical attraction to the ministry, claiming they felt "a tug in my spirit," "an unnatural emptiness inside," or "a deep hunger for something deeper in God." Others spoke more simply of "unctions" or "aspirations about the ministry."

Many ministers describe these feelings as building over long periods of time. A common theme among these ministers was the sense that they had been gradually drawn into ministry with congregants that were similar to them in some way. Dana, who had survived a number of operations following a nearly fatal accident, drew on this experience as God's preparation for a particular kind of ministry: "From what I've been through, I'm more into the sort of hospital or nursing home ministry, deliverance and healing. I really feel that this is where God has really been preparing me to have an impact. I believe God's telling me that I was being prepared for something down the line."

Men, who were more likely than women to describe an "urge" into ministry, often drew on their personal experiences with addiction or the penal system as their entry point into ministry. They usually described being attracted to ministering to other men who were homeless, drug and alcohol addicted, or former convicts. They usually framed these attractions in a basic way: that God had delivered them from these issues and they felt a responsibility to reach back and pull other men out as well. As many of these men were drawn into the church by their church's outreach ministries, joining these ministries became an outlet for those responsibilities. As a result, being given opportunities to channel these interests compounded their sense that God was pulling them in a particular direction. Curtis's comments suggest that his passions for street-evangelism were recognized by his pastor; given opportunities to pursue those passions, he found them growing as a result of positive experiences:

> [My pastor] automatically understood my drive and my calling to street ministry, so that's where he placed me. . . . I was able to develop a sense of responsibility that the Lord had called me to minister to those who wouldn't ordinarily walk into the church. There was a spiritual high that I would get every time we would conclude a street ministry. I began to build a real confidence . . . that that was my true calling, because the more I put my foot forward in that ministry, the more people tended to respond. There was a sensitivity to those who, you could say, was traveling the same road that I think confirmed the fact that this is the area of ministry that God had chosen for me to participate in.

Although Curtis attributed his call to God's choices, you can see the more natural influences—his own drive, his pastor's direction, his emotional responses to his successes—that played a role in his ultimate pursuit of ministerial credentials. Like many of the men in my sample, Curtis' background enabled him to find common ground with the people he ministered to. His own history with drug addiction attributed to his "sensitivity to those . . . traveling the same road." By being given a platform through which to channel that sensitivity, he found himself pulled into ministry conventionally rather than having the kind of blitzkrieg moments that some of his peers would experience.[28]

Other men described concomitant sensations of being drawn away from one ministry and drawn into another. Bill, who had been handpicked to serve as a junior deacon, described his growing dissatisfaction with that role and his sudden sense that he was supposed to switch gears:

> I did it for maybe 2 or 3 years. I was very good at it. But shortly thereafter I began to be very discontent with it. For some reason I didn't feel I should be there. And I felt a real tugging on my heart to do something else, but I had no idea what that was. Then the Lord dropped it into my spirit—and it really wasn't from a message or anybody prophesying to me—just literally one day He just dropped it into my spirit that He wanted me to preach and teach His people.

Calling Narratives among Black Pentecostals | 53

While these urges were usually felt over long periods of time, some ministers described blitzkrieg calls in which they suddenly felt an urge, often described in physical terms, to pursue ministry. The catalyst for this sensation was often not directed at them, but they still described the urge as key to their belief that they were to become ministers. They described situations in which a pulpit speaker would prophesy, to no one in particular, that God was calling someone in the congregation into the ministry. Bob explained: "It was crazy. Like someone had punched me in the gut. I knew that God was speaking to me right then and before I even knew what was up, I was at the altar crying like a baby, giving up. Giving in, you know?"

Voices

The descriptions that follow may seem hard to believe. I shared some of these stories with a colleague who laughed and said that if someone presented such stories in his religious tradition, that person would be laughed out of the church. This is not far from the early experiences of certain world-renowned Pentecostal preachers like Oral Roberts. As a teenager, Roberts had been diagnosed with tuberculosis. On the way to a meeting with a faith healer, Roberts claims to have heard God speak directly to him, saying, "Son, I am going to heal you and you are to take My healing power to your generation." In his description of Roberts's subsequent healing and call, the historian Leigh Schmidt says that Roberts's "very intimacy with divine speech proved a two-edged sword, imperiling his standing in the wider society and ultimately turning him from evangelist to laughingstock."[29]

Lily Tomlin once asked, "Why is it that when we talk to God we are said to be praying, and when God talks to us we're schizophrenic?" Fascinatingly, my respondents described their experiences with a sense of awe and with no hint of embarrassment or shame. These experiences of hearing God speak were only surprising to most of them because of the unexpected message. They believed God could speak to them; they just didn't expect this to be something He'd say.

Like the urges that other aspirants felt, hearing God's voice took different forms. Some callees described hearing God speak audibly. For many, this blitzkrieg moment of their call is one of the only times that God has spoken to them this way. Unlike those who felt God call them inaudibly, those who heard an external voice always describe that voice as masculine. They also used similar language, often describing the voice as a "still small voice," a phrase that would be known to them because of its use in a well-known story of God speaking to his prophet Elijah (1 Kings 19:12). The voice was never described as yelling, a principle that is surprising because the voice was often heard in the midst of a religious service in which music was playing or someone was speaking. In spite of the noise that might have enveloped the callee, they claimed to have heard the voice as clearly as I could hear them speaking in the quiet interview spaces. Monique described her encounter with the voice this way: "While I was in Schambach's tent meeting, the Lord spoke to me. The Lord spoke to me as clear as I'm speaking to you. And I would even say clearer. Because in the midst of the people praising and worshipping God, I heard God say to me, 'I have called you to be an evangelist.'"

Monique's account contains many features common to other accounts of audible voices. While all of these accounts did not happen in the midst of a service (e.g., some heard voices while reading the Bible or babysitting), they all knew immediately whose voice they were hearing. They also volunteered this idea that the voice was audible and described the voice's statements as clear thoughts. For example, Joel said, "I heard an audible voice from God . . . in my left ear, Doc. I heard a voice that said, 'Look at the pastor that's upfront preaching.' Then the voice said, 'that's going to be you.'" Again, there were no hints, in either their expressions or their tone, that they felt awkward detailing these remarkable experiences. They also did not feel the need—as was recognizable both in callees who described urges and "internal" voices—to defend the call as something not born out of their own desires. Their conviction that they heard a clear and audible voice was all the sense they required that this was not of their own creation.

For every callee who described hearing an "outside" voice, there were two who described hearing God speak inaudibly either "in [their] spirit" or "in [their] head." Those callees who reported hearing an "inside" voice had the most difficult time describing their experiences. As Mark, an Aspiring Minister, explained:

I heard God speaking to me. Not aloud or anything. Some say they heard audible voices. Me personally, I don't believe in that dispensation of God. An audible voice, like you can hear me now, I don't know? But there is an inaudible voice by God that happens inside where I don't think that the ears play a part. I can understand it clear, but I don't hear it audibly. I hear it within from God during my quiet time.

Like their peers who heard an audible voice, those who heard God speak inaudibly described a voice that spoke specific words to them. They could recount actual phrases that they heard. Some of those phrases were fairly rudimentary, but others were as specific as those Oral Roberts described hearing.

Most could not describe what the voice sounded like. Instead they resorted to metaphors to describe the sensation, suggesting the difference between hearing an audible voice and an inaudible one was similar to reading a book aloud and reading it silently. Ultimately, both voices they could "hear" while reading were their own, but one would be processed by the eardrum while the other was processed only "inside the head." This feeling that the voice they heard was their own led to a higher level of defensiveness than was present in other callees' stories. Some, like Yvonne, described hearing the voice telling her what she was to do and then explain how she knew it wasn't just her own imaginings and desires: "For me it meant that He had shown me where He wanted to use me. I kept checking back to make sure it wasn't me making this up. I know I would've never in my wildest dreams wanted such a thing. I think that's how I knew that it really was Him and that scared me a bit." Appealing to a similar argument, Julian made the case that his response to his call was contrary to who he was and therefore evidence of God's involvement:

> In the midst of this service we were in praise, and I heard God say clearly in my head, "I want you to preach." And I broke down crying like a real kid. I was head of the deacons. I wasn't thinking about being a minister. And I broke down crying for about 10 minutes. I know the entire church looked at me because I wasn't that type of person. I still cry thinking on that time because it was a time that took me out of me. You know, hard guy, tough guy, Brooklyn cat, and somebody who was in full control of my life told me what they wanted me to do with my life. And it was the first time in a long time since my father that I ever felt that way of a person speaking to me.

Some callees made a point to differentiate themselves from people who had only felt an *urging* into ministry but didn't share their experience of a literal *call* into ministry. Abigail described feeling the Lord leading her to pursue the clerical credential. She was already actively involved in her church's shelter for homeless women but says she had an urge that kept coming back, reminding her that God wanted her to do something more: "I feel like it was in my spirit, but it was also strong enough for me to hear it." She went on to explicitly make the comparison, "I know some people talk about feeling something, but I think in my case, God saw that moving in my feelings wasn't getting us anywhere, so He had to be more clear by calling my name and telling me what He needed me to do." But when pressed on this, Abigail said that she never heard an audible voice. Instead, she described hearing God speak to her, "in her spirit," while praying.

Dreams and Visions

Apparently, God's use of the senses to reach out to potential ministers is not restricted to feelings and hearing. The most fantastical biblical stories of God's interactions with future patriarchs, prophets, and kings involve sight as well. Callees also speak of experiencing dreams and visions as the catalysts for their pursuit of ministerial credentials. While the terms "dreams" and "visions" might carry different connotations—visions, unlike dreams, occur while the person is awake and fully conscious—my respondents use the terms interchangeably. Gail describes one such vision that incorporated both sight and sound as she found herself in a conversation with God:

> It was the most amazing thing. I was sitting in my room and all of a sudden I could see these little, you know, the neon signs on Broadway where they move, that sort of thing, and I said, "I'm not going to remember all of this," and a voice was like, "Go get a pen and paper." So I went and got paper and pen and wrote what it was and said, "What do I do with this now?" The voice said "Go show it to the bishop and the pastor," so I did.

It was the rare interviewee who, like Gail, indicated that he or she was awake during these experiences. Only three callees described a lucid experience, one of which occurred (by the callee's own admission) under the possible influence of a number of postsurgical pain medications. Of the twenty-three other ministers who spoke of visions, it was clear from their descriptions that they were sleeping, even if only briefly.

While callees describe what they believe they are called to do in many ways, no one ever dreamed of doing what many refer to as "servant-ministry" or other ministries that are often associated with lay-members' religious work. For example, while Shana believes she is called to do missions work in foreign countries, she dreamed of herself ministering to an audience that, from her description, sounded like any other American Black congregation. No one spoke of dreams involving praying for people, doing street ministry, or working with children, in spite of these tasks being named as the primary focus of their specific calls. Instead, the dominant meme in callees' dream narratives is their speaking in front of an adult audience in some kind of sanctuary. The size of that audience varied, as did the location in which the moment occurred.

Men were far more likely than women to describe themselves speaking from a pulpit. This makes sense given the church's restrictions on women's involvement in pulpit ministry. Surprisingly, given our usual sense of male preachers in robes or other accoutrements marking them as playing a priestly role, it was the women who most often mentioned being in some kind of uniform in their dreams. Women in COGIC ministry wear different uniforms marking their credentials. These range from a simple black-and-white dress to a white dress with a small lace headpiece. Female callees described themselves "standing at the podium wearing white" or "in the whole Evangelist habit in the section where they sit."

While most visions are like these, some dreams are more oblique. In those dreams, which are usually repetitive enough to be experienced as a pattern, either a recurring image or recurring events leads aspirants to approach a spiritual leader at their church. Some images are obvious metaphors for ministry. George describes a vision of himself on a ship. People around him are drowning in the water and he has a lifesaver that he is throwing out to them. Fishing metaphors are common and in some cases quite vividly described. Luke relates a recurring dream of "deep sea fishing" where he kept catching fish he didn't recognize, fish "that you see on those wildlife shows, and every time I thought I had an easy catch—we even had pulled some of them onto the boat—they slipped off the hook or out the net." Only when he jumped into the water could he keep the fish he found himself trying to catch. He believes that was reflective of a call to foreign missions, explaining the fish as natives of other countries and having to jump into the water as having to "leave the ship in order to be effective at what I need to do."

Other dreams are much less clear. In these cases, clarity comes as a result of conversations with a trusted spiritual mentor. Joi, who believes she is called into the "ministry of deliverance," shared a set of troubling dreams:

> I had this dream about Satan in the church. The devil was walking around in the church, but the people didn't know it was the devil. At some point in this dream, he began to chase me around this table and he grabbed my arm. My arm was oiled, slicked, and I yelled "Jesus is stronger than you" and my arm slipped out of his hand. I woke up afraid, but I could still feel the devil's grip on my arm. Then I was having a second dream—like part

two—where he was walking around the church, and everyone was greeting him like he was just any other person in the church. He would look over at me, and cut his eye and smile, like "ha-ha, they can't see me." It scared me so much I went to Evangelist Myers and she connected it to other things I had told her. She showed me God was telling me that's what I was supposed to be doing. Deliverance is the area I'm supposed to be in.

Joi's account, as vivid as it was, could have meant anything. But she found the dreams decidedly clear as a message, both because of their repetition and because of their religious overtones. Everyone who spoke of having these metaphor-laced dreams and visions, which included dramatic stories of giant doves or rainbows sprouting from their chests, saw the images within them through a religious lens. Their religious community gives them a means of contextualizing what might just be treated as any other dream by the unchurched. Even when they described having these dreams as a child, they "remember" the experiences as being part of God's attempts to reach out to them.

Signs and Wonders

While most calls to ministry, like voices and even dreams, are depicted as fairly ordinary direct communications from God to the individual, some calls to ministry seem to suggest that God has a flair for the dramatic. One account of a pair of dreams is useful as a transition to the final set of narratives: stories about signs and wonders as calls. In this account, the dream was not the callee's. Instead it came from two unexpected sources. Carl described:

So one night my wife woke up, and she said, "Carl, I just had a dream that you were in a room with all these men, and you were preaching to them. You were a minister. You had the robe on." I didn't give it any thought. People dream things all the time and Tracey knows I'm into men's ministry. When I came home from work, she was on the phone with her girlfriend, an Evangelist from another church whose husband is a pastor. While she was talking to her girlfriend, her husband came in and said, "Babe, babe, let me tell you about this dream I had last night about Carl." She said, "Wait a minute, Tracey is on the phone telling me about a dream *she* had about Carl." So the husband began to talk and it was the exact same dream. My wife dropped the phone and was screaming because she and this guy had had the same dream on the same night.

If Carl accurately remembers the sequencing of these events, this is a fairly dynamic example of God reaching out to him. It isn't just a convincing example of a call for Carl but presumably is convincing to anyone else he tells. In fact, Carl describes this story as a confirmation of an urge he had already felt. As he indicated, he was already being urged into men's ministry. This sign was the moment that prompted him to approach his church leadership and begin the work of becoming a credentialed minister.

Other people would speak of confirmatory signs that pushed them to pursue a ministry they already felt an urge to consider. Donald spoke of wrestling with a call to ministry and being unable to sleep or keep food down for nearly a week. At the end of that week, a Saturday night, he turned on the television and at that very moment, a televangelist was looking at the camera and proclaiming, "My brother, God is telling me right now that He has called you, that He is pulling on you with the loose leash. Don't wait for God to bring out the choke chain. Give up and give in. The kingdom can't wait any longer." Donald said he jumped to his feet and called his pastor immediately. That Donald could so clearly remember the details of that evening, particularly the two kinds of leashes, makes this retelling more persuasive than if the televangelist had merely said "God is calling someone into ministry. Answer." The physical struggle he had that week seemed to confirm the message and, he argued, was key to prompting him to respond.

While they did not have the kind of middle-of-the-night resolutions Donald had, a number of other ministers also spoke of health or financial problems that they felt were signs from God that he wanted them to move into ministry. From lost voices to lost jobs, these signs were almost like threats from God, forcing them to make a decision. Adrienne pointed to where she had seen this approach from God in the Bible: "I knew how He had struck Zephaniah [sic] unable to speak until he agreed to name that baby John. God did that kind of thing then. He does it now too."

While many signs are as full of wonder as those I've just described, some people experience calls that we might consider very basic, calls that seem more "sign" than "wonder." For example, some people describe circumstances in which their Bible always falls open to the same scripture(s). In most cases, they feel that these scriptures are clearly aimed at directing them into ministry. For example, every time Alexis opened her Bible, it fell open to Isaiah 61:1, "The Spirit of the Lord God is upon me, because the Lord has anointed me to preach good tidings to the poor. He has sent me to heal the brokenhearted, to proclaim liberty to the captives, and the opening of the prison to those who are bound" Mylisha "felt the Lord" drawing her to 2

Timothy 4:5 ("But you be watchful in all things . . . do the work of an evangelist, fulfill your ministry.") while Dana was drawn to John 15:16 ("You did not choose me, but I chose you and appointed you that you should go and bear fruit . . .").

In a number of calling narratives, God seemed to use confederates to communicate or confirm a calling. Courtney describes a Sunday morning when two strangers (a man and a woman) came up to her and asked her if she wanted to be in the ministry. She never saw them again, but she believes that they were a sign that she was called; she didn't accept the call then because she was in the midst of a divorce. She describes being in a revival and the preacher said, "Somebody is here and God has called you to the ministry, but you're telling God I want you to do this and this and this and God told you He wants you to do this first." At that point she began praying about the earlier experience with the two strangers. Days later, a third sign came when her mother called, anxiously demanding to know why she didn't tell her that she was called to the ministry. Surprised, Courtney asked why her mother believed this. Her mother informed her that a family friend (a minister) told the mother not to worry about Courtney because "God was taking her through a test [the divorce] because she was called to the ministry."

Struggling with the Call

In whatever way the main calling experience happens, it is seen as a significant moment in the callees' lives. A number of ministers described the sensation of being "knocked off their horses," an allusion to the experience of the apostle Paul when he was called to do ministry. Even those ministers who were already doing ministry and drifted into the credentialing process found the decision to pursue clerical credentials to be a very big deal.

While my respondents differ in their descriptions of the way God reached out to them, there is a great deal of consensus on how callees' respond to the call. The emotions expressed are almost unanimously negative, ranging from fear and anxiety to anger and doubt. For example, Victor was fairly blunt in his recollection of his immediate response: "I think this call is something that I really fought against because I kind of had an idea of what it entailed and I really didn't want to do it."

A 1995 survey of aspiring White ministers shows that these responses are fairly common among aspirants to the ministry.[30] William Myers also describes this period, when ministers resist or struggle against the call, as a prevalent part of the calling narratives of Black ministers.[31] Common concerns include being forced to leave one's comfort zone, worries about being able to meet financial obligations, feelings of unworthiness, fear of the unknown, and having to deal with family objections and concerns.

The first of these—having to leave one's comfort zone—was best exemplified in my conversation with Gail. She was in her sixties when she felt God telling her to change cities, abandoning her long-standing relationship with her church, and go to seminary:

> [God] just said, "Go get some [religious] schooling." I'd been told three times, but didn't want to leave my church to go to school. That day when He called me, He said, "Do you love me more than these?" I remember that. And I said, "What?" And then I heard again, "Do you love me more than these?" And I said, "These who?" And then it occurred to me it was the church because they had been such a support to me. I cried. I never forgot it. I made such a racket crying. They had to take me in the bathroom. Eventually, I came back in and just continued crying quietly, and I said, "Alright, I know that I can leave them. I can leave anybody. It doesn't matter." And the next week I got the [admission] letter from the school and started at the Bible college that semester.

Gail's story has all of the trappings of the kinds of dynamic, blitzkrieg calls described in the earlier section. Nevertheless, she resisted, primarily because giving in would have disrupted her life. It would have been difficult enough to pick up and leave her life behind had she been young and just starting out on a career. But at this point, she had already retired and now felt God leading her to take a dramatic step with no sense of where it would ultimately end.

Some ministers found the call disruptive to their lives in other ways, complaining that they felt that God's timing was off. As Justine describes it, "I was coming out of one job, just had a car accident, and I began to hear a call, not the audible voice, but a voice in my spirit actually in the subway station and, I'm in tears, and I'm praying, but I'm feeling a sense of joy that there's something else about to happen." Numerous women concurred, pointing out that trying to pursue a ministerial call as a single woman was difficult. In fact, some even went to religious leaders with the hope that they would disconfirm the callees' belief that God was calling them into ministry. Men worried that pursuing a call, especially if it had educational requirements, would handicap their ability to use their time and financial resources in the pursuit of more lucrative opportunities. As we will see in chapter 5, these concerns were unwarranted.

Many callees felt that going this extra step, pursuing clerical credentials, wasn't necessary at all; they were fine doing ministry without them. Adam initially expressed deep ambivalence about pursuing a ministerial license and ordination. Only his desire to broaden his ministry prompted him to move in that direction:

> Like, I'm called to ministry, but I wasn't trying to get no license. I didn't have time for all that. What motivated me to go after it is when this guy told me about his ministry. He had just became an Elder and he shared that the opportunities open, that by becoming a Licensed Minister or Elder, the opportunities are bigger for you to do ministry. God confirmed in my spirit that this is not about a piece of paper or man ordaining you. It's about enlarging your territory so that you can have the liberty to minister in other areas, not just shelter or prison ministry but maybe marital counseling and stuff like that.

Adam believed that he was fully capable of doing ministry without having to pursue the clerical credential. He didn't need a license in order to be a success; his sense of a call was enough. For others, one of the biggest barriers to pursuing their call was their own doubts about their capacity to be successful in spite of it. These doubts resonated in different ways for callees. Some worried that they could not live up to the high level of moral responsibility credentialed ministry implied. Ministers spoke of not being ready to give up some habits or relationships in order to begin the credentialing process. Not only did they envision having to be more transparent with church leaders as part of the process, but they believed that any lingering issues would negatively impact their ability to minister effectively.

Juanita described having to be critically honest with herself, taking stock of what she would have to give up in order to claim to be a representative of COGIC's staunchly conservative doctrine:

> I couldn't have no hidden issues in my life because the Lord knows it and the enemy knows it and he will use that thing to trip you up. And when he screws you up, it's always in front of someone who has been watching your life and right there at the point in making the decision for Christ, they see me do something wrong. They will always see me that way. I've seen it myself and didn't want that kind of pressure.

Seth, an Elder and the son of a pastor, echoed Juanita's assertion, explaining that he didn't want to be a hypocrite in the pulpit, a pattern of behavior he had often seen in his father's associates, "I have seen too many of them in my life. I know I have things to work on and I'm not saying I'm waiting to be perfect, but before I go all the way with this, I need to be serious about what it's going to require."

Others made the case that they didn't have what it took, whether skills, personality, or even interest, to do what they felt God was requiring of them. Whether pointing to their distaste for public speaking or their desire to continue in the ministry they were already involved in, both men and women expressed their contention that God had made a mistake. Deana struggled because she couldn't see herself working with adults as effectively as she worked with children. Vance was so nervous about speaking in public that he had gotten an ulcer when even his secular job responsibilities required him to make weekly reports to his supervisors; a successful ministry as a preacher seemed out of the question.

Ironically, these beliefs that the callees weren't equipped to do ministry at a different level or in a different role strengthened their eventual belief that the call was divine in origin. Again and again, they pointed out the necessity of a divine push into ministry, arguing that they would never have made the kind of choice they felt they were being compelled to make. Adrienne appealed to conflicts between her call and her personality to make the case:

> He showed me a vision of me as an Evangelist, and for me I am very shy, very quiet. I have not ever liked attention, liked people looking at me. I was comfortable doing background work. Even though I know that He showed me that vision, I just kept thinking it couldn't be. You want to be obedient and all, but at the same time, I was petrified at the thought because I never looked at them and considered doing whatever they did. But I know that I didn't make that up. I wouldn't have fantasized that even if I was going to fantasize something.

Although Adrienne went on to become an effective leader, her initial doubts caused her to resist pursuing the clerical credentials for two years after her dynamic—and in her mind, quite clear—experience of a call to ministry.

In contrast to women, who tend to express their apprehension in terms of doubt, men frequently adopt the language of fear to describe their responses to the call. Asked what advice he might give an aspiring minister, Elder Chris responded, "A lot of people don't understand it's not the glorified position. It takes sacrifice, a lot of painstaking sacrifice from your families, from your friends. You've got to really know that God called you to do this because you're going to be left alone a whole lot and you're going to wonder 'God, is this really you that called me?"

Reverberating with the themes of difficulty, sacrifice, and loneliness, Chris' comments echo the sentiments of many of these men. The men were particularly fearful of pursuing a call to ministry because of their sense that it was a particularly serious undertaking. For men, this seriousness was heightened because, in due time, credentialing would lead to ordination and maybe a pastorate. This, of course, was not the case for women; they were restricted to leadership positions within churches and could never assume leadership positions over churches. The men worried that God held them to a higher standard, a standard that superseded not only one set for lay-members, but also one set for their sisters in the gospel who were also credentialed with Deaconess and Evangelist licenses. So when they felt themselves being led into ministry, they feared the responsibility, claiming that both God and man expected more of them and would hold them more accountable for failure (moral or otherwise). This idea was addressed by the pastoral theologians Howard Sugden and Warren Wiersbe; they stated that "the work of the ministry is too demanding and difficult for a man to enter without a sense of divine calling."[32]

It was not unusual for men to speak in very serious terms about how difficult they believed accepting the call would be. Carl, for example, stated that "for the rest of my life, I would have to know without a shadow of a doubt that what I said out of my mouth came from God. People could live or die from the things that I say because of the position I would hold." He went on to describe being a minister as "an enormous responsibility," saying if he could counsel himself as an aspiring minister he would say "be ready for whatever happens because it's going to be a long journey, it's going to be a tough journey, and it's not going to be easy." Bryant, now an ordained Elder, drew on a biblical example to describe his apprehension when he considered talking to his pastor about his call: "I felt like the sons of Zebedee when their mother asked Jesus, 'can my sons sit on your left hand and your right hand.' Jesus asked the woman if she knew what she was asking. That's how I felt. Like I was about to bite off a whole lot more than I could chew."

Labels and Leadership: Making Sense of the Call

Given this book's emphasis on people who claim a call to be clergy, but ultimately either can't or don't serve as leaders of congregations, it is useful to understand *what* my respondents believe they're called for. Zikmund and her colleagues state that "all contemporary understandings of ordained ministry are grounded in the tradition that clergy are 'called' by God, as well as the church, to assume 'holy' or 'priestly' responsibilities, such as sharing God's message through preaching and officiating at the sacramental rites of the church."[33] These men and women share a conviction that they are called to "holy" responsibilities. Understanding how they express that call is fundamental to understanding how they might continue to legitimate their identity as ministers in the absence of full or even part-time ministerial employment.

It is important to remember that for many COGIC ministers, the actual ministry that they do could just as easily be done by people who did not claim a call to ministry. Even after receiving licenses or ordination certificates, most of these men and women continue to serve alongside uncredentialed lay-members. In fact, as we learned in the section on people who drifted into credentialed ministry, some were serving as uncredentialed lay-members for years before recognizing and accepting a "call to ministry." This was especially the case for those who felt called to evangelism, exhortation, prayer, administrative, and teaching ministries. As a result, few ministers can claim their call gives them unusual access to religious labor; the work is shared with the "uncalled" and uncredentialed. Instead, they speak of being called for a particular purpose, being assigned a different position, or being given an unusual passion.

Purpose

For most of these ministers, the primary message received during the calling experience was instructions about the new direction God was leading them into. This was less often the case for those who drifted into ministry. These persons were already actively involved in ministry, and the clerical label was attached to their tasks. But for the majority of the callees, the charge was given at the time of the calling. That charge, as they describe it, was usually focused on a broad task such as preaching or evangelizing. While most can find their place in the five offices listed in Ephesians 4—apostles, evangelists, prophets, pastors, and teachers—don't always describe themselves in those terms. It was even more rare that someone said they were called, specifically, to one of the titles (e.g., Elder) used by COGIC to designate clergy. In fact, some weren't certain they were supposed to pursue ordination at all. Frank, an Elder, said, "I had always felt as though I was supposed to preach or be out front. Whether that was to be an Elder or not I'm not sure" indicating his clarity about the task he was to do, but uncertainty about the credentials.

Aspirants who had recently declared their belief that they were called to the ministry were just as certain about what they were supposed to do. Jonell, who had only recently received a call in spite of already being actively involved in multiple church auxiliaries, revealed that "being called means I've been set apart and I'm special and I have a job that I believe God has called me to do. We're all called to the ministry of Christ, but when I use that term for me, it is about preaching and teaching the Word of God, elaborating on the Word, about sharing the Word of God." Jonell drew a line between herself and other members of the church, recognizing the more general call "to the ministry of Christ" but explaining, in some detail, the tasks she feels called to perform. Men did this as well. For example, Vance differentiated himself from the uncredentialed members of the church's street evangelism team by saying, "I'm called with a different calling, with a special purpose and special assignment. Not just the ordinary mandate that we're all called to be ambassadors, but the mandate where I've been assigned a task to spread the gospel and to minister salvation to people."

Many ministers spoke like this, suggesting that all believers share a general call, but that those with a clerical call have specific assignments. Sharon expressed this idea directly: "I think the calling is specific, a calling to take on a role. I think we are all called to ministry but I think God has specific people He has in mind to take on a position in the body of Christ to do specific things that He ordained them to do whether it be preaching, a prophetic ministry, pastoring and He specifically called you out to specifically focus on that ministry that He's given to you."

The theologian Steven Croft makes the case that there are three dimensions of ministry: *episcopos* (the ministry of enabling other leaders), *presbyteros* (the ministry of the word and the sacraments), and *diakanos* (the ministry of the servant).[34] For the vast majority of these men and women, the call to ministry was synonymous with Croft's second dimension: a call to the "ministry of the word." In spite of the fact that the Church of God in Christ states that women are only authorized to "teach" (a distinction that is almost universally ignored in practice), both men and women use the word "preach" to describe the primary task of their calling.

That said, while most of the ministers considered themselves to be preachers primarily, only a fraction could be characterized as serving in that role in any consistent way. Because of local-church restrictions on Licensed Ministers and Deaconesses, they preach only when allowed to by their local pastors. Even licensed Evangelists and ordained Elders, both of whom are authorized to run religious services outside the local church, did not report having numerous opportunities to stand behind a pulpit with a prepared message at either their local church or any other. Preaching opportunities were rare, so callees usually added related responsibilities—that tended to use the same skill sets—to the list of tasks they were called to do.

There is a slight gender component to those additions. Men are more likely to speak about preaching in prisons and on the streets as street evangelists. They are especially likely to frame their calling as a "ministry to men." While ordained men are allowed to administer the sacraments, none spoke of that as a key component of their calling. More surprisingly, they also do not mention praying as something they feel called to do. This is in spite of the fact that, for most of these men, praying with congregants either at the altar or at their homes is the task most consistently assigned to them.

While women are nearly as likely to list "preaching" as a part of their call, they are more likely than men to operate in some teaching capacity. Women often express calls to teach that have some of the same specificity about audience as men. In their case, they often feel specifically called to teach children or women. They are less likely to have dreams or visions of themselves preaching at or behind a pulpit and are, therefore, more likely than men to reject pulpit ministry as their goal. Monica's comments exemplified this, defining her calling in terms of an Ephesians 4 office: "I know I'm called because I had a yearning, maybe even a revelation, something strong within me saying that this is what I had to do. I feel as though I am called to the ministry, not necessarily to be in the pulpit to preach, but into the ministry as a capital-T Teacher."

While many ministers focus on preaching or teaching as their primary mode of ministry, another of Steven Croft's three dimensions of ministry is reflected in people's calling narratives—the *diakanos*, or "ministry of the servant." Both male and female callees speak of this kind of ministry as something different from the preaching/teaching ministries, but just as valuable to the overall effectiveness of the church. In many churches, Deacons (and their female counterparts Deaconesses) are usually expected to carry out these responsibilities while Licensed Ministers, Elders, and Evangelists are presumed to carry out the *presbyteros*, or "ministry of the word." In fact, some women are satisfied with remaining Deaconesses, choosing to avoid the steps required for promotion to Evangelists. In their descriptions of the tasks they feel called to do, they give priority to the "helps" and service-oriented tasks rather than the preaching or teaching tasks we normally associate with clergy. In defining the idea of a call to the ministry, most callees speak of leadership in the ways I've described earlier, but some are insistent that the idea should be expanded.

For example, Tasha made the case that ministry could be "so many things." She spoke of having a special destiny related to "upbuilding God's kingdom" and that one's ministry could be "absolutely anything that you're called to do." Others echoed that idea, for example, Alesha, who believes that "ministry can be anything, from cleaning someone's home, to going to the hospital, to feeding the sick, to just sharing the gospel, so it's quite vast."

While a number of the ministers described other people's possible calls to "helps" ministries, only a few claimed a call to do that themselves. Nichole, an Evangelist for many years who serves on a jurisdictional ordination committee, spoke of this broadening of the idea of calling:

> There are some people who the Lord called and said your ministry is going to be dealing with the sick. It doesn't have to be teaching or preaching ministry. To me your call can be anything that has to do with the upbuilding of the church. It could be a ministry to keep the floor clean. It definitely does not necessarily mean preaching. But I was called to preach.

Position

When they were not speaking in specific terms about their key assignment, callees spoke more broadly of the position they saw themselves taking in church organizations. While only men can officially serve as head pastors of churches, both male and female ministers (at all four licensed/ordained stages), are considered clergy in their congregations. These titles come with similar authority and, depending on the actual role played within the church (e.g., youth pastor), many of the same responsibilities. As a result, many callees made it clear that they saw this additional distinction between themselves and lay-members: they were called to be leaders. Justine, the only woman in my sample who felt a call to pastor, may have summed up this idea best: "It's the difference between being a spiritual leader and a spiritual needer: someone who gives to the church and someone who takes from it."

In some cases, callees use terms that reflected how they were once just a church member, but now are members of a kind of church elite. Ramona says "people who are called have been led to be a part of God's *called out*." Jordan relies on common religious imagery to explain the difference between herself and others: "It's different than just being saved because He specifically called you out from among the sheep to focus on that ministry that He's given you." Ministers also described being "sanctified," a term that points to the Durkheimian idea of being set apart from the "profane" as something "sacred" and available only for God's use. Katherine describes herself as "chosen" but sees *herself* as responsible to do the sanctifying: "I'm called to the ministry to really separate myself from what is known as the norm, what is known as the layperson in the church." In some ways, this is also reminiscent of the biblical injunction "to whom much is given, from him much will be required" (Lk. 12:48), an idea more commonly known as Spider-Man's credo—"with great power comes great responsibility."

While most ministers seem to embrace this heightened visibility and status, some express a degree of anxiety about the call to leadership. Dwayne, who indicated a sense of distress when he felt God calling him, explains why he was fearful. His comments especially capture this sense that being in a leadership position carries some costs as well as benefits: "I was worried because I think the call to ministry, I would say it is more leadership-oriented. You're taking a role of a leader, of someone who is going to be held in high esteem many times and looked [up to] at a higher level from those in the congregation and lay persons. It's being called to a higher level of discipline and I don't know if I was ready for all that."

Passion

Finally, the ministers set themselves apart from lay-members by reporting a higher level of passion for ministry than their unlicensed compatriots might have. Misty spoke of ministry this way, as an irresistible impulse to do ministry, an impulse that not all believers shared. She said, "I think in a certain way that we're all called to do God's work, to do the same stuff, but some have a deeper drive than others. It's both what I do and who I am. When you're truly called, you just live, eat, breathe, sleep God and want to minister to people wherever you go." Misty attributes this passion specifically with the calling experience. While other ministers suggest that being called sets them apart to do uniquely different tasks, Misty states that the tasks are the same but the motivations to do them are different.

Numerous ministers concur with Misty's assessment. They resist the suggestion that God has low expectations for the uncalled, preferring instead to say the encounter with God left them with a higher level of commitment to the work than others might have. Owen, who describes himself as being "set on fire the day God called me," states that God's call charged him with a special yearning to do church work, something he says he didn't have for the many years he served as a member of his church's choir. This newfound enthusiasm led him to start his church's successful Ironman men's ministry.

He now spends twenty to twenty-five hours a week in this ministry since he retired from his job as a postal clerk. While Owen serves as the leader and spiritual guide for the auxiliary, he counts on four other men to organize the components of the auxiliary's programmatic offerings. None of these men have expressed a call to ministry, but Owen describes them as an invaluable resource who are "as committed to nurturing these other brothers as I am." Yet in a response to a later question about the authority of pastors, he described these men as having their primary allegiance to *him* as a leader, stating that he has to be careful to "give them their due" for fear that they'll get offended and abandon the ministry. He stated that ministers should be less thin-skinned because they claim to answer to God alone.

In the end, most callees claim a heightened commitment to the work of ministry, attributing that enthusiasm to something they see as more sustainable than just "interest in ministry." Penny, a Missionary, describes this best in her reaction to questions about noncredentialed teachers who join her in teaching the youth at her church: "Maybe laypeople see teaching children as something they desire or just enjoy doing. But being a Missionary? I see it as something I *need* to do." Kelly, an Evangelist, describes the difference in terms of having a gift and having a calling: "The difference I think between a gift and a calling is that a gift is something you can choose to do or not. A calling is something that you have absolutely no choice in. God will make it happen regardless of man's organization or structure and regardless of your feelings or maybe even your plans."

3

"All the World's a Stage"

How Congregations Create the Called

Then Moses answered and said, "But suppose they will not believe me or listen to my voice; suppose they say, "The Lord has not appeared to you."

Exodus 4:1

I believe the evidence of a call to ministry comes in the results. I don't mean a bigger crowd. I don't mean people jumping up and saying, "Girl, preach, man" because they'll do that anyway. I believe in people's lives being changed.

Michelle, Evangelist

When I asked ministers to tell me about their call to ministry, it was clear that they considered the most important social actor in their story to be God. From most callees' perspectives, just having God call them was enough to birth the ministerial identity. Even those who were already doing some form of religious labor as lay-members did not consider themselves to be "ministers" until the moment of the call. They certainly consider the work they did to be "ministry," but the labels "minister" and "clergy" were not something many applied to themselves until they experienced something they recognized as a call to assume one of those labels.

It is not enough to merely claim the "called" or "minister" identity. For that identity to become fully realized, it requires social interaction to give it meaning. In some ways, callees get this social interaction from God. For some of my interviewees, God's endorsement was all they needed. When asked why it took her so long to move from accepting her call to seeking any kind of licensing, Erika argued that she didn't feel a need to have anyone else legitimize what she felt, joking that "God said it, I accepted it, and that's all to it." While we can take very seriously callees' beliefs that God's labeling them as "minister" is all they require in order to assume that mantle, the fact is they aren't called to minister to God. Even in the case of those who describe themselves as "ministering to God" as "worship leaders," the very fact that the word "leader" is in their description suggests there is more to ministry than the interaction between themselves and the divine. The vertical call may be necessary to send someone into ministry, but it isn't enough. Ultimately, someone has to accept that ministry—making it a social identity—if being a "minister" is to truly mean anything.

I refer to this process of acceptance as "the horizontal call." Like the vertical call, it is a social interaction. What makes it different is that the other actor(s) make "minister" a positional designation rather than just a nominal one. While ministers tend to describe the calling primarily as a personal process, it is clear from my observations that there is a great deal of social strengthening of the "called" identity. The horizontal call brings the callee into relationship with a set of human actors, setting off a process in which the label "minister" is defined, refined, and confined in the meaning-making interactions that result.

There is a considerable amount of scholarship on how religious institutions shape the horizontal call.[1] Just declaring oneself a "minister" does not give an aspirant automatic access to people primed to be the "ministered to." Religious institutions constrain access via licensing and ordination processes. Examining the various ways denominations order these constraints is outside of the scope of this book. In some ways, understanding episcopal mandates about ordination does not get us very far anyway. John Calvin was never ordained, but his religious influence, exercised first as a theologian and then as an unordained pastor, made him a leading voice in the Protestant Reformation.[2] Likewise, Dwight L. Moody, the late nineteenth-century Chicago revivalist and pastor, never sought ordination and was lambasted as sinful for preaching as a layman because laymen "are accountable to no-one and may preach false doctrine with impunity."[3]

The fact is, most of the action of affirming one's sense of a call to ministry, credentialed or not, happens at the congregational level. An aspirant presents his or her sense of a calling to members of their local religious community. What direction that conversation takes is shaped by, but not totally determined by, denominational rules or regulations. For example, a Roman Catholic woman's or married man's call to the priesthood may not be accepted, but both can certainly be groomed for religious labor that ultimately finds them leading a parish. According to recent changes in church law prompted by the shortage of priests, diocesan bishops can entrust the pastoral care of a parish to someone who is not ordained; they are not Pastor with the capital P, but they do pastor. As we will see again and again in this book, it is the work of the calling and the call itself, not the labels associated with it, that are key to maintaining one's sense that he or she is a minister. This issue will be especially relevant when we focus on women in ministry.

Therefore, instead of focusing on denomination-level certification of callings, we examine the ways local congregations respond to someone's belief that they are called to do the work of ministry.[4] Like the examination of the vertical calls, this look at horizontal calls is intended to flesh out the circumstances whereby these men and women come to believe that God has called them to do religious labor. Recognizing the role one's congregation-of-origin plays in strengthening his conviction that he is called to religious labor is an important part of understanding how callees maintain that conviction in the absence of a paid position as religious laborer.

Dramaturgical Analysis of the Route to Credentialing

In George Orwell's essay "Shooting an Elephant," he describes an audience's power to shape one's identity and, ultimately, his behavior. His narrator, while fundamentally opposed to the British imperialism he represents, finds himself compelled to play the role of powerful representative of the British government. As he describes in this excerpt, he does not kill the elephant because of his own desire to assert an identity. Instead, he feels compelled to do so by the Burmese crowd's expectations of what he, a British police officer, should do:

> Here was I, the white man with his gun, standing in front of the unarmed native crowd—seemingly the leading actor of the piece; but in reality I was only an absurd puppet pushed to and fro by the will of those yellow faces behind. I perceived in this moment that when the white man turns tyrant . . . he becomes a sort of hollow, posing dummy, the conventionalized figure of a sahib. For it is the condition of his rule that he shall spend his life in trying to impress the "natives," and so in every crisis he has got to do what the 'natives' expect of him. He wears a mask, and his face grows to fit it.[5]

Orwell's use of theatrical imagery—"the leading actor," "posing dummy," "a mask"—serves as an effective metaphor to describe the way identities, even those we'd rather not have, are crafted and performed. In fact, many sociologists and social psychologists have come to understand people's portrayal of their identities, their "presentation of self," in dramaturgical terms. The impetus for this framing comes from Erving Goffman's use of a theatrical metaphor in his influential sociological study of impression management.[6] Goffman describes us as performers who have to maintain "front stage" performances, often contradicting those performances in "back stage" behaviors, and depending on other cast members (our "team") to effectively portray our characters. We are, at once, performers and characters, with the one being the subject of a performance and the other being the object of it.

The character, in Goffman's terms, is the identity (or self) the audience experiences. While he describes the character experienced in these performances as temporary, a "virtual self" tied to the specific situations we find ourselves in, attributes of these performances often follow us off the stage. Other social scientists suggest that these performances operate in a kind of feedback loop.[7] We perform an identity. Our audience then responds to us as performers of, and fundamentally, holders of that identity. These responses lead to a hardening of those identities into our understanding of who we are. Essentially, we become committed to that character. This is especially likely if the audience is large and carries some emotional significance.

A similar process takes place for Aspiring Ministers. In their efforts to understand this identity the vertical call has awakened in them, they seek out some further validation or confirmation of that identity. Once accepted, various components of the credentialing process give them more opportunities to perform the role, gain experience in the role, and ultimately be successful in the role. These experiences, as described in interviews and observed at their churches, carried many of the same dynamics of auditioning, costuming, staging, rehearsals, and audience interaction that I saw as an actor in and director of theatrical performances. It is through this lens that we examine the horizontal call to ministry.

The Acting Resume

Resumes are intended to highlight the most important and relevant characteristics of an actor's life story. They tell casting directors what they need to know about the actor's background that makes them appropriate for the role being sought. When asked how he likes to learn about the background of an actor, the casting director Danny Goldman said, "I like a resume. I like to see the background and training. I can tell an awful lot about an actor by the resume."[8] In many ways, the collection of experiences expressed on an acting resume can give directors a clear sense of who that actor is.

Like an acting resume, the best way to communicate one's suitability for the role of minister is to present a calling narrative. It is not enough for someone to want to preach or even be capable of preaching. The COGIC manual states that when someone expresses a desire to preach, his pastor must first determine the "sincerity, soundness or authenticity of his calling." It goes on to say that he should "be able to convince others that God called him."[9] Having a convincing account of one's calling is the primary qualifier—or in its absence, disqualifier—to begin the credentialing process in the Church of God in Christ. Nichole, an ordination committee member, confirms the importance of a narrative, mentioning some components that must be present in order for her to be convinced: "I would look for you to have been in close contact with the Lord and He had spoken to you through a dream or through a vision or through something to get your attention to let you know that there is a work specifically designed for you by the Lord."

Being able to tell this narrative seems to come to my respondents as easily as it might be for an actor to list her stage or film credits. In every case, ministers were as capable of explaining how they were called to the ministry as they were of explaining how they happened into the secular jobs they currently hold. In some cases, they even got ahead of themselves in telling the story, having to backtrack to ensure that salient bits were not lost in the retelling. These stories were as real as any other experience they may have had. That said, these were still accounts of that experience, put through the filter of a cultural context that has expectations for what those accounts should communicate.

Some actors pad their resumes in order to give casting directors what they think the directors are looking for. The most common advice in acting circles, regarding resumes, is to tell the truth. Mike Fenton, the casting director of *E.T.* and *Back to the Future,* warns, "in putting your resume together, use your head—because if you prevaricate on your resume, it can come back and bite you in the bottom, and if it does it leaves teeth marks."[10] The veracity of a resume is easily determined. A calling narrative, on the other hand, is less easily challenged. That is not to say that callees are lying per se, but it is unlikely that every story accurately depicts what happened in these defining moments. Remember, the calling experience is just another piece of their biography, a slice of their life story. The narrative, the means by which that story becomes a social experience, is shaped by the circumstances of its telling. William Myers explains it this way:

When the claimant comes to the community of faith, they come for confirmation and their story (the content) is transformed into a narrative (the discourse—how it is told) in order to persuade the community of the authenticity of the call. This isn't about error or deception, but is as much about the individual's attempt to wrestle with God and self in their story and then use the narrative as a way to make sense of this to other people.[11]

There is always a complex mix of truth and fiction in the stories we tell *about* ourselves, even if those are only stories we are telling *to* ourselves.

If we leave the acting metaphor for a moment and reconsider clergy as professionals, this idea of crafting a narrative about one's professional interests is not unusual. Prospective medical, law, and doctoral students spend considerable amounts of time struggling to craft the perfect narratives explaining how and why they became interested in those professions and how committed they are to them. A crafted narrative of interest and "calling" is a key component of the gatekeeping mechanisms for some professions. For many, creating these narratives is not just a hoop to be jumped through. These narratives come to define who they are once they begin their training. In fact, some have to actively resist being pigeonholed by the intellectual histories they've offered their future colleagues. These "statements of purpose" become just that, statements that define who they intend to be as professionals in that field. They do not see these only as descriptions of what they will do; they are, in many ways, descriptions of who they are.

In this way, resumes, statements of purpose, and calling narratives play a role in the construction of social identities. People make sense of their lives through autobiography. The psychologist Jerome Bruner describes this as "life making," an idea seconded by his colleagues George Rosenwald and Richard Ochberg. They say that "personal stories are not merely a way of telling someone (or oneself) about one's life; they are the means by which identities may be fashioned. It is this formative—and sometimes deformative—power of life stories that makes them important."[12] In being required to describe the moment when God redefined them, the callee's conviction about that moment is strengthened. This is especially the case if, as most of my interviews showed, those stories were responded to positively.

Getting the Part

Danny Goldman, the casting director cited earlier, mentioned a factor not only important in "getting the part" in acting but in being able to move forward in the clerical credentialing process: "If I know the actor, I certainly don't need to read the resume."[13] While calling narratives play a major role in the credentialing process, they were always given to a church leader who had already formed some opinion of the person expressing a call. How these

leaders responded became an understandably important component of aspirants' belief that they should pursue the credentialing process.

Of course, anyone an aspirant approaches with claims of holding the identity of "minister" can either accept or reject that identity. In fact, some ministers did experience an early rejection, usually from family members who knew
them as holders of an identity that seemed contrary to the ministerial one. In
some ways, this is a problem of typecasting. Both Henry "The Fonz" Winkler
and Leonard "Mr. Spock" Nimoy found it difficult for people to believe their
portrayals of other characters because audiences could see them only as Fonzie
and Spock. Similarly, some people who have experienced a callee's past as a
womanizer, alcoholic, or convict might find it difficult to accept the Aspiring
Minister's claim to be called to ministry. But with some persistent, believable
performances of the identity, even those naysayers may be persuaded.

Andrew, for example, described how emotional he felt the day his Evangelist mother, who had initially rejected his call, affirmed his call after hearing
him preach. His mother's acceptance of his performance strengthened his
belief that he held the identity that undergirded it. If he hadn't had an opportunity to perform as a minister, the identity might have atrophied in spite
of his having experienced the vertical call—a dream of him preaching—that
triggered that identity. Like Nimoy, who has played more voice-parts than
non–Star Trek acting roles, he may well have used his talents in a different
venue. But Andrew received a horizontal call, from his pastor, who affirmed
his vertical call and gave him the opportunity to pursue the clerical credential and identity.

Few ministers had to come as far as Andrew did, but they all went through
a similar process that started with approaching a church leader. Many report
going to the leader with some trepidation, but still feeling certain that they
would get the part. As a Deaconess, Amanda stated, "Mother knew my heart.
She already seen me doing God's work, that I could be trusted with small
things and now God was trusting me with big ones." They expected their
calls to be positively received, and they were rarely disappointed. Damian's
description of his announcement was repeated many times in my interviews:
"I went to the head Elder at the time and I told him what my call into ministry was. His response was, 'I already knew that. What took you so long?' I
was a little irritated with him actually because I was, like, well why didn't you
tell me?" This is often the norm for people who have already been serving
in some role—either as lay-leader or in some lay-ministry—in the church.
Unless there are considerable, and widely known, flaws in the person's character, their call is usually affirmed.

While most aspirants went to their church leaders understanding their call and just seeking entry into the credentialing process, a significant minority went hoping for more clarification, and even denial, of the calling moment itself. Church leaders report that one's calling story is rarely rejected and accommodations are usually made to begin the credentialing process. This norm works against those callees hoping their interview with church leaders would disconfirm their calling.

When Erika went to her Church Mother, she saw it as "putting down a fleece." The phrase, "putting out a fleece," is a commonly used metaphor for testing God, drawn from the biblical story of Gideon who used a sheep's fleece to have God prove that He would use Gideon to bring deliverance to Israel (Judg. 6:36–40). Erika's struggle with a call to ministry came to a head in her first year of law school: "I felt like I was being called, but I was saying, 'You gotta be kidding me, God. I'm jacked up. I'm in school right now.' The timing was all off and everybody I knew who went into ministry, their life just gets crazy." She struggled long enough that she missed the annual deadline for any Aspiring Missionaries to have spoken with the pastor's wife about their calls. She took that as a sign, but she still approached the leader hoping she would be denied a seat in the new class. That didn't happen:

> For some reason, in her mind, I had already spoken to her. I told her about my call, but that I felt the timing's all wrong. I must be hearing wrong cause I'm being pulled in all of these directions. She looked at me and was, like, "No. I can see why God wants you here right now. The timing's not wrong. Your learning curve is just going to be different from everybody else's." And I'm looking at her, like, I knew you were going to shut me down because I had to be wrong.

Erika was formally recognized as an Aspiring Missionary that night.

While most aspirants encounter an enthusiastic yes, others report receiving an answer that, while not a complete assent, was experienced that way. One tactic that leaders described using, particularly for newer converts, would be to offer "wait" rather than an outright "no." Soon after Damian experienced what he considers "a miraculous deliverance from drug dependence," he began to feel a call to ministry. He wondered, "why am I getting this desire to want to—now that I've been, as they say, set free, delivered, or healed—this desire to want to help others have the same freedom?" At the age of thirty-six and only recently converted, he wasn't sure what to make of these feelings:

I was explaining to my pastor that this is what I believe the Lord wanted me to do, to help others either through counseling or whatever the case is. He didn't shut me down. He had me sit on the front row and observe what the ministers do. So I sat and observed. And as I was observing, pastor was observing me and seeing whether I was worthy, looking at my faithfulness in coming to church, my faithfulness in participating as a servant. Apparently, I met those requirements and he licensed me.

Few men reported having this particular experience, but an appreciable number of women (who usually had to go through another woman as a gatekeeper) reported being told that the first thing you do when you're called is "wait and watch, sit and learn." This was especially the case for recently married women and women with small children. They were told that this response was a function of wise timing and that the delay should not be seen as a denial. While leaders may assume they are communicating a "no," the callees engage in selective perception, that is, they attend to cues that support the called identity (e.g., being allowed to sit in the front row and observe ministry) while ignoring cues that don't (e.g., not being able to participate in some activities as an Aspiring Minister). This interpretation of the situation is furthered by supportive statements suggesting that their time would come.

Whether they receive an enthusiastic "yes" or a tepid "wait," callees experience anything but a "no" as a sanction of their calling. Pastors, committee members, and other spiritual leaders argue that it is not their responsibility to tell people they aren't called. They state that God will inform them, and those people will naturally remove themselves from the process. This perspective does not take into account the tremendous power the leader's affirmation has in strengthening the aspirant's sense that he is called. Our sense of self is shaped in large part by our interactions with other people. If individuals experience social support for identities they are claiming, that identity becomes more prominent. This is particularly the case if the support they receive for the identity (or in Stryker's terms, role-identity) comes from people with whom they have strong and deep ties.[14] In this case, having the called identity legitimized by one's spiritual leader strengthens their commitment to that identity. This identity, which may have been relatively low in the aspirant's long list of important identities, is given a boost once it is (a) supported and deemed legitimate and (b) done so by individuals who aspirants depend on for spiritual guidance.

Costumes and Staging

In the Tony Award–winning musical *Spring Awakening*, the director Michael Mayer decided to seat members of the audience onstage, intentionally breaking down the physical barriers between performers and spectators. This blurring of boundaries is further enhanced in those moments when the leads in the cast, dressed in late nineteenth-century German school clothes, sit near and among the onstage spectators. Of course, this blurring is incomplete because of the unmistakable period-dress the actors are wearing, outfits that mark them as members of the cast and not just members of the onstage audience; costuming matters. For much of the first act, it is always clear to spectators who is who on the stage because the young actors do most of their actual performing away from the bleachers situated on either side of the stage. This all changes when four members of the cast, dressed in street clothes and also seated among the onstage audience, stand and join the cast in singing one of the songs. This moment is often surprising to those spectators sitting near them as well as to the larger audience because their clothing and their positions on stage hide their true identity from onlookers. It is only when the directors desire it that their true identities as characters in the drama are revealed.

Just as the director of a play might use costuming to signal actor's roles, churches do the same with ordained clergy. In many religious traditions, it is customary for religious leaders to dress in liturgical vestments (e.g., a cassock or robe) when serving in their formal, ceremonial role as priest or pastor. When serving in less ceremonial roles, e.g., visiting parishioners in hospitals, they tend to mark themselves as ministers in other ways, the most common being the wearing of the black clerical shirt with a white clerical collar. These "costumes" make the men and women who wear them visible on any stage they find themselves. They also communicate something—about status or purity, for example—to congregants and even secular audiences. Even when ministers "dress down" by wearing casual clothing while preaching, instead of formal robes or suits, they do so with the intent to communicate a message, either about themselves or the religious community they serve.

Clothing and costumes can constitute what Goffman refers to as an "identity kit," a set of symbols that we wrap ourselves in to create an image of who we are.[15] He gives an example of perfume clerks who put on white lab coats in order to provide customers with a sense that "the delicate tasks performed by these persons will be performed in . . . a clinical manner."[16] The key to this messaging is the shared meaning that both actor and audience have for the clothing as a symbol. In early Westerns, a white hat indicates the good cowboy and the black hat indicates the bad one. These fronts, as Goffman calls them, are not intended to deceive the audience. Often, they are accurate depictions of who the person wearing the costume actually is.

Clothing has always been important in COGIC doctrine. Modesty in dress, particularly for women, has been a defining characteristic of Holiness churches. Until recently, injunctions against makeup, slitted dresses, and even the color red were taught in Purity and Young People Willing Worker classes. The clergy were held to a set of standards as well.

The COGIC manual has two sections titled "The Dress Code," which treats uniformity in dress as a spiritual injunction, pointing to Philippians 3:16 which reads "let us walk by the same rule, let us be of the same mind." The first section focuses on "the clergy" (i.e., men) while the second section offered both a dress code for women in ministry and short admonition for laywomen to "return to the old-fashioned standard of dressing as becometh holiness."[17]

Unless given specific permissions to do so, an Aspiring or Licensed Minister cannot wear a clerical collar. Both the "Brother's Collar," as it is officially called, and the ceremonial cassock/robe are reserved for use by ordained Elders only. Yet "as an *indication* of his apprenticeship in the Ministry and to *signify* his Candidature for Ordination," these men are required to wear black suits, white shirts with black neckties, black shoes, and black socks.[18]

Because women cannot be ordained, they wear neither collars nor robes/cassocks to distinguish between the levels of licensing. Aspiring Missionaries usually wear a uniform that distinguishes them from both laywomen and licentiates. That uniform is often something as simple as a black skirt with a white blouse. Once licensed, a Deaconess wears a white skirt with the white blouse. Evangelists wear a specially made pleated and belted white dress, called either a habit or, officially, "The Saint." Also, in keeping with biblical injunctions that women should have their hair covered (e.g., 1 Cor. 11:5–6), women wear a "doily," a small white lace worn on the hair. Evangelists may also wear a white bonnet-type hat when in their habit.

While these "costuming" distinctions are considered real and meaningful by those charged with overseeing the credentialing process, the distinctions are not always clear to the congregation. The following excerpt from an interview demonstrates some of the difficulty congregants have in discerning the difference. Sheba attributes this difficulty to the similarity in uniforms:

I had just crossed over to become a deaconess. Back then we were still mainly just helping at the altar, but we could wear all white instead of looking like an usher in the black and white dress. And after service one day, this woman grabbed me when I was leaving and wanted me to pray for her daughter back in the vestibule because she thought she had a demon. I didn't know what to do because I didn't have any training for anything like that. I told her I had to get one of the ministers and she asked wasn't I one. I didn't know what to say.

Both in interviews and in my own observations, it became quite clear that Sheba's encounter was not an isolated incident. Her experience with her white dress is reminiscent of many medical students' experiences with the shortened white coat they receive in their second year of medical school. In a similar way, the different style of coat worn by students and physicians has no meaning for patients. As the physician and author Ellen Rothman suggests, the coat itself carries the important meaning: "While not the long coat of a physician, the white coat signaled our medical affiliation and differentiated us from the civilian visitors and volunteers. To my patients, the white coat denoted the authority and trust ascribed to physicians by the general public. Most patients were not attuned to the medical hierarchy designated by coat length. A white coat is a white coat is a white coat."[19]

Just as Rothman's patients prematurely promoted her, members of Sheba's church promoted her and other aspirants, referring to them as "minister" before they had earned the title. For men, the actual title "(Licensed) Minister" led to similar confusion. Even Aspiring Ministers reported having people mistake them for ordained church leaders just because of their titles and costumes.

This visibility, premature as it might be, plays a role in strengthening one's commitment to the "called" identity. The more people who interact with us as holders of an identity, the stronger our commitment to that identity. If we receive intrinsic rewards (e.g., status) via those interactions, our commitment to the identity grows even deeper. So it goes in this case. The more people confuse the costume of the aspirant with the costume of the credentialed, the more likely they are to interact with aspirants as if they have been fully confirmed as clergy. These interactions work to increase aspirants' sense that they are called to the ministry. Their costume communicates this to an audience and that audience responds accordingly.

But costumes don't just communicate who we are. They also play a role in shaping who we are. The acting coach Joanna Rotté describes costumes as, by their nature, provoking a response: "It compels the actor to move, walk, and sit different from his habit, in the manner appropriate to the costume."[20]

She goes on to say that "whether a crown or an old sweater, each element of the costume takes the actor one step toward becoming the character."[21] In some ways, the claim that "clothes make the man" is much more than just an empty cliché. Tequia described it as a "big deal" when she wore the doily for the first time because "now I looked like what I felt like." Wearing the white dress didn't have the same impact because in her church's annual Women's Day, *all* women wear white dresses. But wearing the doily, one of the most distinctive attributes of the female minister's uniform, strengthened her sensation of being a minister.

Just as costuming affects the way audiences respond to both actors and aspirant callees, staging also plays a role. We come to expect people serving in particular roles to be located in particular spaces. Choirs are situated in choir pews; ushers are situated in the aisles. Clergy and other church leaders (e.g., deacons) are usually situated in special areas as well. Even if they are not placed on an elevated pulpit, there are usually unmarked, but nevertheless clearly designated, areas where they are seated. No signs need mark these areas; they become recognized as special areas based on who sits there week after week. The space takes on meaning, a meaning that can be transferred onto anyone who resides in the space. If you're on stage, we assume you're an actor. If you're sitting "in the audience," we assume you're not. In the same way, these spaces mark those sitting there as leaders—either as "the called" in the case of clergy or "the chosen" in the case of lay-leaders like deacons.

Both aspiring and licensed trainees are expected to serve in some capacity during services. At the aspiring level, a person's level of commitment to ministry can be determined by having them attend to basic functions during service. They are often seated in the front of the church on the days they are assigned to serve. Even if not actively participating in the administration of religious ordinances, trainees are still seated among those who have been elevated to full clerical status. These seating arrangements mark them as something different from lay-members, but may not distinguish them from fully credentialed clergy.

Rehearsals

Once licensed, while serving as clerical apprentices, both male and female licentiates are likely working "on stage" in ministerial positions. A Licensed Minister, for example, is still officially a lay-member in his local church, but he has the "authority to preach, conduct worship services, and visit jails and hospitals."[22] The major difference, in capabilities, between a Licensed Minister and an ordained Elder is the Elder's ability to administer the ordinances of the church (e.g., the Lord's Supper, marriages) and, ultimately, to pastor. The local distinctions in tasks or responsibilities of Deaconesses and Evangelists are even less clear.

In some churches, Aspiring Ministers are put through a task rotation. For those churches, this is a key component of the preparation aspirants receive to fully express their calling. A sample rotation at one church requires licentiates to participate in each of the following ministries over the course of two years: prison ministry, hospital visitation, morning prayer, street witnessing, Christian education, nursing and convalescent home ministry, and assisting with Communion and Water Baptism. At another church, they were also required to give ten-minute sermonettes during Sunday morning services. These rotations are intended to give aspirants an opportunity to experience different kinds of ministry in the hopes that they would find one that fits their calling.

Most Aspiring Ministers found the rotation to be a useful exercise, usually because it gave them a clearer sense of what they were not interested in doing in the ministerial role. For some women, the rotation into ministries with primarily local reaches (e.g., ministering to the church's convalescent members) moved them to abandon plans for promotion; they chose to remain Deaconesses. All of the men found external ministries, particularly those with a preaching component, more appealing. When required to rotate through ministries, they were especially drawn to prison ministry and street witnessing.

Therefore, at all levels—aspiring, licensed, and licensed-ordained—people who claim a call to ministry are actively put to work doing ministry. Aspirants worked alongside fully credentialed Elders and Evangelists in ministries both outside and inside the walls of the church. While distinctions between aspiring clergy and the others are made in their ceremonial service (e.g., during Communion), these distinctions are almost irrelevant outside of those tasks. Some callees who were Aspiring Missionaries or Aspiring Ministers continued in the ministries (e.g., street evangelism) they served in before accepting their call. The status of "apprentice" assumed by the titles "Aspiring Minister" or "Licensed Minister" was barely experienced by people who retained their roles as, say, Sunday school teacher or director of the singles ministry.

Like the costuming distinctions discussed earlier, the distinctions between training and fully credentialed clergy are not always obvious to other members of the congregation. Their prominent position in the sanctuary, coupled with their continuing service in nonsacramental but nevertheless ministerial roles, obscures the fact that they are still trainees.

Does this matter? In many ways, it does not matter anymore than universities allowing graduate students to teach courses or medical schools expecting students to suture wounds. Trainees and apprentices have always been given opportunities to practice their crafts before being fully credentialed as practitioners. But in this case, two important issues are at stake.

The first is the religious credentialing authority's desire for those who are not "truly called" to abandon their belief that they have been, in fact, called. As we discuss later in this chapter, pastors believe that aspirants who don't actually have a call to ministry will discover their mistake and abandon the pursuit of credentials; they hope the identity won't mature and the aspirant won't become committed to it. As with costuming, positioning trainees on stage in positions of spiritual leadership or ministry prompts congregants to treat them with the same authority and trust they ascribe to fully credentialed clergy. While undergraduate students may call a graduate instructor "Ms." instead of "Dr.," they still consider her as their "Professor" because of the role she is playing. Acting out the identity is more powerful than just claiming it. Performing a role and then being affirmed in one's performance of that role acts as a one-two punch when it comes to strengthening one's commitment to it.

The other issue is the presumption that engaging in or, even worse, merely observing a task is always adequate training for that task. No wise attending physician would assume that a second-year medical school student should be left alone to insert an IV line because he or she had completed an anatomy course. In fact, they may not trust them to do any number of seemingly basic tasks until they had proven themselves adept at doing them under supervision. Conversely, PhD programs often allow novice graduate students to supervise undergraduates in labs or even teach introductory courses. The question is, are religious congregants more like hospital patients or young scholars?

Learning the Lines

If it is the former, the words of Adrienne, a thirty-six-year-old Deaconess, are particularly significant. Her words capture the dissatisfaction she and other young trainees expressed when discussing their premature exposure to "the performance space":

When I was an Aspiring, all you were allowed to do was sit on the front row and "work the wall." When people were brought to you, you took them in the back, and you signed them up. You couldn't talk to them, you couldn't ask them anything. You simply filled out the paperwork. So, one day they wave the magic wand, and now you're called "Deaconess," and they have you on a schedule to bring [the short sermons called] God's Promises. Then they're saying, "Well, now you can pray for people," and I suppose they can ask you to preach, if they wanted. I have been asked to bring the Word in smaller settings, and I feel like, when did you train me on how to put together a message? What do I do if somebody comes up and says they are filled with demons, or if I detect that they have demons? When did we get training on how to operate in that?

Adrienne's complaint about training is important. No actor can effectively portray a character if she doesn't know her lines. Even if actors have mastered the choreography or fully understand where they are to be situated on the stage, without learning the play's words or the musical's lyrics, the emotions, perspectives, and values of the characters cannot be communicated. Hamlet isn't Hamlet without his "to be or not to be" and Scrooge isn't Scrooge without his "Bah, humbug." It is not enough to be able to act; one must know the material.

The Church of God in Christ desires that all of its licentiates and ordinands have some grounding in biblical, theological, and practical ministry. For example, they strongly recommend that women aspirants to the ministry "study the Word of God as her rule of faith and practice, seeking knowledge from the Higher Power and training through Institute Classes, Bible School, etc. This will better equip her to serve God and His people."[23] Similar recommendations are made for male aspirants.

In order to facilitate this, COGIC formed the C. H. Mason Jurisdictional Institutes, local "academies" where students could develop basic competencies in Bible, church administration, and theology. The two-year certificate program offered at these institutes includes ten courses including Old and New Testaments Surveys, Principles of Effective Leadership, Homiletics, and Christian Counseling. In addition to lectures and discussions, the courses often have role-play components where students practice delivering sermons, evangelizing, and practice performing the ritual ceremonies of the church.

Because so much of our understanding of ourselves—our self-concept—is tied to appraisals of some sort, learning environments like these can be particularly influential in helping that process along. It is in the course of taking these classes that the strengthening of and legitimization of the calling continues to happen. There are three ways this happens.

The first is tied mainly to one's self-appraisal, i.e., the minister's sense of him or herself as a competent minister. Without these courses putting boundaries around the necessary knowledge base for someone who is called, it might be difficult for a callee to determine when they've learned enough. We saw that in the previous section with Adrienne, who had completed only her jurisdiction's Old Testament Survey at the time she was licensed as a Deaconess. Without the successful completion of all ten courses clarifying what successful ministry requires, she had nothing to point to as evidence that she could be effective doing the work required of a Deaconess. This left her wondering how she could feel confident that she could perform effectively when called upon. If she had completed the ten-course certificate before being licensed, her sense of her own capabilities could be grounded in, at the very least, the knowledge made available in those courses. By learning the knowledge that she would eventually need as a practicing minister, she would become (even if only in her mind) a more effective performer of the ministerial identity. She would have acquired what we call "self-efficacy," that sense that she has the ability to produce the desired ministerial outcomes. Even if she didn't achieve mastery of all of the material, learning what she could of it would strengthen her sense that she might be effective in at least some avenues of ministerial practice.

The second way training helps to strengthen trainees' identities as ministers is much more social. Classes, even if taught by correspondence or online, offer opportunities for the appraisals of others, specifically the course instructors. We then reflect those appraisals in our sense of who we are. An actor in Arthur Miller's *Death of a Salesman* may know the line "you can't eat the orange and throw the peel away—a man is not a piece of fruit," but if his director criticizes his performance of that line as unemotional, it may negatively affect his sense of himself as an effective Willy Loman.[24] In these courses, trainees are evaluated by the instructors and those appraisals, in turn, shape their appraisals of themselves. "Shape" is an important term here because the trainees' evaluations of themselves are not direct reflections of the instructor's appraisals. They closely approximate what the appraisal might be intended to communicate but are ultimately filtered through the callee's perspective, their respect for the evaluator, or their desire to protect their identity as a minister.

Obviously, these filters aren't as necessary when the trainee shows him- or herself capable of performing at the required level. They are more likely to come into play when these appraisals conflict with or threaten their belief of themselves as competent ministers. For example, when Angelo gave a practice sermon, his pastor said, "the best thing about that message was that you brought it to a close." Instead of experiencing that statement as a criticism of his calling, he described it as a "teachable moment" in which God was critiquing his focus on his own abilities. If there was a failure, it was that he had prepared *too much* and, as the voice of God, didn't depend enough on God for the message. He interpreted the appraisal more mildly than it may have been intended, framing criticism in a way that made even failure serve as further evidence of a calling. In the end, he argued that God blessed the sermon, and its message wasn't hindered by his failure.

The third way that people determine if they are effectively performing a role is to use some reference point as a basis of comparison. An actor might answer the question "am I a good Hamlet" by comparing himself to other actors who have played the role. Because we tend to try to protect our identity, we are likely to choose a basis for our comparisons that enables that preservation. The actor doesn't pick a Tony-winning actor's portrayal of Hamlet; he picks either someone like himself or someone much less effective than himself.

These courses, particularly when taught in a discussion format, enable some callees to do this same thing. This was especially clear when female ministers described their experiences. Women talked about the ways the classes showed that they, as a group or as individuals, were as qualified (and, for many, more qualified) to be ordained as were the men. They often spoke of men's lack of biblical knowledge, frequently adopting a stance that the ability to perform in class was further evidence of a call to ministry. In describing her experience of her church's COGIC doctrine course, Ramona lambasted the men in the class, "It was almost ridiculous the level of ignorance of the Word—of just basic Bible—the men showed in that class. In classes where you could get away with just talking off the top of your head or from life experience, they were fine. Well, some of them were fine [laughs]. Others were still bad. But let a scripture be required and they don't have anything to contribute."

She followed with an attack on the theological arguments against ordaining women and then summed up her discussion with, "So that's how it goes. They'll make him an Elder and then turn around and say I can't even preach from the pulpit and have to preach from the floor? If the decisions got made based on those classes, they'd make me an Elder and tell him to sit down somewhere." Numerous women concurred with Ramona's perspective, often pointing out that most of their Jurisdictional Institute's classes were taught by experienced *women* in ministry. While their argument was usually intended to communicate their broader belief that God called women into ministry, their experiences in these classes convinced many of them that their own calling was legitimate. Ultimately, both women and men found these courses to be great opportunities to prove to themselves and others that their calls to ministry were real. As Adrienne suggests, undistinguished and even mediocre performance still led to the receipt of the desired credentials. In some ways, just being in the class and holding one's own among more experienced scholars and practitioners was enough to strengthen an aspirant's belief that he was on the right track.

The Performance

In the end, all of these preparations—getting the part, fitting the costumes, rehearsing movements, learning lines—are intended to prepare an actor for a credible performance as the character they aim to portray. In theater, the weeks of practice perfect an actor's ability to stand on the stage and *be* Andrew Lloyd Webber's Phantom, Lorraine Hansberry's Walter, or Jonathan Larson's Angel. They have been trained to do so, they look the part, and they assume that they are capable of pulling this performance off. Either the person can be the character or they can't; opening night will test that.

Aspiring clergy also have their versions of opening night. Whether it is Alesha, who claims a call to teach, being assigned a class of preteens for Vacation Bible School or Marcus, who claims a call to preach, being asked to give "Words of God's Promises" at his church's morning service, these ministers eventually find themselves in a situation that tests their ministerial identity. The twenty-three former Aspiring Ministers and Missionaries are all licensed today, so presumably people pass these tests: they appear to be called. The other eighty-five people who were credentialed already must have passed the test as well.

That said, in the interviews, ministers regularly spoke of peers whose callings they doubted. Ministers' critiques of each other are tied to their belief that a calling *must have evidence*: people must have character appropriate to a calling, must show commitment to the work of a calling, and must be able to perform the responsibilities of the calling. Diane, an elderly Evangelist, summarized her own measuring stick: "I would expect a different lifestyle, different behavior, a love of the word, being in the prayers and the service. But really if you're answering the call of the Lord on your life, you just need to do whatever your hands find to do in that ministry and do it in a spirit of excellence." While character was the most commonly mentioned reason for people to question their peers' callings, the most damning criticisms were reserved for incompetent performers of the ministerial identity. The evidence offered to support these assertions was often secondhand but, coupled with my own observations, is still useful in helping us understand how some aspirants might not experience their failed "opening night" as anything other than a great success.

For example, in some COGIC churches, sermons are followed by an "altar call," a period in which congregants can come to the front of the church and be prayed for. In churches with a large enough body of ministers, the responsibilities to pray for people are distributed among the ministers. Praying for someone is a primary, and consistently performed, task for COGIC ministers. Presumably, most ministers perform the task capably, but it is clear from my conversations that some ministers fall short of this challenge.

Both peers and congregants describe a number of ways someone can "fail" as a pray-er: mumbling through the prayer, praying with no emotion, "babbling but never actually saying anything," not showing sympathy for the congregant's situation, and (most commonly mentioned) not addressing the prayer request at all. Character certainly plays a role as well. As Tabitha, a congregant at one of these churches, said, "OK, even though this might sound judgmental, I choose who prays for me because of the person he is when he isn't wearing that robe. I don't expect ministers to be perfect; they are human. But if I don't feel good about you as a pretty decent and upstanding person in everyday life, you can't put your hands on me." Wanda, one of the Evangelists pointed out that congregants "won't even go with [some ministers] to pray, or they'll come back and say, 'That minister now, I don't want her to pray with me no more. She can't pray.'"

Failures are not limited to prayer services. On a separate occasion, I sat in an adult Bible class and the teacher, an Evangelist, claimed to have received a revelation while preparing the lesson on Jesus' temptation at the start of his ministry, a story located in Luke 4. That revelation—that Jesus and Satan were brothers—was stated unequivocally in the class containing a mixture of lay-members, lay-ministers, and other credentialed clergy. As a credentialed Evangelist, she describes herself as a preacher and someone who "carries the Word of truth." No one I asked after leaving the class considered her statement to be true or biblically sound. She, ultimately, failed in her responsibility to preach her church's doctrine. In spite of this, the "revelation" went unchallenged as the class sat there quietly taking notes.

Finally, I watched and recorded a number of what can best be described as "trial sermons." Many of these sermons and, in many cases, short sermonettes were not billed as trial sermons. They were simply opportunities, often in the aforementioned training rotations, for aspirants/licentiates to craft a message and deliver it to the congregation. Some sermons were given during the church's early Sunday morning services while others were given on weekday auxiliary services (e.g., youth service) and holy days (e.g., Good Friday). In one case, the sermons were specifically treated as the ministers' "initial" sermons. In that case, the church assigned six Licensed ministers and Deaconesses to preach a fifteen- to twenty-minute sermonette as a test of their ability to effectively minister through preaching. At first blush, it would appear to be easy to determine—and describe—when this test was not proceeding well. There are certainly objective standards that one would apply to measure one's competent as both a speech maker and a deliverer of a speech. Of the fourteen sermons I observed and analyzed, most would be considered successful sermons. But there were some that were clearly poorly executed. The following excerpts from my field notes illustrate some of the problems:

> He moved away from his written notes and told a story about an encounter he had with his mother. The sense of anticipation for the punch line of the story was palpable in the room. The audience, with the exception of the occasional "yessir" and "well," was mostly silent. At the conclusion of the story, he declared, "I just wanted to say that" and moved on to the next point on his outline. The lengthy story took up nearly seven minutes of his fifteen-minute allotted time such that soon after reading the scripture for his next point, the musicians were playing music chords intended to signal that he should be wrapping up the sermon. He moved immediately to "tuning up," never actually finishing the sermon.

> The minister misquoted the scripture reference. Apparently he hadn't turned the page to catch up with his current point in the sermon. As he read the incorrect scripture, members of the congregation were still saying "yes" and waving their hands at him. He then realized (about a verse or two in) that he was in the wrong place and said, "wait that's not where I want to be. My bad" and paused, fumbling to find the appropriate place in his Bible. As he looked through the Bible for the actual scripture, the cheers and encouragement (e.g., "take your time preacher") continued enthusiastically.

> The audience was mostly silent while he struggled to read the difficult-to-pronounce names in his scripture reference. Occasionally voices could be heard saying "that's alright" or muttering a pronunciation. Once he got to a part of the scripture without names, or that the audience seemed to recognize, more members of the audience started saying "amen."

In each of these cases—altar prayers, Bible studies, trial sermons—there is some evidence that a successful career as clergy is unlikely for some aspirants. Clearly, congregants and their peers experience people in these ministerial roles as failures, but do the poorly performing ministers recognize this? According to my interviewees, probably not. The main reason for this is the congregation's failure to communicate these failures.

Dennis Brissett and Charles Edgeley, both social psychologists, suggest that our awareness of how well we are performing in any given role depends on the "tolerance of the other. Some audiences are very enabling; while others are very critical and challenging."[25] In most cases, audiences are quite tolerant and are as committed to the successful performance as the speaker is. Goffman says that audiences have a tendency to want "to help the performers save their own show."[26]

Audiences attempt this in a number of ways, but the most relevant in the case of the calling is their tendency to "ignore" flaws in the performance. This happens in two ways in a religious context, particularly in a Black Pentecostal one. In the first example, of the altar call prayers, people have negative experiences with ministers. Some of those experiences are not even based on competency; some interviewees mentioned that their colleagues have objectionable breath odor but refuse mints or gum when offered. Instead of recoiling from the minister or, worse, refusing to be prayed for by them, a congregant may stay to be prayed for, get up quickly, and choose to never go to that minister again. Nothing is communicated to the minister who moves directly to the next person in line. The same dynamic happens if that person asks for the minister to pray about something specifically and the minister ignores the prayer request and simply prays a generic prayer. My interviewees roundly reject that kind of behavior as a "fail," but the congregants do not generally tell the minister that. As they do with the breath issues, they simply get up and never return to that minister again.

In some ways, the congregant is playing a role as well, as tactful and reverent audience member. She responds to the minister's performance, as Goffman suggests, with the "elaborate etiquette by which individuals guide themselves in their capacity as members of the audience."[27] She, like any other audience member is governed by a "desire, above all else, to avoid a scene."[28] Unfortunately without any feedback, the minister assumes he performed sufficiently, grades his own performance as a "pass," and becomes all the more committed to the ministerial identity. Similarly, in the case of the Evangelist's "revelation," the audience's silence communicated an endorsement of her abilities to "preach" a direct, new message from God even though the audience recognized that this message is flawed. In a way, the maxim *qui tacet consentir evidetur* (silence gives consent) is especially germane to horizontal calls. The audience's inaction still has an impact; it affirms the minister's sense that she or he is performing adequately.

Silence is one way congregants affirm a minister's performance. The other is to actively voice support for a performance that, measured objectively, fails. Each year, one of the most eagerly awaited television moments of the year is *American Idol*'s broadcast of their national auditions. Millions tune in to watch people who, in more cases than one might think, sincerely believe that they hold the identity this show is intended to highlight: singer. We marvel at the scores of aspiring but tone-deaf contestants who stand in front of the judges, prepared to demonstrate the evidence of their singing identity. The judges let them know, often quite harshly, that they've failed. A more dramatic version of this has been taking place at the historic Apollo Theater in Harlem since 1934. The mostly Black audiences in the Wednesday "Showtime Amateur Night" competitions come prepared to ignore all of the aforementioned rules of tact. Instead, they arrive primed to loudly "boo" poor performances until the "executioner" literally sweeps the failed act off the stage.

Trial sermons, like opening night or an Apollo Theater performance, are opportunities for one's community to make clear—in case other "failures" did not—that the performer cannot competently pull off his character. The likelihood that audiences will register dissatisfaction with a flawed sermon is reduced because the deck is often stacked against that possibility. Many of the people who come to trial or initial sermons are avid supporters of the central project of the event: they want the person to move from aspirant to licentiate or licentiate to ordinand. It was obvious, at each initial sermon, that the loudest "yeahs" and "amens" came from family members. But they weren't alone. The Black Pentecostal congregation is as primed to yell supportive statements like "yeah" and "alright," in response to a sermon as the Apollo audience is primed to yell "boo." As a result, instead of being silent during confusing or disjointed or even incomplete sermons, church audiences essentially reward "failing" performances with the same positive reinforcement a "passing" performance might receive. Consider, for example, the impact of the phrase "take your time, *Preacher*" on the minister who lost his place in the middle of his sermon. Referring to him as "Preacher," even in the midst of a flawed performance, is a strong statement of audience support for his attempt. In instances where an aspirant's performance slips, the audience either ignores the mistake or provides an excuse for it.

One of those excuses, often provided when preachers either lost their place or seemed to have difficulty getting their thoughts together, was to blame failures on the devil. For example, when an enthusiastic Deaconess had yelled herself hoarse, members of the audience shouted "take your hands off, Satan." This suggestion that the aspirant's difficulties getting through the message were an attack on her by the devil himself could only have one outcome: a strengthening of the called identity. An attack by the devil during her trial sermon added an additional confirmation of her calling. Not only did she have God's endorsement, but her audience was telling her that the devil saw her as a threat. What further evidence could an aspiring minister need than that?

Of course, all audience members were not complicit in these overt signs of support. Some congregants remained seated or did not voice any words of encouragement. But in every case, there was enough social support of the performance that some aspirants could blame their failure to reach those congregants on the unmoved congregants themselves. A common accusation voiced by preachers was "I guess some of y'all ain't ready for this Word." This accusation was inevitably cheered by the already supportive audience members and always had an impact: more congregants would stand or join in the positive verbal responses. In this case, silence was viewed as intractability, a failing of the intractable rather than a failure of the minister himself.

Counterfeits and Confusion

The *Newsweek* reporter Joshua Alston, in describing people's motivations for going on *American Idol*, submits that "the idea that you can be unspectacular, boring, marginally talented, lazy, and still achieve your dreams, is an alluring and insidious one."[29] While the fault for this phenomena may easily be placed at the foot of the reality television industry, shows like *American Idol* and "Showtime Amateur Night" can escape some of that blame. They go much farther than most at challenging the self-deluded's sense that he or she is a talented performer. When I began this project, I recognized the possibility that Alston's "alluring and insidious" idea may be present in clerical aspirants, but I also expected to find *American Idol*–like barriers to a fully realized minister's identity for those who weren't "called." Instead, I discovered the complex mix of identity-strengthening interactions, *the horizontal call*, described throughout this chapter.

Being accepted by one's home or originating congregation, especially if that congregation is the primary location for one's service, is a powerful mechanism for enhancing an aspirant's sense that they are called. This horizontal call certifies the vertical one. As a result, most people who start the credentialing process make it at least to the first intermediate licensing stage, and of those who endeavor to receive the terminal credentials (i.e., Elder and Evangelist), the vast majority of them do so successfully. When pressed, both church leaders and ministers found it difficult to name someone who dropped out of the process because the aspirant determined that he or she was not called. If anything, many of those who abandoned the process at one church did so to pursue a faster route to licensing or ordination at a different COGIC church or in an "easier" process in another denomination. In spite of pastors' beliefs that a mistaken sense of calling would eventually be undermined, either by the process or by God directly, nearly everyone who claims a call to ministry gets an opportunity to serve as a licensed or ordained minister.

Is this a problem? What wrong can come from licensing or ordaining someone who has found an accepting audience, is committed to the identity of minister, but may not be truly committed to (or right for) the work of ministry? My answer comes from a statement made by a member of one jurisdiction's ordination committee. Anna describes having to deal with some clergy *after* they've received the credential:

> When I used to try to get some of the men to go out with me to minister to the homeless, they would say "that's not my ministry" and I would look at them and say, "how can you say that's not your ministry?" If you're called by God, that's part of what you do. Most people talking about they're called to the ministry don't have a heart for going out in the streets and doing the work. They want to stay in the four walls, but that's altogether wrong as far as being a minister or missionary or whatever. We have some ministers now that don't even want to go out and serve communion to members who can't come to church and that's the most sacred ordinance of the church. If you love people, you don't mind helping people. But a lot of people who talk about being called to preach don't have that kind of heart. They got the paper and the collar for the wrong reasons.

From Anna's perspective, there are people who have found an accepting audience but should not have been credentialed as ministers; she does not believe they're called.

The Bible warns against people who do not actually come with a calling from God but who are able to find acceptance from audiences. While some of the warnings seem to point to people coming from outside of the religious community, most examples of false teachers, prophets, or leaders are actually credentialed members of that religious community. It was, for example, Moses' spokesman Aaron who built the golden calf at the base of Mount Sinai (Exod. 32:1–5). The sons of two priests, Eli and Samuel, were appointed to leadership positions and "turned aside after dishonest gain, took bribes, and perverted justice" (1 Sam. 8:3). Whether voiced in Old Testament warnings of leaders who judge for bribes, priests who teach for a price, and prophets who tell fortunes for money (Mic. 3:11) or New Testament warnings of men who arise from within to distort the truth in order to draw away disciples after themselves (Acts 20:30), the Bible authors seem to recognize the dangers of less-than-careful credentialing processes.

History is full of stories of men and women who, upon being accepted as a minister by some community, served with the kind of characteristics a true calling might require. But there are also stories of people who received credentials and used them to bring great harm to the people they attracted. In fact, one of the major areas of inquiry in the study of clergy is the examination of clerical malfeasance.[30] Much of that work looks at the ways religious structure may be complicit in ministers' seeming betrayals of their calling, creating what historian Philip Jenkins calls "a culture of clergy deviance."[31] All too often, it is only after an incident of malfeasance that followers (and credentialers) begin to question if that person was truly called.

One of the most infamous examples was Pentecostal minister, James "Jim" Jones. According to the historian Catherine Wessinger, Jones experienced a call to ministry at a Pentecostal convention when a minister declared, "I perceive that you are a prophet that shall go around the world . . . and tonight ye shall begin your ministry."[32] He later founded the People's Temple Full Gospel Church, a church that became officially affiliated with the Pentecostal denomination Disciples of Christ and had, at one point, an estimated three thousand members. Church members were not the only ones who held Jones in high esteem. Even when former members called for an investigation of Jones prior to the Guyana incident, Willie Brown, at that time a California state assemblyman and later mayor of San Francisco, "labeled the attacks 'a measure of [the church's] effectiveness.'"[33] Before the Guyana massacre in November 1978, Jim Jones was "revered as a good Samaritan" and as the "charismatic pastor of one of the largest interfaith churches in California." After the massacre, Jones was labeled a "mind-bending cult leader" whose name appeared with the likes of Charles Manson and Adolf Hitler in mainstream analyses.[34]

The Jones example, while stark, is a useful examination of the extreme consequences of having what sociologist Anson Shupe calls "wolves within the fold."[35] Many church leaders confess that there are indeed "wolves" who have slipped through the church's filters and are currently serving as credentialed clergy. The church officials certainly do not suggest that these "wolves" will one day lead hundreds of their members to commit suicide. In fact, they don't even consider them to be false teachers (i.e., teachers of a false doctrine). Instead, they argue that the motives that drew, and still keep, some people on the path to clerical credentials were flawed. Some spoke quite frankly of men who used their positions as Licensed Ministers and Elders to attract women into sexual relationships. Others described women who followed their friends into the ministry, describing their motivations as Jordan did, "They just see it like a sorority. My girlfriend is wearing white. Now I want to wear white."

Most concerns about fraudulent callings were like Anna's. Ministers and pastors alike believed that some people sought ordination for the status that comes with the credential. As Chris said when describing the challenges of ministry, "a lot of people don't understand it's not the glorified position. They look at the bigwigs like T. D. Jakes and think that's where they need to be, like he just arrived where he is." The suspicion that people might seek leadership positions in church for the prestige it might bring has some support from social scientists. For example, the psychologists Joseph White and William Cones suggest that

> despite dead-end jobs and low-status positions in mainstream America, many Black men and women have found a sense of somebodyness in the church. Black males . . . could be somebody in the church. They could aspire to become deacons or trustees, they could be elected to represent their church as delegates to state and national religious conventions.[36]

In addition to their concerns about people with "counterfeit callings," many ministers complained about aspirants who are "in the wrong lane." They argue that these people mistakenly believe they have a call to ministry when their talents are better served in nonclerical roles. Many ministers who spoke of "people in the wrong lane" worried that these "confused callings" might get people into situations that God never intended them to be in and thus they would be either ineffective or, worse, detrimental to the people they seek to serve.

A number of ministers go even farther, citing a story from Acts 19, which is a useful example of what might happen. The author of Acts of the Apostles tells of a group of itinerant preachers, the sons of a chief priest, who went through town claiming to be able to exorcise demons. They invoked both the name of Jesus and of the apostle Paul, saying, "We exorcise you by the Jesus whom Paul preaches." Then one day, the evil spirit in one man called their bluff, saying, "Jesus I know and Paul I know; but who are you?" (Acts 19:13–16). The demon-possessed man then jumped on the seven men, beating them until they were naked and bloody. The ministers worry that trained, but uncalled, clergy may find themselves in the same kind of situation. While some specifically suggested that callees might have to face down demons, Mona, an Evangelist, spoke of having to minister to "drug addicts or other desperate people, and you ain't gonna be able to pull out something you learned in a book. You're going to need some power."

Loss of Pastoral Authority

The problems posed by "counterfeit callings" and "confused callings" point to one of the biggest paradoxes of the horizontal call: the way ministers make sense of pastoral authority. The primary gatekeeper for entry into clerical training is either the pastor or, in the case of women in some churches, the Church Mother. It is this endorsement that allows aspirants to be trained, to operate in certain roles in the congregation, and ultimately to be licensed or ordained. Understanding this, ministers at all credentialing stages believe that pastors should be, at the very least, cautious about giving that endorsement. For example, Eric asked, "Does the man of God have a right, maybe even a responsibility, to say, 'son, you need to examine yourself'? Definitely. I think that's the discernment of whoever is the leader. He has to have that discernment."

"Discernment" becomes a crucial part of the formula for accepting someone's call, but ministers were uncertain about how it should operate. In describing people they deemed unfit for ordination or licensing, ministers often pointed to observable characteristics as evidence. They focused their attentions on a callees' lack of character, lack of commitment, or lack of competence. They often attributed both aspiring and credentialed callee's failings in these areas to a lack of a true calling. Maria, who coordinates her church's Deaconesses, argues that "today people say 'I'm called' and we let them through without paying attention to their character or their gifts or their anointing or their fruits or anything."

Ironically, while they considered an absence of these characteristics an easy marker of a false calling, ministers also argued that pastors' affirmations of "confused callings" were too strongly based on the presence of these observable characteristics. This, ministers declare, is not discernment.

Maria argued this position as well: "So there's the other danger of people saying, 'I see your fruit, I see your character, I see your commitment, I see your dedication,' and then they assume if you have all those things, like any good Christian should, that you have a calling on your life. But every good Christian is not called to preach."

For the most part, none of the ministers believed that observing a callee's behavior was the best way to verify the authenticity of their call. They maintain instead that pastors should have a supernatural ability to determine whether someone is right for the ministry. Ministers' beliefs that these men might have that ability are shaped in large part by their faith in their pastor's ability to hear from God. Shaunda, an Aspiring Missionary, voiced her sense of this ability to discern a call: "God authorizes our pastor to lead this flock. I believe God speaks to him and God would tell him that. Once God gives it to him, then he's responsible to share it." Shaunda referred to her own interview with the Church Mother who affirmed Shaunda's call with a suggestion that she, the Mother, already knew about it.

The common response of "I knew it already" carries more meaning than just a simple affirmation of an individual's call. It implies that pastors, and their proxies, have an ability to discern such a call in members of their congregations. Even in the absence of those specific words, a pastor's endorsement of someone's calling inadvertently signals some precognition about that call. Most callees, and particularly men who hope to be pastors, consider this supernatural ability a critical piece of a church leader's spiritual toolbox. When asked if they believed their pastors had such an ability, nearly all of my informants responded affirmatively.

Given the seemingly widespread belief that church leaders can, and must, discern if someone is called, how do "noncalled" people find themselves in the clergy? While the ministers and likely other congregants believe that their pastors have a responsibility to discern one's calling, pastors and other church leaders maintain that they do not in fact have that responsibility. On one hand, pastors simply do not believe that they have to, arguing that they only acknowledge the person's belief that they are called. The confirmation of a call has to come from the one who, supposedly, initiated it: God. Therefore, they place the responsibility for disconfirming a confused call at God's feet, deeming it inappropriate for them to make that decision. On the other hand, if someone is pursuing the credential for the wrong reasons, claiming a "counterfeit call," the pastors believe that God will uncover their motives. As one pastor said gravely, "they'll just wind up hanging themselves. That's one thing you don't want to mess with, saying you're called by God and you're not, because eventually the truth will be known." In both situations, pastors expect aspirants to get the message that they are not truly called and then abandon the ministerial identity. Of course, as we've seen, the process itself works against those ends.

Church leaders also do not feel comfortable relaying a negative response to aspiring callees because they don't trust their own ability to make that judgment. When I asked Kasim, an Elder and aspiring pastor, how he would determine if someone wasn't called, he replied, "I would have to seriously know that that person was living like a heathen to tell him he wasn't called. Seriously, I would have to labor before God before I knew I had it right." Because the call—unlike character or commitment—is unverifiable in any documentable way, church leaders prefer to err on the side of caution. This is especially the case in larger churches where gauging even character and competence, let alone calling, can be difficult. As Mona said,

> See, back in the day, in the little church I grew up in, they could say, "I been watching your life, and God has called you." But in a church like ours, with three and four hundred people showing up every Sunday, you get people coming in two and a half years saying they're called, but you don't know nothing about them. You ain't been watching anything.

Rather than deny someone's call, leaders take a "wait and see" attitude, letting aspirants move through the process and deciding along the way if they have any promise.

Of course, "along the way" is an indeterminate span of time when there is no clear rubric for measuring someone's success. If leaders come to believe the person is not effective in ministry, they deny their calling in an implicit but effective way: they eventually stop using them. Apparently, this occurs quite commonly. When asked how callings should be discerned, an instructor in one Jurisdictional Institute complained, "The awful thing is that it's done after the fact. Instead of telling him when he's an aspiring, they go ahead and give him a license and then never really use him for anything. They just waste people's time." The instructor went on to explain that unused licentiates become jealous and resentful of other ministers who are given opportunities to minister. This resentment in turn creates new problems for other leaders.

The unverifiable nature of a calling raises another challenge for church leaders. Angelo, the chief of protocol at his church, is responsible for shepherding aspirant ministers through the first phase of the credentialing process. He describes an important weak point in his pastor's authority over an aspirant: "I see it all the time in our jurisdiction. If I can go to my pastor and he tells me I'm not called, and then I can go down the street to another church and that church says I am, who's to say which church is right?" The possibility of going to a different congregation and finding success, however measured, calls into question the originating pastor's wisdom and discernment. Basing a decision to reject someone's calling on observable characteristics, which can change or be unknown to a new congregation, is a risky proposition. Few pastors seemed willing to take that risk.

I was surprised to discover that some of the leaders' fears were warranted. While ministers believed that their pastors had the authority and responsibility to confirm people's callings, their own responses to that authority would be mixed. Even though Eric believed that pastors "definitely" had the right to reject someone's calling, he made room for callees to prioritize their vertical call over their pastor's authority to deny them a horizontal one: "I think it would be on the individual to accept that or reject it. In terms of operating as a part of the larger body of Christ, if you believe God had called you then I believe you would have to pick yourself up, and mosey on out the door, and find some pastor that would raise you up." This was another paradox. While all the ministers deemed their pastors capable of constraining someone else's ministry, believed he had ultimate authority over their own.

In my conversations about their pastors' authority over them, aspiring and recently licensed women were more likely than men and their advanced peers to defer to their pastor's authority, within limits. Each person was asked how they would respond if their pastor limited them in some way that felt contrary to their sense of their call. Some, like Adrienne, would accept those constraints initially: "Well, I think first I would be obedient because that's the person God has over me. I would still go into prayer, and follow whatever leading God gave, whether it would be to stay or to go to a different place where he can allow me to be used." Many new female callees spoke like Adrienne, claiming deference to the pastor's authority, while still turning to God for confirmation. Even at this early stage in the development of a ministerial identity, they struggled with possible external resistance to it. Erica, another aspiring missionary, found it difficult to even consider what it would mean if her pastor had denied her calling: "I don't know. I know for sure I would have to go and pray. Especially knowing all that God done said to me and then for [pastor] to say something like that? I would need God to help me. I really would because that would be tough."

Conversely, men at all stages and women who had been credentialed for at least a few years were less likely to take on a deferential pose. Some explained that they would argue their case. Justine, for example, said, "I would sit down, discuss it with them, tell them 'no, that's not where God wants me to be.' I would explain to them why. [If they disagreed], my next thing would be to say I know this isn't the place that God would have me work." Others would seek some divine confirmation, but did not suggest any likelihood of submitting to their pastor's authority in the absence of that confirmation. Jonell made the case that God would speak to her first, as he did when he gave her the call, before telling her pastor what constraints should be put on it:

If he came to me and told me that I'm not called to do what God told me I was called to do? I would need to hear God say that to me. Sure, God will give it to him, but if God can speak to him, God can speak to me. He's not going to speak something to you about me, but not tell me to my face.

The most common response was to reject their pastor's statements and leave their local church. Eric relied on a metaphor to explain what he might consider a difficult, but ultimately necessary, decision:

I would never choose to go against the pastor in terms of not being able to serve in this particular house. I believe this is the house the Lord has placed me in for this season and I believe that my rearing is not over in this house. But if he told me that I wasn't called, I would have to leave. I wouldn't want to leave. It's warm here. The food's good here. It's family here. But knowing that my Father in heaven has called me, I would be forced to take my conviction with me.

Eric, like nearly every other minister, made it clear that the fears pastors and credentialing boards express have some validity. The power of the aspirant's conviction of a calling can be so strong as to render a pastor's criticisms meaningless. This possibility is heightened by the likelihood that Eric, and any other aspirant, can find *some* congregation to accept his vertical call and grant him a horizontal one. The one chance pastors may have to diminish the aspirant's sense that he or she is called is at that moment when they are approached. Once they endorse the possibility that someone is called, there is no turning back, especially if the credentialing process has already moved forward.

PART III

Being the Called

4

"A Stutter and a Stick"

The (Non-) Value of Educational Credentialing

Then the Lord put forth His hand and touched my mouth, and the
Lord said to me: "Behold, I have put My words in your mouth."

Jeremiah 1:9

Moses delivered a nation with a stutter and stick. I think I can
do what I'm supposed to do whether I hold credentials from
men or not.

Kasim, Elder

The economist Robert Reich refers to professionals as "symbolic
analysts," experts who use specialized knowledge to solve problems.[1] The
sociologist Andrew Abbott describes the work of the professional in three
parts, stating that professionals make "claims to classify a problem, to reason
about it, and to take action on it; in more formal terms, to diagnose, to infer,
and to treat."[2] The autonomy and authority, which also characterize the professions, flow to a large degree from their abilities to deliver on these claims
in ways that nonprofessionals cannot. This expertise makes them accountable only to their peers while also earning them the trust and compliance of
their clients and supporting paraprofessionals.

These so-called experts make a claim to a professional jurisdiction, an
arena of labor, that cannot be encroached upon without going through their
gatekeepers. They do this by monopolizing knowledge through a credentialing process, a process intended to reduce access to the social and economic
benefits that possessors of that knowledge claim.[3] Although there are no
secret methods of suturing a wound or giving a persuasive religious speech—
two skills that one can learn in minutes online—the skills and the often cog-
nitively indeterminate theoretical underpinnings of them have become the
intellectual property of the medical and religious professions, respectively. In

order to practice medicine, law, or theology, one must have the imprimatur of senior members of the medical, legal, and clerical fraternity.

It is not enough to be taught, or even to master, the knowledge. Consider the scores of bright and capable scholars who, after years of study, languish in the liminal category referred to as "ABD" (all but the dissertation) until a panel of experts in their field deem them acceptable to carry the title "Dr." Even more starkly, those trained in medicine or taught to make legal arguments can practice neither craft without passing a medical board or a legal bar exam. Training at even the top medical school or law school does not make one a professional: receiving a license does. We have come to understand professions—particularly the classical "learned professions" of medicine, law, and theology—as closed labor communities, where considerable amounts of training in the art and the science of the craft are normal and essential.

In 2001, the Black Pentecostal pastor Thomas (T. D.) Jakes appeared on the cover of *Time* magazine as part of an article asking if he was the next Billy Graham.[4] In addition to pastoring an eighteen-thousand-member church, Jakes is a best-selling author of more than thirty books, an owner of a gospel record label, a movie producer, and the organizer of one of the largest evangelical ministry events in the country, Megafest. He's a remarkably successful religious professional. He's also a college dropout. And he's not alone.

The Potter's House's T. D. Jakes, Church Without Walls' Paula White, Lakewood Church's Joel Osteen, Calvary Chapel's Bob Coy, and the international televangelist Benny Hinn lead some of the largest and fastest growing ministries in the United States. None of them has a bachelor's degree, let alone a master of divinity degree or any other degree from an accredited seminary. Yet they pastor a combined total of more than one hundred thousand congregants, not including the other hundreds of thousands who follow them on television. They clearly have considerable power and prestige, traits that accrue to occupations, nay professions, whose members have "special competence in an esoteric body of knowledge."[5] In the absence of seminary or Bible college training, where do ministers like these claim to get this "special competence"?

A General History of Religious Educational Credentialing

In the United States, professional knowledge was first learned while in the employ of a practitioner in the field. For example, aspiring physicians learned their craft working with and for mature physicians. Similarly, those men who sought training as ministers learned theological practice and theory through apprenticeships with practicing ministers. Before the advent of the American college or professional school, these apprenticeships were the access point to most occupations. These apprenticeships, which included some study of pertinent texts, were likely to focus more on practice than theory. Students learned by doing, a system that was markedly unsystematic in the way novices were exposed to techniques or to the theoretical ideas that might undergird those procedures.[6]

While most apprenticeships were individualized, some enterprising ministers began to accept groups of students for training. These "schools of the prophets" were precursors of the religious professional schools, remedying some of the inconsistency in training that ministers were otherwise encountering.[7] Like their biblical namesakes,[8] these academies sought to routinize piety, inculcating religious principles with moralizing lectures and rehearsed catechisms rather than the more earthy, but disorganized, apprenticeships. The turn to fully integrating the two in a systematic way occurred when Congregationalists sought to combine the practical training ministers received in apprenticeships with the more theoretical training—and attendant professional prestige—that others acquired in religious academies. The creation of Andover Theological Seminary in 1807 (now Andover Newton Theological School) marked the beginning of an experiment in professionalizing the clergy. By 1850, seven other denominations had joined the Congregationalists in creating forty-three more seminaries.[9]

Faculties at Andover and other seminaries helped to concretize the image of a professionally educated clergy. Like any other professional school at the time, these seminaries began to systematically establish jurisdiction over the knowledge that aspiring practitioners would need. As the historian Brooks Holifield explains:

> Seminaries promoted the vision of ministry as the "noblest of professions." They aimed to elevate their students into a "learned profession" by providing a body of knowledge and the principles for applying it. A clerical professional was, according to the ideal, a person of "sound scholarship," a person "learned and accomplished," capable of scaling "heights of knowledge."[10]

The academics in these schools trained aspiring ministers to do more than represent the voice of man to God. As preachers, they were becoming more responsible to serve as the voice of God to man, which required more than knowledge of ceremony and ritual. It required the kind of intellectual spirit that elite education could instill in these religious professionals. Just as the master craftsman served as the gatekeeper for apprentices, seminaries and Bible colleges became the portal through which acceptable ministers needed to go.

Competence in ministry became tied to one's educational pedigree, and that pedigree could be earned, in certain religious traditions, only by attending these institutions. These schools were attractive to many Congregationalist ministers who were losing their hold on local congregations and being forced to become itinerant preachers. Without the status inherent in being head of a congregation, they needed some other way to separate themselves from the laity. The seminaries gave them "new bases of professional status; where revivalists distinguished themselves from the laity by fiery preaching, the new breed of Congregational ministers would seek this distinction in a learned and autonomous elaboration of theology."[11] The belief in seminary's importance was so strong that when their status was threatened by itinerant preachers, seminary-trained clergy succeeded in passing laws making it illegal for parishes to call a pastor without a college degree.

The Resurgence of the Untrained Revivalist

This practice of requiring a degree was effective when most colonists were members of presbyterian, congregational, and episcopal congregations; in 1776, 55 percent of religiously active Americans belonged to one or the other of these denominations.[12] As new religious sects born in the late eighteenth and early nineteenth centuries—the Methodist Episcopal church, the Baptist Triennial Convention, the Latter-day Saints, and others—began to blossom and challenge more established denominations, the preeminence of seminary training began to falter. These new sects ballooned in size as a result of the ministry of effective, energetic, but uneducated itinerant preachers. This brought them into open conflict with mainline clergy such as Timothy Dwight, the Congregationalist president of Yale College (1795–1817) and founder of Andover.

Dwight denounced followers of the upstart denominations, using an argument that equated the clergy with other classical professions. He said:

[T]hey demand a seven years apprenticeship, for the purpose of learning to make a shoe, or an axe [yet] they suppose the system of Providence . . . may be all comprehended without learning, labour, or time. While they insist, equally with others, that their property shall be managed by skilful agents, their judicial causes directed by learned advocates, and their children, when sick, attended by able physicians; they were satisfied to place their Religion, their souls, and their salvation, under the guidance of quackery.

In spite of the charges leveled against them, the new denominations decried the need for formal religious education well into the mid-nineteenth century. They argued that seminary education would "make them dependent on their books and written sermons rather than the movement of the Spirit which was central to the revival experience."[13]

There were clear benefits for not depending on seminary-trained ministers. At the organizational level, denominations could grow quickly without the lag between someone's professing a call and their ability to start operating in it. Clergy shortages were almost unheard of. Training for new preachers occurred in short apprenticeships, often while those preachers co-led smaller units of larger local congregations. There were also benefits to the ministers themselves. Men from non-elite backgrounds could claim a calling and pursue ministry, with all of the authority and autonomy that comes with the title. They assumed the status of professionals, at least within their own religious denominations, without one of the most important trappings of professionalism: formal religious training. Most importantly, they seemingly maintained some level of effectiveness at their craft, which enabled them to continue to attract adherents.

While the Baptists, Methodists, and other new denominations fought credentialing for many years, once their prominence made them the new protectors of the clergy's professional status, these now-mainline institutions began to turn to seminaries as a means of patrolling the borders of that status. Today, a non-seminary-trained member of the clergy in the mainline denominations is the exception rather than the rule. If not a requirement, seminary or seminary-like training is becoming a clear expectation for ordination in these formerly "new" American sects. In the contemporary mainline denominations, ordination usually follows some evidence that the aspirant has mastered specialized knowledge. While internships in a local congregation or chaplaincy position along with some kind of denomination-sanctioned examination may constitute part of that evidence, neither is a strong substitute for an advanced degree in religion. Consider that there are seventeen seminaries or schools of theology affiliated with the United Methodist Church and its predecessor denominations. Similarly, twenty seminaries are affiliated with three of the largest Baptist denominations. Not surprisingly, like their nineteenth-century antagonists, these denominations are beginning to experience the very clergy shortages they warned against.[14]

Both the memberships and the clergy pools of many mainline denominations (including former upstarts like the Methodists) are being dwarfed by sects born in the latter part of the nineteenth century. These include the Jehovah's Witnesses and Pentecostal-Holiness sects. Zikmund's study of clergy determined that less than half of the ministers in (predominately White) Pentecostal denominations attend seminary.[15] While not being stridently anti-seminary, these denominations have returned to the apprentice-style of training that characterized early versions of practically every new American religious tradition.

Joining them have been what sociologist Donald Miller calls "new paradigm" congregations: nondenominational churches and innovative religious movements like the Vineyard Church and Calvary Chapel, which train their ministers in similar ways.[16] In Miller's study of the leadership of these predominantly White and moderately charismatic ministries, he encountered the kind of emphasis on calling above all else which was present in my interviews with Pentecostal ministers. Rejecting the need for seminary, the founder of the Calvary Chapel network is quoted as saying, "God does not call those who are qualified, but qualifies those who are called."[17] In listing the kinds of qualities that guide the selection of leaders, Miller points to characteristics like "passionate commitment to God" and "a Spirit-filled life" as the only prerequisites for effective ministry according to these movements. "After all," he adds, "they say, Jesus used a group of fishermen to establish his kingdom."

The Black Church and Educational Credentialing

Formal religious training has been a factor almost from the beginning for the Black church in America. In fact, barely three years after its founding in 1816, the African Methodist Episcopal (AME) Church had created a publishing house that produced study materials for young ministers. Soon, they began to develop Sunday school programs, a development that helped to solidify the Black church's position at the heart of many Black communities.[18] In the absence of opportunities to do so in any other way, former slaves and their descendants were learning to read in these classes, with the Bible as a counterpart to the "New England Primer."

In 1844, while the AME's White Methodist peers were still debating the Congregationalists about the value of seminary training,[19] this new sect created the Union Seminary in Ohio. The seminary's objective was explicitly to educate "young men who propose to enter the Christian ministry."[20] Soon after Union Seminary became what is now Wilberforce University (the oldest private degree-granting historically Black university), the church organized the Payne Theological Seminary. Alongside Atlanta's Gammon and Turner seminaries, which were also founded by AME bishops, Payne is one of the oldest historically Black seminaries in the country. In many ways, the AME church has been the only one of the Black denominations to fully embrace the value of formal religious training as an important component of credentialing. While there has been a considerable increase in the numbers of Black clergy graduating from accredited divinity schools or seminaries, much of that growth has been in the AME denomination, which has the highest percentage (48–51 percent) of "trained" clergy.[21] They are also the only historically Black church that has made the degree of master of divinity a requirement for pastoring.

The majority of Black clergy do not have seminary training. According to most studies, it is believed that about one-third of all black clergy have had some religious training beyond the college level. Only 10–20 percent of Black clergy are estimated to have completed their professional training at an accredited divinity school or seminary.[22] Of the largest Black Protestant denominations, the Church of God in Christ has the smallest percentage of ordained clergy with graduate degrees (19 percent).[23] Certainly some of this trend is a function of cost and time. Many Black pastors are bivocational, splitting their time between full-time secular employment and part-time pastoring. But there is also a cultural angle: as in the "new paradigm" congregations, most of the religious talent in Black Pentecostal and Baptist churches is homegrown. For the majority of clergy in these denominations, apprenticeship training with a senior pastor is often the only educational requirement for ordination.[24]

Specialists without Spirit, Sensualists without Heart

In many Black denominations, the same arguments that White Methodists and Baptists used to reject training at Andover are still being used to reject seminary degrees today. These arguments, when based on scripture at all, are often drawn from passages like 1 John 2:27, which reads "the anointing which you received from [Christ] abides in you, and you do not need that anyone teach you . . . the same anointing teaches you concerning all things." The message implicit in this warning about false teachers, a label occasionally used to describe seminarians, is that anything a religious leader needs he can get directly from God; everything else is counterfeit. The historians C. Eric Lincoln and Lawrence Mamiya explain that contemporary efforts to mandate seminary training collide with these long-held attitudes:

The educational issue is problematic for most black churches because the historical evangelical background of the Baptists, Methodists, and Pentecostals did not have stringent educational demands but only required evidence of a personal call from God to the ministry. The anti-intellectual and fundamentalist strains of that tradition have made it difficult for innovative church leaders and bishops to make professional seminary education a requirement for the ministry.[25]

These anti-intellectual strains are evident in statements made by Black congregants in the recent past. In Melvin Williams's book *Community in a Black Pentecostal Church*, the author quotes COGIC congregants: "Jesus chose common men, everyday men, men used to the sunshine, men used to the rain, not seminary men or college men" and "You may be trained, but not have the Holy Ghost. Education is trivial."[26]

The AME bishop William DeVeaux points to "an interesting phenomenon that occurs in some churches. When a guest preacher is introduced, the following comments are often made. 'She may have a BA, Bachelor of Arts degree, but what really matters is her 'BA,' her born again credentials. Some African American Christians go a step further by saying, 'As you get the learning, do not lose the burning.'"[27] This milder denigration of educational credentialing points to the continuing suspicion that education is good, but being directly led by God is better.

The fear that too much (religious) education does damage to one's ability to preach with "power" or conviction finds some resonance among Black preachers and their congregations. This belief was displayed quite prominently in a 2003 forum on the role of the church in Black America. In his introduction to a conversation about Black clergy and religious credentialing, the talk show host Tavis Smiley led with "there ain't nothing that's messed up the minds of black folk like crack and Harvard. You put too much education in the minds of black preachers and black pastors, too much spirit exits."[28] In the conversation that ensued, the tensions that still exist among Black clergy were evident.

Some argued that new challenges pastors face—administering larger churches, counseling congregants with more complex problems, learning to recognize less overt incidents of racial disenfranchisement—require pastors to have more training than may have been necessary in the past. For example, one of the issues attracting considerable attention by those studying Black churches is the criticism that those churches are no longer interested in either social justice or social service activism. To this end, the United Church of Christ pastor Jeremiah Wright spoke in response to a question posed to him about why Black preachers "preach until we shout" but don't have any services serving Black people. In particular, he was asked to address why Dr. Martin Luther King endeavored to put theology into practice as a social activist. To cheers, this former professor at the Chicago Theological Seminary replied, "Dr. King was seminary trained, my brotha. So that's where you get the intersection of the social and the theological hermeneutic. Ninety percent of African-American clergy persons are not seminary trained." He paused while the audience loudly cheered and then continued, echoing the sentiments of Timothy Dwight spoken centuries before him, "I cannot be a lawyer if I don't go to law school. I cannot be a doctor if I don't go to med school. But all I got to do is turn around my collar and 'hallelujah, I got the anointing' and I got fifty thousand Negroes following me."[29]

Dr. Jacquelyn Grant, a professor of theology at Atlanta's Interdenominational Theological Center, who also spoke at the Smiley conference agreed with Wright, arguing that:

> seminary for the African-American pastor or preacher is in fact crucial. Today our congregations are more educated and it seems then that what is required is an educated pulpit in order to be able to address the needs of educated people. I see no discord between education and preaching. They both are necessary. Other professionals have to go to school to be properly trained and we would expect no less of persons who are called to do the work of God.[30]

In Dr. Grant's comments, another important factor in arguments supporting religious credentialing can be found. Today, the ministry remains the only class of Black professionals where most practitioners do not have graduate training.[31] In many congregations, this puts the heads of those religious bodies far behind some of their congregants in terms of educational attainment. The historian Jackson Carroll states that "in denominations that have not previously emphasized clergy education, the rising tide of educated laity has had what might be called a 'push-up' effect on clergy, with an educated laity pushing for better-educated pastors. Simply put, educated laity generally expect more of their pastors."[32]

This consideration may be especially important for Pentecostal churches. While, historically, Black Pentecostal churches were considered the province of poor, southern Blacks, the migration of well-educated, well-heeled Blacks from the North to the South is causing dramatic shifts in the demographic makeup of many Pentecostal congregations. In her study of sixty-six black megachurches—all of which were Pentecostal or neo-Pentecostal in their worship style—the political scientist Tamelyn Tucker-Worgs discovered that these predominantly urban churches have overwhelmingly middle- to upper-middle-class memberships.[33] It is very likely the case that Black congregants *want* their religious leaders to be educated. Many studies of Black Americans point to the Black community's appreciation for education, particularly at the postsecondary level. In fact, Mark Chaves argues that African American congregations are more likely than their White peers to engage in programs that encourage, and even facilitate, congregants' pursuit of (nonreligious) educational opportunities.[34] That said, the desire to have an educated clergy does not necessarily mean they desire a *religiously educated* clergy.

Pastor Marvin Winans, who was raised in the Church of God in Christ and now pastors a nondenominational Pentecostal church in Detroit, spoke to this point at the Smiley conference. He argued that there is a danger to depending on seminary training:

> I believe we should be trained. I believe we should be taught. But can you imagine what educational institutions would have charged for us to receive eternal life or the knowledge of Jesus Christ? How much tuition would it cost us to be filled with the Holy Spirit? How much would they charge us for us to be healed from our diseases?[35]

Winans gives voice to the Pentecostal (and likely Neo-Pentecostal) perspective that the important components of ministry cannot be taught in a seminary.

COGIC and Educational Credentialing

While the current leader of the COGIC, Bishop Charles Blake, has earned a master's and a doctoral degree in divinity, no other COGIC Presiding Bishop has earned more than a bachelor's degree. The founder of the denomination, Bishop C. H. Mason, was admitted to and attended the Arkansas Baptist College. While considered a talented student by the college's leaders, Mason withdrew after three months because of frustrations with both non-scripture-centered teaching methods and the doctrinal perspectives of the faculty.[36] In spite of this, Mason was a strong advocate for education, encouraging education-leader Dr. Arenia Mallory to found the denomination's Saints Industrial and Literary School (now Saints Academy) in 1926 in Atlanta. His successor, Bishop J. O. Patterson Sr. later established the C. H. Mason Seminary and the system of jurisdictional colleges that have since become the Jurisdictional Institutes discussed earlier.[37] The jurisdictional college for the Memphis area became the All Saints Bible College in 2002 and offers a bachelor's degree in religious studies.

The COGIC denomination now owns both undergraduate and graduate institutions designed to train aspiring ministers but still has no requirement that aspirants possess degrees of any kind. While some of my respondents have taken at least one Bible college or seminary course, many ministers maintain a fairly negative appraisal of seminary and seminary-trained clergy. This is not to say that COGIC ministers are anti-education; nearly two-thirds of those I interviewed have some college experience. In fact, the educational range of these ministers is a broad, and likely surprising, one. A little more than a third of the ministers have no college experience at all. Three of those—all women—have less than a high school diploma, with one having attended formal schooling only to the fifth grade. Even if they wanted to, these ministers (half of whom have terminal clerical licenses) would not qualify for seminary admission because they don't hold bachelor's degrees.

About 43 percent of the ministers are college graduates.[38] Only two of my respondents have undergraduate degrees in religion or theology. Consistent with the norms for Blacks, the men in my sample are less likely to have gone to college or received bachelor's degrees than the women. One in every five ministers has received some kind of post-baccalaureate degree, but most of these degrees are in something other than religion: either business, education, or social work.[39] Two female ministers were pursuing law and medical degrees. Only eight ministers—five men and three women—have master's degrees or doctorates in divinity. In addition to these eight, twelve other ministers report spending time in some kind of formal religious training.

Hidden in these numbers is a more surprising finding. Half of the ministers without any college experience currently hold either an Elder's or Evangelist's license. One of these is a pastor. Of all the ministers who have these terminal credentials, only one-quarter indicate having spent any time in a seminary or Bible college; less than half of those have degrees. Of the pastors I interviewed, only half have seminary degrees. These numbers make clear the role that educational credentialing plays or, more precisely, doesn't play, in the ordination process of Black Pentecostal ministers. Not only is seminary or Bible college training *not* a requirement of ordination, it could not even be considered normative. It is the rare COGIC minister who has pursued or completed such training. There is a structural reason for this.

The most likely explanation would be that most Black ministers, regardless of denomination, come to recognize a call to ministry late in life. These "late-career" clergy are, understandably, less likely to pursue seminary degrees. While this trend is especially prevalent in Black churches, studies of other religious communities suggest that many clergy decide to pursue callings at a later age than in the past.[40] Compared to their counterparts who have been in ministry for ten to twenty years, clergy in both mainstream Protestant and historically Black denominations are getting ordained six to seven years later. According to religion Jackson Carroll, the median age at ordination was thirty-nine for Black clergy who have been in ministry for less than ten years. That number ranges from twenty-one to thirty-two for clergy who have been ministering longer than that.[41] One can see from my sample that many COGIC ministers are also late-career clergy. The average age of Aspiring Ministers and Missionaries is forty-five, with men claiming a call to ministry two years later than women.

Concomitant with their late-career decision as clergy is that every one of my respondents would be considered second-career clergy as well. Accordingly, for many of them, their educational training is more closely aligned with their pre-call occupation than with a clerical one. This too is becoming the norm, regardless of race and denomination. While young men and women are still coming into the ministry directly from college, they are in the minority. Most new clergy, including those who have attended seminary, are coming to ministry from another career path. While the second-career trend is not abnormal for mainline and conservative (White) Protestant denominations, where nearly half of the clergy are second-career, it is more significant in Black churches. Almost 80 percent of Black pastors had a different occupation before actively pursuing a call.[42]

In terms of both late-career and second-career entrants, the clergy is quite different from medicine and law. The age for entry in these professions still hovers around twenty-four to twenty-six; the decision to pursue a law or medical degree generally happens at age twenty-one. The average age at which aspirants seek ordination is thirty-one.[43] Compare that number to the average in my sample (forty-five years), and it is clear that pursuing a call by seeking additional educational credentials is prohibitive, based on the disruption to one's life that decision might cause. This disruption is exacerbated by the twin challenges of finding—and affording—an appropriate seminary.

While the structural barriers are quite real, the church does not see them as insurmountable for someone claiming a call to ministry. The pressures to have appropriately trained ministers weighs heavily on many congregations, especially those in urban areas. As COGIC leadership changed, they launched new priorities for the church as it moved toward the new millennium. One of those priorities was responding to the need for a more professional clergy.

In 1995, the COGIC Assembly mandated that anyone seeking professional status via ordination must complete the denomination's two-year certificate program. Part of the curriculum for the certificate can be found in the *Understanding Bible Doctrine as Taught in the Church of God in Christ* textbook and workbook.[44] The book is "designed to acquaint the candidate [for ordination] with the biblical teachings which constitute the doctrines of the Church of God in Christ." Aspirants are trained in eleven doctrinal areas: the Bible (Bibliology), God (Theology), Christ (Christology), the Holy Ghost (Pneumatology), Angels (Angelology), Demons (Demonology), Man (Anthropology), Sin (Hamartiology), Salvation (Soteriology), the Church (Ecclesiology), and the Last Things (Eschatology). In addition to doctrine, the other pillars of training (i.e., those tested in written/oral examinations) for ministers are church history and organization. They are required to know COGIC history, COGIC polity and structure, and church protocol. Some training is also offered in Bible study techniques and homiletics (sermon preparation and delivery).

The assumption (stated in the introduction to the handbook) is that "all candidates for ordination *must* complete the catechism before receiving ordination." In spite of this mandate, few of my sample's recent licentiates or ordinands had even seen, let alone completed, the catechism in the back of the training manual. As with many mandates in the Church of God in Christ, the decision to require completion of the seventy-six-page catechism belongs to the Jurisdictional Bishop alone. If he does not require the catechism as part of the credentialing process, it may or may not be used. In larger COGIC churches, the training in catechism is facilitated by in-house courses overseen by a, usually, seminary-trained Elder or Evangelist. The courses themselves are often taught by clergy, but many churches draw on expertise wherever it may reside in their congregation. As a result, licentiates and ordinands may be taking courses taught by lay-members and lay-leaders.

In order to receive a terminal license or to be ordained, female Deaconesses and male Licensed Ministers must pass both an oral and written test created by each jurisdiction's ordination board. The jurisdiction's Commissioner of Ordination uses these tests as the key qualifiers for his recommendation to the Jurisdictional Bishop (and for women, the jurisdiction's Supervisor of Women) that the aspirant be given their final credential. This test, based largely on the catechism, can be a stumbling block for some. Ordination committee members gave examples of ministers who could competently give stirring sermons and served the church passionately, but could not pass the written test. In some cases, the minister had to retake the test multiple times until he or she could pass it. Again, as with most COGIC mandates related to training and credentialing, the final decision resides in the hands of the Jurisdictional Bishop. If the recommending pastor can make the case, as one ordination committee member quoted, that "no number on some test should get in the way of this young man's destiny," the bishop may waive the test as a requirement.

It is important to note that these are requirements for *ordination*. In most cases, the local requirements for *licensing* (which are entirely controlled by the local pastor) are much less structured. In addition to offering some suggestions for aspiring licentiates (e.g., "write one message or lesson each month and present it to your pastor"), one jurisdiction's training manual for aspiring ministers informs them of how the process might proceed:

> Wait for the day that your pastor tells you that he will bring you before the church to be licensed. The process may differ from pastor to pastor. You may desire to ask your pastor to tell you his manner. This is not to question his manner or to tell him how someone else does it. You are asking that you man [sic] know how best to wait with patience. Some pastors will have you preach on a given evening and after you have preached he then will go forth to issue you the license. Other pastors will license you based on your faithfulness alone. The manner is left to the local pastor and you will be licensed based on your fitting into his system.[45]

This description is a very real example of how imprecise the local-licensing process is for Licensed Ministers and Deaconesses.

Much of this flexibility is a result of COGIC's (and, more broadly) Pentecostalism's tensions with what historian Grant Wacker refers to as a "primitive" otherworldliness and a very practical and realistic "pragmatism."[46] Pentecostalism, more than any other Christian religious tradition, is practically defined by nonpredictability and lack of standardization—a sovereign God demands the freedom to act, unconstrained by human rationalism. However, Pentecostal religious leaders are working under the same pressures to maintain professional standards of competence that their less Spirit-oriented counterparts are. These pressures have created long-standing tensions, with which Pentecostalism has had mixed results.

Weber's Priests, Prophets, Charisma
Priestly Professionals

To some degree Wacker's description of those two poles—the pragmatic and the primitive—finds a corollary in Max Weber's description of two kinds of religious leaders. The clergy can be divided into two ideal types, priests and prophets, the first being the pragmatic professional and the latter the primitive personality.

Weber suggests that "priests" are, essentially, religious bureaucrats whose primary duty is to patrol the borders of religious ideology. They protect religious institutions by sacralizing certain actions, texts, and interpretations of those texts, drawing clean lines between the traditional values of the community and the tendencies of laity to reject that orthodoxy. The danger here is amplified as religious communities interact with other communities or expand via conversion. Whether labeled priest, pastor, or cleric, religious professionals represent the religious establishment. Their professional status is intrinsically bound to the success of the "corporate enterprise of salvation" they protect.[47]

Like any professional, Christian priests' claims to authority are tied to their monopoly of some body of knowledge and the practice associated with it. This is not just a question of claiming exclusive rights to mediate man's communication with God. Weber argues that not only do they claim to "monopolize the regular management of Yahwe worship and all related activities" but they also claim "a monopoly in the employment of certain oracular formulae, priestly teaching, and priestly positions."[48] In essence, they seek to control the methods by which God communicates with mankind.

Of course, in order to control knowledge, a professional group must standardize that knowledge. In this way, people who stake a claim to knowledge can be tested and deemed legitimate. Physicians have done this by embracing empiricism, moving farther away from seeing medical practice as "art" and beginning to depend more on the efficiency produced in scientific and technical discovery. This move has been effective. Beyond first aid, few laymen would consider themselves competent to meet their own health care needs. "Priests" have been less successful, even with the advent of professional schools, at retaining a monopoly over the arcana of religious practice. Inasmuch as most Protestants take seriously the New Testament principle of the "priesthood of all believers," the doctrine of priestly mediators between man and God loses much of its meaning. As a result, mainline churches are losing members as congregants find themselves fully capable of meeting their own religious needs.

Consider, for example, one of the most sacred religious traditions in the Christian church: administration of the Eucharist. While still mystical in some ways, its management by contemporary priests has become as rationalized as any other priestly duty. Many churches use pre-filled communion cups advertised as "a communion wafer and grape juice in one sanitary, single-serving container." Laymen can buy these in the same stores where they purchase other paraphernalia once reserved for clergy. In fact, the book by the Pentecostal evangelist Perry Stone, *The Meal That Heals*, encourages readers to take communion at home as a kind of prophylactic against illness.[49]

The idea of a trained clergy, already firmly embedded in largely bureaucratic organizations, points to the rationalization of ministry. It might be argued that such training promotes the rational over the traditional, a preference for logical answers over mystical ones. Thus the work of religious professionals becomes formulaic: evangelizing a new convert? Just teach them their "*ABCs*"—A(dmit your sins), B(elieve in Jesus), C(onfess Him as Savior). A congregant is ill? Just "*PRAY*"—P(raise), R(epent), A(sk), and then Y(ield). Preaching? Wash your mouth out with "*SOAP*"—S(cripture), O(bservation), A(pplication), and P(rayer). This development has the potential to lead to the kind of "too much education in . . . and too much spirit exits" phenomena that Tavis Smiley warned about at his 2003 conference. Weber, too, warned of this possibility when he spoke of "specialists without spirit."[50] While he was speaking of any worker who gave into the bureaucratization of life, the larger context of his comments make this relevant to the question of religious professionalism as exemplified in "priests."

Charisma and Prophets

While the priest still plays a critical role in religious communities, he is not the only game in town. While much of the priest's influence is tied to his position in the church, that position and its authority rides on the personal holdings of the priest himself. Weber describes these as "his professional equipment of special knowledge, fixed doctrine, and vocational qualifications, which brings him into contrast with sorcerers, prophets, and other types of religious functionaries who exert their influence by virtue of personal gifts (charisma) made manifest in miracle and revelation."[51] In this summary, Weber introduces readers to another trait held by religious leaders—specifically, prophets—a trait whose meaning is as contested as that of the word "professional."

Indeed, charisma has the power to make a lowly carpenter the "savior of the world" even more than two thousand years after his death on a cross. It made a German shoemaker able to take a distorted version of that cross and make it the most hated symbol in the world. Its power took four young musicians from Liverpool and gained them crowds of crying, fainting followers in America and around the world. For Weber, the chief distinction between priests and prophets is the prophet's holding of "charisma," which he defined as

> a certain quality of an individual personality, by virtue of which one is "set apart" from ordinary people and treated as endowed with supernatural, superhuman, or at least specifically exceptional powers or qualities. These as such are not accessible to the ordinary person, but are regarded as divine in origin or as exemplary, and on the basis of them the individual concerned is treated as a leader.[52]

Those endowed with charisma gain legitimacy as authority figures because people believe them worthy of being followed. As a result, churches led by charismatic leaders are initially characterized more by follow-ship than by fellowship. The charismatic prophet's authority is freely given to him or her, and this legitimates them in a very different way than the traditional or bureaucratically determined authority of the priestly professional.[53]

Weber argues that the legitimacy of true charismatic personalities resides in the followers' belief that the leader just has "it" and that it is their duty to be devoted to the individual. There is rarely any evidence of this kind of genuine charisma, that is, charisma not catalyzed by some evidence supporting a belief that the person has exceptional qualities. Weber focuses more on the kind of charismatic authority granted as a result of one's magical abilities, prowess on the battlefield, or ability to enthrall and manipulate. In order for these actions to legitimate someone's leadership, they must be perceived as worthwhile or important themselves.

In this way, most charismatic communities are, at least initially, governed by an emotional action orientation. Unfortunately, emotional social action is tenuous and is easily undone. If there is a weakening of the evidence of charisma, the followers may rescind their "offer" of legitimacy and the charismatic's following would minify. Traditionally, this evidence was based in some magical or heroic ability that was usually not sustainable. Defeats in war, droughts, and locust attacks were easy proof that the charismatic leader may have fallen out of favor with the gods. Today, something like a terrible selection of songs or poor reviews of a movie can just as easily bring a charismatic leader down.

Studies of charismatic leadership have reduced charisma to a set of personality traits (e.g., visionary, energetic) or abilities (e.g., a command of rhetoric) likely to be found in both secular and religious leaders.[54] Even as our redefinition of charisma has expanded the number of people who can be considered "charismatic," the concept has been stripped of much of the meaning Weber initially gave it. Certainly, Weber is himself partially responsible for this expansion of the "charismatic authority" to describe secular leadership. He places it alongside "legal authority" and "traditional authority" as the means by which secular leaders might legitimately maintain control of social and economic organizations.[55] But his definition of charisma, in its purest form, is a religious phenomenon tied much more explicitly to the supernatural. Again, his charismatic prophet is believed to be "endowed with *supernatural, superhuman,* or at least specifically *exceptional powers* or qualities."[56] These powers—or the assumption that they exist—are what distinguishes the professional priest from the more divinely inspired, and empowered, prophet.

Weber goes to great lengths to describe the resources charismatic leaders—prophets—bring to bear in their efforts to gain acceptance and a following:

> It was only under very unusual circumstances that a prophet succeeded in establishing his authority without charismatic authentication, which in practice meant magic. At least the bearers of new doctrine practically always needed such validation. It must not be forgotten for an instant that the entire basis of Jesus' own legitimation, as well as his claim that he and only he knew the Father and that the way to God led through faith in him alone, was the magical charisma he felt within himself. There was always required of such prophets a proof of their possession of particular gifts of the spirit, of special magical or ecstatic abilities.[57]

While my respondents refer first to their vertical call as the source of their spiritual authority, they also make a claim to the kind of supernatural powers that characterizes Weber's charismatic leader. Along with the vertical call, these abilities set them apart from talented (and maybe even gifted) rhetoricians like Barack Obama or visionaries like Bill Gates, both of whom might be considered charismatic leaders. These men's abilities to lead are considered notable even exceptional by my respondents. But ultimately their abilities would be considered ineffective in a religious context; talents and gifts are inadequate for religious labor. My respondents argue that one must have the kind of abilities that Weber describes: powers that "are not accessible to the ordinary person, but are . . . divine in origin." Ultimately, charisma is "made manifest in miracle and revelation" and it is on the basis of these powers that charismatic ministers are treated as leaders in their churches.

Congregants and ministers both demand "charismatic" works if they are going to give any credence to a congregational leader's claim to religious authority. They don't follow their pastors because these men are professionals who can apply logic and reason to situations. Instead, they argue that in the kinds of situations they encounter, natural and supernatural alike, reason fails. What good is reason when their child has just been in a car accident? Can reason pay their bills when their boss employs a "last hired, first fired" rule unexpectedly? No. They find the kind of reason represented in the solidly trained, professional priest unsatisfying. Instead they require their pastor to have the supernatural capacity to speak to their situation and do what would be considered *unreasonable* and maybe even impossible, and that is to effect change in their circumstances. Of course, ministers don't just apply these expectations to other religious leaders. Many ministers claim these same powers for themselves. Surprisingly, given their assertions to have what, at first blush, appeared to be charisma, no one used that term in the interviews. Instead, these ministers describe their authority as being tied to their holding of a charisma-like quality called "the anointing."

The sociologist Margaret Poloma speaks of terms like "revelation," "being baptized in the Spirit," and "being slain in the Spirit" as rhetorical phrases that have meaning in Pentecostal circles but may not be understood at all by non-Pentecostals.[58] The "anointing" may be one of these. In the *Time* article that profiled T. D. Jakes, a former editor of the Pentecostal magazine *Charisma* was asked to explain how this country preacher has managed to gain such success. Incapable of extolling Jakes's educational credentials, the editor, Lee Grady, did not turn to the word "charisma" to describe the source of Jakes's prominence. Instead, he said, "We talk about someone being *anointed*. Jakes knows he's got a special trust."[59] While we might consider the Pentecostal televangelist Oral Roberts's effectiveness as a preacher a function of his "charisma," Roberts himself claimed an anointing as the source of his oratorical prowess: "I become *anointed* with God's word, and the spirit of the Lord builds up in me like a coiled spring. By the time I'm ready to go on, my mind is razor-sharp."[60] Upon the death of the renowned pastor (and college dropout), even the *Economist*'s version of Roberts's obituary referred to the "heavy anointing" that enabled him to preach across the world.[61]

Weber describes the prophet's powers as the source of his appeal, his charismatic authority. The "anointing" may operate in this same way, granting one the ability to perform in the prophetic role, making the absence of priestly "vocational qualifications" irrelevant. But what is this "anointing" and how does it function?

The Anointing: Defined

The clearest description of "the anointing" comes from COGIC Missionary, Kenya. She describes it as "a special impartation through the Holy Spirit to give you the wisdom, the know-how, the revelation to do what it is you need to do from a spiritual perspective. The things that I go forth to do, I know that me and my own ability wouldn't come up with the ideas, the creativity, the understanding that I have. That doesn't come from a natural ability." Kenya's description of her abilities as unnatural are, in some ways, surprising. From an outsider's perspective, one might look at the religious labor she does—teaching in and helping to administer the church's youth Bible study— as fairly routine and manageable. This is especially the case given her secular training and employment as a program coordinator in the local school district. She says she has a gift to teach and a gift to administer, but in order to be effective in her calling, she must be anointed to do it. She explains:

> Like with [Vacation Bible School], a curriculum was set before me. So now I need the anointing from the Lord to tell me how to teach this so it would fit this particular group of people. I don't perceive me getting that from just regular intellect. I need the direction and guidance of the Holy Spirit who knows the needs of the people, who knows how it needs to be set up, who knows what needs to be done. The Holy Spirit gave me the creativity on how to map it all out.

Even though a minister might appear to have the requisite skill set to perform church tasks, they downplay those skills. Kenya certainly has the ability to organize a classroom and teach a set of materials given to her by her church's education coordinator; she does similar tasks every day as a middle-school administrator. But from her perspective, religious labor requires some skills she does not naturally have. When she speaks of needing to know how to "teach this so it would fit this particular group of people," she's referring to something other than being able to teach at a grade-appropriate level. She is speaking of needing a kind of supernatural insight into what approach might best be used to have an impact on her students. This "revelation to do what it is you need to do" is attributed to divine intervention via this anointing that she describes.

When this anointing is activated, the ministers claim to be supercharged. Again and again, they used the word "power" to describe what they felt the anointing gave them. Their abilities to do ministry are not just unnatural; they're supernatural. For example, Amy goes farther than Kenya in describing what she is capable of doing when anointed. She is not just more creative or more capable of understanding complex theology. When in "preaching mode" she says, "even the state that I'm in at the time is not a normal state to be in because I'm hyperaware of my surroundings and what's going on in the room. I can hear things I couldn't normally hear, I can see things that I couldn't normally see. And so that's not me. I know that that's not me."

In the absence of any seminary training to perfect their skills as preachers or teachers, ministers pointed to the impact of their anointing. Even when they described working for hours on sermons, ultimate credit for the success of the sermon went to the anointing. Consistently, ministers described the anointing as empowering them to preach. As Carl says, "Right now, if I were suddenly asked to preach, I feel the Lord's anointing will come on me to be able to preach. That's the power of God that comes on you and allows you to do whatever He calls you to do." At the time Carl said this, he had been an Aspiring Minister for just one year, and yet he believed wholeheartedly that, with very little training, he would be capable of successfully preaching a sermon on the spot. Nothing in his professional training as a baker could prepare him to do that. Prior to having a call (and having it endorsed by his pastor), he likely would not have considered himself capable of such a thing. But he understands the calling and the anointing as a package deal. With one, he has access to the other.

Because most ministers serve in some capacity alongside people who neither claim a call nor claim to "operate under an anointing," they must have a way to distinguish themselves from other religious laborers. One way they do this is by speaking of the anointing as something different from talents, skills, and gifts. Essentially, they argue that someone might have a set of gifts or talents—which they are as likely to attribute to hereditary origins as divine ones—that enable them to be effective as a religious laborer. But, they explain, the gifts or talents can be absent, and the anointed person can still be effective. The most common example used to explain this phenomena was musical ministry. The comments of one Evangelist, Katherine, capture this idea:

See, the calling and the anointing go together, but a gifting and an anointing may not. I can be gifted to sing, hitting all the right notes. And you're the person that cannot sing. But if God has anointed you, I believe God does something not just to the giver but to the receiver. Although you sound like junk, because the anointing is on your life, they're not even hearing your bad notes. What they're hearing is what you're singing and the message that you're giving. But if I can sing, but there's no anointing there, I believe that nobody's receiving anything from that.

While many describe the anointing as enabling them to do the kinds of tasks one might be otherwise trained or skilled at, like teaching or singing, they also describe its importance in managing other tasks. Many COGIC ministers, both men and women, ordained and licensed, are expected to do more than preach sermons, teach classes, and administer the sacraments. Additional responsibilities that some ministers claim to be anointed to do are drawn from a list of gifts found in Ephesians 4:11–13 that includes serving, encouraging, contributing to the needs of others, giving, leading, and showing mercy. Like teaching, many of these responsibilities are shared by laymembers in the COGIC church. Ordained and licensed ministers participate in these tasks but don't consider them the exclusive domain of someone who is called. That said, many believe these tasks are important enough that anyone doing them should be anointed. Essentially, they believe that everyone who does ministry, including what many might consider lay-ministries like choral music, ushering, and hospitality, should be anointed for it, even if they have not been called as a minister.

There is another set of tasks, though, that COGIC ministers argue requires both a calling *and* an anointing. In some cases, both COGIC doctrine and the Bible explicitly charge clergy with these tasks. According to the COGIC manual, the church believes in and practices divine healing. It describes scriptural commands for spiritual leaders to heal, pointing most directly at the quotation compelling a sick church member to "call for the elders of the church, and let them pray over him, anointing him with oil in the name of the Lord. And the prayer of faith will save the sick, and the Lord will raise him up." (James 5:14–15). Healing is still practiced widely and frequently in the Church of God in Christ and, according to the manual, "testimonies to healing in [the] church testify to this fact."[62] My respondents believe that the list of supernatural abilities enumerated in 1 Corinthians 12:8–10 and other places—which include giving prophecies, discerning and subduing evil spirits, speaking in or understanding unlearned languages, and having special insight into or knowledge of circumstances—are real and actively practiced by COGIC clergy. In fact, many ministers listed one or more of these attributes as a function of their own call to ministry.

While one might imagine not needing any supernatural powers to give a sermon or distribute meals to the homeless, these forms of religious labor would certainly require something more than a course in homiletics. Believing themselves responsible to carry out these tasks, ministers find in those responsibilities their biggest premise for requiring an anointing. For example, Paulette describes her ability to heal parishioners:

> The anointing of God comes in and empowers you to do certain aspects that He has called you to do. I couldn't lay hands on the sick and they recover if I didn't have the anointing of God. If He calls you, He's going to empower you to do what He's commissioned for you to do. The anointing is when it is not you yourself operating. You realize that you could not have done that and it's not you. You are now operating at a point that you know it is only God himself.

Anointing Carriers and the Anointing Infused

When it comes to understanding how the anointing operates in their lives, ministers seem to come in two types. While some ministers blur these distinctions in their descriptions, the vast majority of them tend to fall into two clear categories. The first, and smaller category of ministers, are "anointing-carriers." They consider the anointing to be something they always have, making them certain that whenever they have an opportunity to do ministry, they will be effective. In light of this, some believe they carry their anointing with them in nonreligious environments, such as shopping malls, as well as religious venues. Some ministers believe that their anointing is useful for what we might consider secular tasks, but which they see through a spiritual lens. For example, Courtney claims to use her anointing when shopping:

> When I go shopping, my thing is I need God to lead me. I pray and ask Him first for the parking space, then I pray and ask Him to guide me to be a good steward over what He has blessed me with. Once, I had to buy something for my daughter and the thing was like $700, but I found it in this little obscure place for $30. I consider He led and He guided me. He anointed me to spend the money that He blessed me with.

For others, the anointing is not used to function in these situations. As Katherine says, "it's not that deep with me. I don't use the anointing in the mall. I'd rather use my natural abilities when it comes to certain things. Not to say that I don't need the Lord or the guidance of the Holy Spirit in my everyday life. Yes I do. But it's just certain things that I feel capable of." Most carriers argue that the anointing's presence within them makes them capable of operating in their calling at any given moment. In fact, some claimed to be anointed during the interview, suggesting that this power would ensure that they said what God needed them to say in response to my questions.

Anointing-carriers tend to describe the anointing as "rising up" in them or "coming out" of them, almost as if it lies dormant until they have a ministry opportunity. Natalie says:

> I would say that there is an anointing on my life, but I don't believe it's activated except when I have to step before God's people to do ministry. Sometimes I can be on my way to prison ministry and just be fleshly Natalie, driving in traffic trying to get there on time, screaming at the other drivers to get out of my. But I know that as soon as I get behind the podium, there's no more flesh there. It's all just anointing then.

Like Natalie, the anointing-carriers describe feeling anointed from the very moment they begin to do ministry. Raquel says, "it's there in me. It's part of me. I don't have to wait to get up behind the podium. It's in me before I even leave the house, so I know it's in me as I'm doing the work."

The second set of ministers refers to the anointing as something that comes upon them during an act of ministry. Like the "carriers," they expect the anointing to operate whenever they are doing ministry, but they were more likely to talk about the anointing as something they can feel descending on them at some point during the ministry act. For example, some would describe being in the middle of a sermon and feeling their "help coming on." This "help"— the anointing—was described as something they could literally feel, either as a flush or tingling of the skin or as a kind of head rush. Often this moment was accompanied by outbursts of glossolalia (or "tongues") or involuntary muscular tics ministers referred to as "quickening." Whatever the particulars of the infusion, ministers claim to know precisely the moment when the anointing is activated. Mylisha described the moment this way:

> God, how can I explain it? I can feel the presence of the Lord and I can feel the change within me and how the Word of God is just coming up, as the

scripture says, "out of your belly shall flow rivers of living water"? I know it's God because of the things that are happening, how the Word of God is coming and coming, and then it's just overflowing. I can tell that the spirit of God is just taking over and I'm operating under the anointing.

It became clear in ministers' descriptions that this infusion of the anointing tended to occur only during acts of ministry they might consider needing to be "empowered" for. The moments most often given in examples were preaching, praying, and teaching—in that order. Ironically, no one mentioned "feeling the anointing" while participating in sacramental tasks (i.e., administering the Eucharist or baptism) reserved only for ordained clergy.

The anointing may also be activated, in a felt way, only during those parts of one's religious service that they feel a particular call to. Tasha, a Deaconess who also sings on her church's praise team, feels called to preach but doesn't describe herself as called, specifically, to music ministry. While she might not feel any particular infusion of the anointing while singing, she describes feeling something when asked to introduce a song to the audience:

It's like this sensation'll come over me. And then I'll get up there, not having practiced anything, and it's like I can just, I'll get to talking, and the words aren't scattered. They're just flowing and they're connecting and they're ushering in the spirit of praise, and by the time I'm done, I'm like, wow, what did I say? When the anointing comes on me, I just know something's happening to me at that moment. I know this level of authority that comes on me, and it just takes me to another level.

Just as they can describe the moment when they receive the anointing, ministers seem to know when the anointing is withdrawn. They describe the circumstances of the anointing's infusion and withdrawal almost as one might describe an adrenaline rush. Amy says that "when that moment passes and that anointing kind of subsides, you're drained, you're tired, you feel like a wet towel." Again, they seem to experience the anointing as something physical and real. Kelly describes this moment the same way: "When you're up ministering and stuff like that, you're highly anointed to do that. And you can go and do stuff like that, sweat like crazy, and don't pass out. And then as soon as you finished, then you're drained. Because that anointing's lifted off you. It's a supernatural ability that comes on you to do something at a particular time."

The Role of Audiences

Just as congregants play a role in legitimizing a minister's calling, they are also part of the process whereby one's anointing is confirmed. In some ways, the audience's response to a minister's preaching or teaching is, at once, a confirmation of both their calling and their anointing. To the extent that ministers believe that an anointing is evidence of a calling, they depend on a response to their anointing to legitimize their sense that they are called. This was not only evident in their statements about their own calling but in their evaluations of other ministers' callings as well.

Many anointing-carriers spoke of "fruit" as an important component of their belief in their anointing (see Jn. 15:1–8). In fact, their past experience with effective ministry seems to have led many of them to the belief that are always anointed. Katherine exemplifies a common anointing-carrier perspective when she explains:

> I know I'm anointed because everything that I do, everything that I set out to do, I see the fruits of it. I see the fruits in other people's lives. And I see the fruit in my life. I see the things that I've done in Christ based on what my calling is and my anointing. I see the fruits. It's like the seed is planted and here's the fruit of it.

A history of positive audience responses to her religious labor strengthened Katherine's belief that she had the ability to be successful in future exercises of her calling. Audiences help give meaning to the ability to do ministry just as they give meaning to the motivation for it.

That said, anointing-carriers didn't always require a response in order to maintain their belief that they were anointed. Some described situations when they would pray for someone and nothing seemed to happen in that moment. These are the kinds of moments described earlier that might otherwise appear to be a test of one's calling and, pertinent to this chapter, anointing. In the absence of positive outcomes, they stated that their belief in their calling and anointing never wavered. They have reasons for this, backing up their claims using examples from the ministry of Jesus himself. While in most cases, Jesus' ministry had "immediate" effects, ministers made the case that his anointing didn't always operate that way.

Their primary argument was that every act of anointed ministry does not have an immediate effect, describing those situations as "as they went" encounters. Most describe these moments in terms of the biblical accounts of Jesus healing ten lepers (Lk. 17:11–19) or healing a blind man (Jn. 9:1–7). In both accounts, the healing did not seem to happen in Jesus' presence. Instead, the lepers were cured as they went the priest and the blind man was only able to see after washing mud out of his eyes in the pool of Siloam. The ministers pointed to similar examples from their own ministry where they might tell someone to go to their doctor to confirm the effectiveness of a prayer for healing. Alternately, they extend the "fruit" metaphor to these circumstances, explaining that they are only "planting a seed" and that it takes time for the anointing to fully produce whatever outcome it is intended to produce.

They also read these two biblical stories as parables about deference to spiritual authority, essentially arguing that the healings required the lepers and the blind man to trust Jesus and follow his instructions. They suggest, for example, that the lepers' healing would not have happened had they not had faith in Jesus' power to heal them. Paulette argued this point exactly, extending it to her own preaching ministry:

> In that same way, God anoints the Word, but that Word has to land on good ground. People have to be receptive to it, and you can't always do something if somebody's not receptive. If they're not open to it, if they're not open to the will of God, you can have all the anointing in the world. It's not going to change their situation.

This is one of the ways that the anointing is different from charisma. Anointing-carriers like Paulette do not require a positive response from the people she ministers to. Charisma requires a response and is measured by its effectiveness at drawing followers. Paulette doesn't measure her effectiveness that way. When followers don't see results, she sees the problem as theirs: she would be more effective if the followers weren't so flawed. In this way, she can still maintain her belief in her anointing even if it doesn't engender a response.

Those who experience an "infused anointing" depend as much on their own physical sensations as the responses of an audience, but even they are clearly affected by audience interaction. In fact, they are more likely than anointing-carriers to speak of outcomes as a determinant of anointed ministry. Justine, a Deaconess at the time of her interview, spoke of the common occurrence of being drafted to do ministry without preparation and how much she depended on the anointing:

So often in my experience I get surprised by chances to preach. There's no real chance to do a lot of study and preparation before I have to get up there. I believe that that's why He does that; so that I don't try to make my whole purpose be to get up and to preach the people crazy. Half the time I'm not feeling anything but fear when I get up there. And I don't always get effects. One time I thought I was a bad preacher because the people just sat there.

This feeling of uncertainty, of wondering if the anointing will (or did) "show up" was described by many as an important, and even desirable, attribute of the phenomena. For example, Joel defends his lack of certainty about the anointing, claiming that this uncertainty keeps him humble:

> Most of the time I know I've been operating in the anointing only when I'm walking away from a time of ministry. Because, see, I think that's where the flesh will come in if you say, "I'm walking in here and I'm going to blow these people away with my anointing." It's not like you can turn the anointing on or off. I have to go in thinking I'm going in here to do what God has me to do. Then whatever happens happens.

Obviously for ministers like Joel, the goal of any ministry opportunity is success at it. These ministers often measured their success both in the degree to which they "felt" anointed and on the level of response they got from their audience. These measures of success were more readily available in certain specific ministry situations.

While anointing-carriers occasionally spoke of their anointing's activation in the absence of an audience (e.g., while praying alone or even doing the dishes), those who experienced anointing infusions almost always gave examples of ministry interactions with other people. In those cases, the audience's response played an important role in confirming their sense that even if they weren't on track with their plans for the lesson or prayer, they were still operating in an effective manner. Reflecting on this, George described how he feels when he comes prepared to minister and God chooses to do something different:

> I have my objectives and all the key points that I want to hit. But when He begins to sidetrack me, make me deter from that, that's when I can see where people's hearts are being touched and the tears begin to flow. It's not me doing it. I don't think I'm saying something so amazing. I don't think it's just emotion either. I consider it the anointing of God working through me destroying that yoke, breaking those chains and those binds in the people's lives.

When the Anointing Falls

While George suggests that he is able to reflect upon his in-the-moment experience of ministry, some ministers claim to be so overtaken by the anointing that they go into a kind of dissociative fugue state. In that state, they are incapable of measuring their success by audience response. They suggest that under the anointing's influence, they are no longer in control of their bodies and have little recollection of the events that took place while ministering.

In some cases, they were very clear that they were lucid when this was happening. In explaining a moment when the anointing enabled her to pray with a congregant, Sharon said, "I don't know what I said to her after that, but I know it was words of encouragement. A whole different tone. I'm not saying I went into a trance or nothing, but God just spoke directly through me like in the movie *Ghost* with Whoopi Goldberg. That's how I knew it was the anointing." While Sharon knew the point when the anointing started to affect her, she had no recollection of what she said after that point.

This phenomena seems to occur in a variety of situations. Monica says, "when I'm speaking, I'm not there. When I'm praying for somebody, I'm not there. I guess I just zone out for lack of a better phrase. I do things and have no idea that I did it. So I know it's not me because I'll have no recollection of saying or doing what people tell me I've done." Monica describes various ministry opportunities where she was overcome by the anointing, experiencing it so powerfully that she describes herself as not even being conscious. A more dramatic version of this was relayed by Jeff who was also required to minister with little preparation:

> We have a model here where you need to be ready when called. One time they just called me up because the guy whose time it was didn't come. I got up there and I didn't have any idea what I was going to say. To tell you the truth, even now I can't tell you what I said. Afterwards I had to ask my wife what I said because I was gone. I remember standing up behind the podium and leaving the podium, but all that in between? No clue, Doc.

The most common element in these explanations of the anointing's function was these moments when ministry was required but the minister had no time to prepare. In a practical sense, this is no different than a lawyer having to think on his feet as his opponent changes course in the midst of a trial or a physician suddenly being called on to render first aid.

But imagine that same physician having to do an emergency procedure and claiming, once done, that he "zoned out" and doesn't remember doing the operation. While our trust in that physician would be shaken by such an admission, similar admissions by ministers are intended to strengthen the hearer's trust in them as someone who is truly dependent on God for their successes.

Just as ministers resisted any suggestion that their calling was self-initiated, they consistently spoke of their actual religious labor as being outside of the scope of their own abilities. Unlike other professions, personal inadequacy and even lack of knowledge or skill authenticates one's membership in the corps of called and anointed ministers. Jimmy spoke of his ministry on the street team:

> To be able to have people crying in the street and accepting Christ? That ain't me. That's when the anointing's going. I'm just being used by God. So you know it's Him that draws everybody to hisself, not me. I'm just there. Like I said, I'm not the smartest guy in the world, but Lord I'm available. Once again, I depend on Him and I trust Him to give me what to say and to do the work.

While charismatic leaders are often assumed to be outsiders—rabble-rousers who seek to usurp priestly authority—that is rarely the case. The prophet is often a member of the traditional organization who, through normal means, probably could not attain a leadership position at all. They could not make any claim to power based on position or purse. So, in a way, the possibility of charismatic authority allows nobodies to rise up and lead. The anointing enables seemingly unqualified men and women to do the same.

For example, Jimmy's assertion that he's not the "smartest guy in the world" is one that was repeated in different ways by many of my respondents. They would often say things like "I know it wasn't me" or "I'm not smart enough to come up with that" as a way to underscore the authenticity of their calling. By claiming non-elite status (i.e., "I don't deserve to be used this way"), they strengthen the claim that their ability to effectively play out the prophetic role isn't a function of origins, training, or even hard work. Instead, they argue, they depend fully on God's favor and His anointing. Success in ministry is not theirs to claim; the credit—or as they describe it, "the glory"—remains His.

When the Anointing Fails

An important rationale for only recognizing one's successes in ministry as a function of an anointing, rather than one's talents, training, or even preparation, is that sometimes the anointing fails. One of the most surprising characteristics of the anointing, and one that makes it quite different from the skills/knowledge one might gain by training, is the possibility that someone could "lose their anointing." For many of my respondents, a person could find themselves dis-empowered.[63] Some had biblical examples for this possibility. The two most common examples were the biblical judge and strongman Samson and the first king of Israel, Saul.

In most cases, people were adamant that disobedience—whether in your use of your anointing or in your character—was grounds for losing one's anointing and that this loss could hinder one's effectiveness even if they are called. Apparently, an important aspect of access to this anointing, this power source, is the required absence—figuratively—of the body. Referred to as "the flesh" by many respondents, the body seemed to be a hindrance to the full activity of the anointing. The body, or "flesh," is considered to be the locus of sinful behaviors and motivations; it is profane. As a result, it must be managed in order for the anointing, a sign of the minister's sacredness, to be fully activated. Amy speaks of this management, "Like at work, I'm having a hard time staying out of flesh. I really got to get that under subjection. When I know I ain't been right all week, I feel like God can't use me. My anointing can't be as high as it should be."

While some speak of having to actively manage their flesh, claiming to tamp it down or bring it into submission, others suggest that the anointing itself does the work of managing their flesh. As Jeff argues, "having the anointing is knowing that the spirit of God is there upon you. You're out of the way. The flesh is out of the way and it's the anointing of God, the spirit of God that has taken over with the power."

Ministers are adamant that even if a person is called to do ministry, there is the possibility that they could fail in that ministry if they haven't managed their flesh. They tend to describe the problem as the sociologist Emile Durkheim did when he described sacred things as "par excellence, that which the profane should not touch, and cannot touch with impunity."[64] It seems that the profane "flesh" and the sacred "anointing" cannot abide in the same vessel. This idea was expressed more plainly by Mona:

I just don't see how God can bless mess. Now understand me. They may look effective. The people might shout and things, but if the ministers' life ain't holy, there's not going to be any real change going on because the anointing won't be there. God's anointing can't rest in an unclean vessel. Even David. He was a man after God's heart, but when he did that dirty thing with Bathsheba even he was praying, "Lord don't take your anointing from me"

Seminaries: Not Really "A School of the Prophets"

My respondents claim to have *supernatural* gifts and talents—an anointing. Why not do what other "prophets," like Jeremiah Wright or mega-pastor Rick Warren did and take those gifts to seminary? Why don't they become priests? The answer came early in the interviews when I asked some of my respondents a seemingly simple question: "Without any additional information, if you had to place your children in a Sunday school class taught by a teacher who claimed to be called to the ministry or one taught by a teacher who also claimed a call and had been trained in seminary, which teacher would you choose?" In every case but one, the respondents paused for a moment and then answered, often shyly, that they would choose the nonseminarian. Their answers came with critiques similar to this one from Deana, a forty-year-old teacher with both a bachelor's and a master's degree in education: "I would say the one who hasn't gone to seminary. Personally, I think if you need to go to school to learn how to do ministry, that's a crutch. You can tell the difference between someone who was schooled by man and someone who was schooled by the Holy Ghost." In different ways, ministers seem to share Deana's rejection of seminary or other formal (i.e., outside of their local church or jurisdiction) training as part of the formula for effective ministry. They are likely advocates for general education, not only for themselves or their children but also for members of their congregations. But while they believe education is necessary for success in other occupations, most see ministry differently. They argue that the important ministerial skills cannot be taught and that people trained in seminaries are either "handicapped" or inauthentic ministers.

Seminaries Can't Teach It

As our discussion of the anointing shows, the primary reason for rejecting seminary is ministers' beliefs that the knowledge required to do most religious labor cannot be learned in the classroom. Claims to be able to heal illnesses, prophesy, and exorcise demons have long been central to Pentecostalism's understanding of itself as distinctive among Protestant religious movements. The historian Grant Wacker describes the testimonials of early American Pentecostals who sought the kind of power my respondents claim comes with the anointing: "Many, perhaps most, spiritual memoirs began by referring to years of intense yearning for an 'enduement of power.' For some it meant the ability to perform apostolic miracles of healing and exorcism, for the others the ability to witness for Christ with extrahuman boldness and effectiveness."[65] What is notable about this description of the Pentecostal's desire for supernatural ability is its inclusion of both "miracles" and of what might appear to outsiders as more natural, and trainable, achievements.

It is not enough for Pentecostals to depend on the anointing to be able to do miracles. They also consider the anointing to be critical for witnessing, preaching, and other tasks that are taught in seminary courses. As such, they find seminary training in these areas irrelevant to one's effectiveness as a minister. While this was consistently voiced by ministers without any seminary training, it was echoed by some who had attended Bible colleges. Kelly explains:

I went to Bible school. I learned the facts about the Bible and the history of the Bible and all that kind of stuff. But there wasn't much that they could teach me that I could really use to change people's lives. The revelation that I get directly from God is something different. When the anointing's there, it's like a supernatural ability to take that Word and really use it.

Seminarians Are Handicapped

Ministers' critique of seminary training goes farther than this. Not only do they consider such training unnecessary but they also describe it as problematic. Thus they would not just avoid prescribing seminary training for aspiring ministers, many offered proscriptions against it. One reason they denounce seminary training is their sense that seminaries hamper effective ministry. They worry that material taught in most university settings, but particularly in seminaries, is likely to be contrary to their beliefs. Their evidence for these suspicions are, in some ways, dependent on their own experience in these environments.

Some point to courses in religious studies, sociology, anthropology, or English literature (e.g., "the Bible as literature") they had taken as undergraduate students at secular institutions. Tanya, a Deaconess, told us that "the professor told us on day one that he wasn't a believer and that we were just studying it as a book just like any other book. I should have known what I was getting into just from that, but I stayed anyway. I admit it caused me to question some things." Some ministers state that they took these courses prior to receiving a call to ministry, and that these courses made them wary of similar training they expected to get in seminaries.

Others, who had taken courses in Bible colleges or seminaries, reported similar experiences. Kathryn, a fifty-five-year-old Deaconess who has gone to seminary part-time over the course of three years, made the case that COGIC ministers need to be prepared to go to seminary. She discussed arguments she had gotten into with Sunday school students who had taken noncredit courses offered by a local Lutheran-affiliated seminary: "I've had some seminary training and I got caught up in it too. There was a way of thinking when I came out that made me look at things different. I think there's a danger in seminary. The Bible says 'lean not on your own understanding' and I think seminary can really take you away from that."

The harshest critiques against religious training came from a third group. Most ministers who criticized seminary training had had no experience at all with religious training outside of either their local church or their COGIC jurisdiction's training institutes. Their apprehensions were based on the testimonies of other ministers or on their own impressions of ministers who had pursued seminary degrees. Sheba, another young Deaconess, says she still occasionally considers taking courses at a local seminary but is skeptical of the benefits that training is supposed to provide. She worries that the courses might "take [her] backwards," a fear based on conversations with a seminary-trained mentor: "My old pastor—who had a degree, mind you—said that when you go to seminary, most of the teaching is contrary to what the Word is and what you believe. So if you're going to go to seminary, you better know your Word."

Curtis, who has been an ordained Elder for nearly twenty years but holds only a high school diploma, is not only critical of seminaries but of their product as well. He, like most of my respondents, maintains a belief that the anointing—more than training or preparation—is the key to a successful performance as a minister. He explains why he believes training is not only futile, but the lessons learned there might hinder effective ministry:

I never prepare a whole lot because I've learned the hard way that you're never going to use that. Why? Because if God gets his opportunity, what he's going to reveal is revelation. It's going to be direct from him. That right there is one of the things you see a lot with people who have been [uses quotes with his fingers] "trained." They try to plan out their whole message. I think a lot of people who been taught in seminary are being taught how to do that and not relying on God to do it. The anointing's coming if you are relying on God to do it.

The emphasis on preaching is perhaps related, to some degree, to the accessibility that both trained and untrained ministers have to that particular form of religious labor. For example, at the church attended by a subset of my interviewees, one of their colleagues had been to seminary to be trained in pastoral counseling. The consensus about that minister was that her roles as preacher and counselor were different. At the time, she was serving as a counseling intern at the church, in preparation for receiving a chaplaincy at a local hospital. They believed that both jobs required an anointing, but the counselor position required the kind of training she received in seminary. In fact, they didn't criticize her at all, even after rendering more abstract criticisms against seminaries and seminarians. The specific *task* her training was being applied to had an impact on their acceptance of her training. Again, this suggests that there is no wholesale rejection of education. Instead, it may be the case that training which is attached to one's professional employment, even if ultimately religious in nature, is acceptable.

Seminarians Are Inauthentic

Curtis's statement denouncing "trained" ministers also points to another problem Pentecostals have with seminary training: it produces inauthentic ministry. Because so much of the called identity is tied to the idea that ministers cannot take credit for their successes, seminarians' ability to claim a learned set of skills seems anathema to their untrained peers. Even in those cases where ministers respect the skills of trained ministers, they still disparage them as less authentic than themselves. Carl, a forty-four-year-old Aspiring Minister with no college experience, does this when he says,

It's not easy to preach. I can share my testimony, but to outline a sermon and really give God's people God's Word? That's not easy. We have some people here who are truly Bible students. They been to school and learned things I would never be able to get. So to stand before them and give them God's word, you have to come correct. But I know one thing, they can't hold a candle to someone really flowing in the anointing. Even without a degree. I know where God guides, he provides.

Untrained ministers, especially those without college degrees, resisted any suggestion that they needed seminary training to serve as ministers. Tequia, who has two years of college but no degree, argues that "ministry can't be like a vocation where you go to school and learn it like a trade, like some skills. I know what I have comes from God. I can't help wondering when some Dr. Such-and-Such preaches what book he got that message from."

This was a common theme among these ministers. They argued that seminary-trained preachers were fakes, mimicking what they learned in classes, drawing on sermons they've read or watched as inspiration for the sermons they deliver. They spoke of religious labor as having technical aspects that accompanied good ministry but which weren't always necessary in order for that ministry to be effective. It was those aspects that they ridiculed as easily learned and copied by seminarians. Eric, a fifty-seven-year-old Aspiring-Minister whose full-time job as a human resource manager made pursuing seminary training difficult, pointed out the difference between his anointing and others' ability:

> I think that someone can have technical abilities to do certain things and not be anointed to do it at all. Like we can learn the mechanics of something and go through the motions of doing it but it doesn't mean that we're really called to do it; it's just that we can mimic doing it. You see that a lot in seminary-trained preachers. They learned how to do the technical work of ministry, how to talk, how to make sure you have three points, but they don't really have any real impact because they're not anointed.

This criticism was not just reserved for seminary training. A number of the ministers complained about being required to go to the jurisdictional courses on homiletics, those courses designed to teach techniques, principles, and standard practices in the delivery of sermons. Angela, an Evangelist with an associate's degree, argued that these classes simply become showcases for ministers' abilities to imitate their favorite preacher: "You can learn to do things in those classes. You can learn all the body language and it's just theatrics to me. I find today a lot of people emulate other big preachers. You'll know who they really like because you can see part of them in their stance or their presentation. God don't make copycats."

The COGIC ministers' reliance on "the anointing" over seminary training as the source of their knowledge or skills need not be viewed as global anti-intellectualism. In some cases, while their defense of the anointing may have left little room for the possibility of training's impact on the core tasks of ministry, my own survey of popular books sold in their churches' bookstores told a different story. Entire shelves were heavy with books on intercessory prayer, expository teaching, counseling, leadership, spiritual warfare, healing, and even prophecy and divination. While these books were likely being purchased by clergy and laymen alike, it stands to reason that some of the clergy were using these books to supplement and reinforce their understanding of these phenomena. Indeed, some of the minister's homes had book collections that rival those of any seminarians.[66]

These books are clearly written as how-to books. For example, there is a hugely popular book by the Black Pentecostal evangelist John Eckhardt titled *Prayers That Rout Demons*.[67] The book claims to teach readers how to preach, prophesy, heal the sick, and cast out demons, the four major tasks my respondents say requires the anointing—not training—to accomplish. The publisher's description of the book says that it "combines powerful prayers with decrees taken from Scripture to help you overcome demonic influence and opposition in your life. It includes an introduction to spiritual warfare and biblical principles for praying along with specific declarative warfare prayers for every circumstance. *Prayers That Rout Demons* is your reference handbook for defeating the devil." The popularity of this book and a host of others points to the likelihood that Pentecostals believe that there is some room for instruction when it comes to even "supernatural" religious labor. It is likely that this belief is played out by my respondents and other nonseminarians in the church.

It is somewhat counterintuitive that having more education might decrease one's status in the minds of these Pentecostal ministers and the congregants they serve. But we see a similar dynamic in the ways self-taught artists and musicians describe themselves and the status given to them. The "authentic" artist is the one whose craft is uninfluenced by the established institutions, born of instinct rather than color-by-numbers-trained sensibilities. By producing this "primitive art," they gain status, not despite their lack of training but because of it.[68] Gary Fine, a sociologist, quotes the art critic James Yood's description of this inverted status system:

> Intuitive [self-taught] art is seen then as the sole art of Arcadia, all else is fraudulent, mired in intellectual corruption, needlessly obscure and pretentious. What was low now becomes high, what was high now becomes debased. New York is Gomorrah, education causes loss of originality, knowledge is insidious and rejectable, and anti-intellectualism is to be defended and made officially viable.[69]

We could easily replace the word "art" here for "ministry" and "New York" with "Harvard Divinity School" and find this an apt description of the beliefs about seminary training that many Pentecostals seem to hold.

While we might expect untrained ministers to use such criticisms to counteract any damage to their own reputation or sense of themselves as serious pursuers of a call, this doesn't explain why even those ministers with religious training or even secular, but relevant, training provide the same appraisals. Again, we see the tension between pragmatism and primitivism, the priest's reason and the prophet's revelation. Although reason and pragmatism may be more valued in non-Pentecostal denominations, that is not the case among members of the Church of God in Christ. If there are only two explanations for a spiritual problem, "we figured out a solution" and "your faith has made you whole," the more appropriate answer in a denomination that considers its leaders prophets and not priests falls into the latter case. It is for this reason that many professionally trained teachers in my sample don't claim the "logical" explanation for their success in Sunday school, claiming instead that their talents would be ineffective without the anointing. In this cultural context, the pragmatic or technical solution to spiritual problems—and every problem is, ultimately, spiritual in nature—is simply insufficient. It would be like trying to fix a crooked nail with a spoon. There's nothing wrong with the tool; it's just the wrong one for the job.

A Caveat on the Value of Seminary Training

It would be unfair to suggest that all of my respondents were ill-disposed toward seminary or other formal Bible training. Some spoke quite eloquently about the evolution in their perspective about seminary training, an evolution that started at the same place that many of their peers remain. In contrast to those who saw seminary training as a handicap, these ministers spoke of the training as a possible asset. Like their peers, they still retained the sense that the ability to do successful ministry was dependent on the anointing. But they also recognize that outside of Pentecostal circles, a profession of an anointing might be insufficient for some opportunities. Angelo, a twenty-nine-year-old Elder, has recently begun to pursue his bachelor's degree in the hopes of eventually earning a master's degree in divinity. The son of a Baptist pastor and a COGIC Evangelist, he is well aware of the benefits of seminary training; his father has a doctorate in divinity.

Angelo, who was called to the ministry as a teenager, originally believed the anointing was all he would need to be effective in ministry. Using the apostle Paul as a model, he described how he came to realize it might not be enough:

Initially I thought there were some things I had to work on like stage presence or people skills. When I was younger, I felt that while I needed to work on that, the anointing would help me through those deficiencies. But I've come to believe there's a greater quantity of people you can reach with the skill that comes from an education. Paul said we need to be all things to all people. He was trained in the religious seminaries of his time. He was a Jew but also had learned the culture of the Greeks and Romans, their language, their culture. Even though he had this undeniable experience with God, he was able to minister to the Gentiles because he had this education. While God can definitely give me the skills without a degree, there might be a need for it so I can identify with a greater number of people. There are some people who won't listen to me preach because I don't have a degree.

In his description of Paul, Angelo draws on a statement in 1 Corinthians where Paul proclaims "to the weak I became as weak, that I might win the weak: I have become all things to all men, that I might be all means save some" (1 Cor. 9:20–22). While Angelo suggests that seminary would be instrumental in enabling him to "be all things to all people," three of the ministers mentioned earlier—T. D. Jakes, Paula White, and Joel Osteen—are experts at shaping their messages to reach different audiences, and none of them learned those skills in seminary classrooms.

Shayne Lee, a sociologist, and the historian Phillip Sinitiere, in describing T. D. Jakes's particular talents state, "Some may call this God's anointing, others may acknowledge it as the preacher's craft; but however one frames it, Jakes radiates the kind of energy that leaves audiences spellbound."[70] Lee and Sinitiere detail moments when Jakes, literally, follows Paul's example by "speak[ing] in the place of those hurting and longing for relief," sometimes reviewing his own struggles before audiences in a way that makes his message more persuasive, more "touchable," more "real."[71] These talents, shared by Osteen and White, are described as effective because of their conformance to sound psychological principles. Yet, we are also reminded that these powerful models of effective ministry, for example Osteen's "simple, pragmatic, and positive message . . . the force behind his mass appeal" come from "unlettered evangelical innovators."[72]

Deprofessionalizing Religious Professionals

It stands to reason that many Pentecostal ministers, and possibly many of those I interviewed, do not give much thought to the professional clergy's "seminary project." The religious labor that most of them engage in on a regular basis does not require study of systemic and philosophical theology, homiletics and liturgics, or even pastoral care and counseling. In most cases, licensed and even ordained COGIC ministers are completing tasks shared with lay-members of their churches. In fact, these ministers engaged in many of these very tasks—from praying for other congregants to directing church auxiliaries—before they ever considered pursuing a clerical credential. Certainly some kinds of religious labor require considerable skill or talent (e.g., instrumental ministry), but to be blunt, most ministry *really isn't* brain surgery. As a result, few ministers see any incongruence between their claims to be called to do ministry and their ignorance of the not-so-esoteric knowledge their seminary-trained peers might possess.

In a way, this approach to credentialing makes the clergy very different from the other classical professions. As noted in the introduction to this chapter, both professionals and paraprofessionals may work in the same environments, contributing to the same cases, and even possessing similar knowledge. The distinction between the paralegal and the lawyer is both training *and* credentialing. The lawyer's educational background is substantially different, and she has earned that legal credential certifying her possession of that knowledge. Can we truly consider even the layman-clergy, let alone deacon-clergy, distinctions analogous to the paralegal-lawyer or nurse-physician ones? Certainly, ordained clergy have reserved some legal authorities (e.g., to solemnize weddings) that are not available to laymen or lay-ministers, but even those authorities aren't tied to a foundation in any truly "esoteric" body of knowledge.

In many ways, the clergy in these "new paradigm" denominations are more like certified public accountants (CPAs) than lawyers or physicians, but barely so. Even CPAs are required to pass a national standardized test (the Uniform CPA Exam) and prove that they have 150 credit hours of post-secondary training in accounting or in a field related to it.[73] In COGIC, the intermediate licenses—Licensed Minister and Deaconess—give possessors of those licenses many of the rights and most of the responsibilities of their terminally licensed peers, the Elders and Evangelists. Because COGIC ministers, like accountants, never have to pursue the terminal license in order to do most of the profession's essential tasks, pursuing either a terminal license or ordination becomes optional. As CPA's do not need to hold an MBA in order to be licensed as accounting professionals, so Pentecostal ministers do not have to hold a master of divinity degree or its equivalent to be licensed (or ordained) as religious professionals. This new reality, at least for this portion of the clerical population, certainly brings into question how *professional* these professionals may actually be.

Because the success or failure of many religious tasks—prayer, evangelism, preaching—is determined by congregant response, ministers can measure one's anointing the way social scientists might claim to measure charisma. If an Evangelist preaches a sermon that moves people, she considers herself anointed. On the other hand, COGIC "prophets" don't have to have big followings; they're not movement starters. They see themselves as people with a message. If people hear that message and are changed by it, they believe they've done the work of the prophet. But in their minds, it isn't charisma that moved the followers. They consider charisma to be a gift, something Barack Obama or the motivational speaker Les Brown might have. For them, the work of the prophet is done through the anointing.

What's particularly fascinating about the anointing and makes it quite different from charisma is that one can continue to claim to be anointed even if no one else believes it; even if there is no response. Charisma is an almost explicitly social phenomena; we know someone has it because people respond to it. In that way, it is like "status." While you can take power, you must be given status. One's charisma is evident only if an audience buys the message. As discussed earlier, though, ministry doesn't always have an immediate response. In fact, sometimes there is no apparent response at all. Congregants move forward with divorces; no one joins the church at the end of a sermon; prayers are prayed, but the child still dies. In these circumstances, these ministers take the same pragmatic response to seeming failure that other professionals do. In spite of years of training, physicians have patients that die, lawyers lose cases, professors have to give some students failing grades. If these situations happen continuously, any professional might doubt his competence. Even if he didn't, others would.

But if these situations happen only infrequently, it is easier to attribute that failure to other culprits. For the physician, it may be the body. For the lawyer, it may be the system. For COGIC clergy, it seems to be the follower himself. They invoke Jesus, Weber's favorite example of prophetic charisma, for support of this decision: "But Jesus said to them, 'A prophet is not without honor except in his own country, among his own relatives, and in his own house.' Now he could do no mighty work there, except that he laid his hands on a few sick people and healed them. And he marveled because of their unbelief." (Mk. 6:4–6). They argue that even Jesus wasn't always effective in attracting a following. In spite of ample evidence of his charisma—or, in their words, anointing—elsewhere, this hometown "prophet" was not received as a religious authority and his usual abilities to do charismatic miracles failed because of potential followers' flawed faith. Jesus was still competent; after all, he laid hands on some people and healed them. But his inability to perform his usual raft of miracles—raising the dead, casting out devils—suggests to some that even anointed leaders have their bad days. Their belief in that person's anointing—and their own when *their* anointing fails—remains unabated.

—————————————————————————————— 5 ——

"Don't Quit Your Day Job"

Redefining Religious Work

And Jesus, walking by the Sea of Galilee, saw two brothers . . .
casting a net into the sea; for they were fishermen. Then He said
to them, "Follow Me, and I will make you fishers of men." They
immediately left their nets and followed Him.

Matthew 4:18–20

I've always thought of missionaries as people who work out in
the missionary field and ministers as people who are out ministering to people's needs. I don't understand why these people
are sitting on the front row of the church instead of being out
there doing that.

Dwayne, Aspiring Minister

Zeni Fox, author of the leading book on Catholic lay-ministry, asks
an important question about clergy, "Is being a minister about what you do?
Who you are? Where you work?"[1] It is still very much the case that most people who pursue licensing or ordination as ministers intend to serve in positions easily defined as "clerical." They plan to be leaders of congregations in
some form, usually as a senior or associate pastor. While new routes and new
entrants (particularly women and older aspirants) into ministry are causing
a rapid expansion of where ministry is done, the bulk of our understanding
of the clerical identity continues to be shaped by studies of people working in
the expected ministerial locations: church congregations and parishes.

There are a number of occupational metaphors used in churches to
describe the work of religious laborers. For some ministers, dreams of serving in these metaphoric occupations—fishermen, farmers, shepherds—
alerted them to their call to religious labor. A commonly stated rationale
for the pursuit of ministry, even among non-ministers, comes from an allusion to farming used by Jesus when he sent a group of disciples to evangelize

nearby towns. Jesus' statement, "the harvest truly is plentiful, but the labor-ers are few. Therefore pray the Lord of the harvest to send out laborers into His harvest" (Matt. 9:37-38; Lk. 10:2) is a charge many ministers consider themselves an answer to. God has called them to retrieve the human harvest, commanding them to win souls through preaching or teaching. Alternately, they are "fishers of men," hand-chosen by God to capture the attention of potential converts with the lure of the gospel message.

Yet, of the thousands of men and women who carry ministerial creden-tials in the Church of God in Christ, only a small portion of them have even part-time employment as heads of congregations, associate ministers, or institutional chaplains. Most COGIC clergy are working full-time secular jobs, and they are represented in all of the major occupational categories (see table 2). While it may be true that the harvest is ripe, many of this church's laborers are busy working in other vineyards as tradesmen, educators, and business women.

With few exceptions, the ministers in this study, whether licensed or ordained, seem to serve two masters. They claim the same compulsion to pursue ministerial credentials that any seminarian might, yet they spend most of their work week serving in secular positions ranging from bus drivers and school teachers to engineers and bank executives. Without the "where you work" or even "what you do" aspects of ministry being clearly defined by pastoral occupational positions, how do they maintain a sense of themselves as "clergy"?

Both men and women see their secular employment as either a means of financial support for their ultimate work in ministry, an extension of their calling, or the mission field for their religious labor. The sociologist Howard Becker and the historian James Carper propose that occupational personali-ties grow out of institutionalized careers and one's relationship to his or her occupational title.[2] In the case of ministers, both the occupational title and institutionalized careers are absent, yet the occupational personality remains. The rhetorics ministers deploy in talking about their secular work and their calls to ministry help them overcome the structural constraints that might otherwise hinder a coherent sense of themselves as religious laborers.

Models of Church Leadership

Most studies of clergy as an occupational or professional category depend on samples of employed clergy. Whether studying job satisfaction or gen-dered experiences of clerical labor, researchers generally seek out ministers who have "full-ministry" via an ordination process and who serve in religious leadership, usually as the head of a congregation. Some scholars even consider the idea that "almost all clergy are salaried employees of organizations (local churches)" to be a taken-for-granted certainty.[3] While on the surface it makes sense to study clergy this way, the approach is flawed by an important dynamic: in practically every denomination, "clergy" outnumber congregations. The much-touted clergy shortage in Protestant and Catholic congregations is perhaps tied more to clergy choosing not to work in certain environments (e.g., rural) than there not being enough qualified clergy to fill pulpits. The sociologist Mark Chaves gives an example of this, pointing to the United Methodist Church that reported having 35,600 congregations and nearly 44,000 clergy in 1999.[4] Even with that imbalance, those congregations were understaffed; only 25,000 clergy were serving in congregations. That said, the norm for most U.S. congregations is for a church to be led by a full-time salaried minister whose primary role is to lead worship services (usually including preaching a sermon of some kind) and to administer the church sacraments.

When pastors serve full time in ministry, they gain these positions in four ways, tied primarily to the kind of polity that governs that church: they can be assigned to a church as itinerant pastors by a bishop (episcopal governance), they participate in an open-matching system managed by a board of elders (presbyterian governance), they can be hired by a congregation through a free-market system (congregational governance), or they can found a church (charismatic). With the exception of the last, each of these approaches requires church vacancies of some sort.

In an itinerant or closed system, aspirants to ministry must agree, prior to ordination, to serve wherever the diocesan bishop appoints them. Upon ordination, they become employees of the denomination and they serve the local church where they have been assigned. In the case of the United Methodist Church, a prime example of this system, pastors are paid by the local church and otherwise cared for by the church. They receive housing through a system of parsonages and are also likely to receive benefits as full-time employees of the religious organization.

In an open-matching system, commonly used by both episcopal and presbyterian churches, the pastorless church informs a geographic board of elders that there is a position to be filled, indicating a range of requirements they seek: years of experience, tasks and programs the pastor will be responsible for, primary skills sets the person has, and even geographic origin. Ordained ministers—who often have seminary degrees—go through a similar process of filling out an information form that includes information about education and experience, church community preferences, skills they bring to bear in their ministry, leadership style, and minimum compensation requirements. In the U.S. Presbyterian Church, where this system is used, a computer matching system is used to connect appropriate ministers to appropriate congregations. Once local congregations receive the ministers' information, they begin to engage these ministers until a decision to "make a call" is made. Then the terms of the call need to be negotiated, and upon the approval of the local presbytery, the match is completed and she or he becomes pastor of the congregation. Usually, these positions come with a salary, a housing allowance, insurance, and retirement benefits.

In the kind of free-market system common to autonomous congregational churches, churches advertise positions and ministers seek them out. In some denominations, clearinghouse lists may become available to facilitate some of the matching but have no real authority to determine the outcome of these searches. Elaine McDuff and Charles Mueller, both of whom are sociologists, argue that this approach tends to be governed by conventional labor market principles of supply and demand.[5] The churches pick ministers based on their holdings of relevant human capital, and the ministers choose church homes based on a combination of economic need and personal fit. The economic considerations that ministers engage in seem somewhat contrary to a professional model, which would assume economic rationality to be anathema to the decisions professionals, and particularly clergy, might make in pursuing employment opportunities. Pay, benefits, and work conditions, rather than divine guidance, seems to motivate the decisions some ministers make about their professional lives.[6]

The final entry point to pastoral leadership is the least studied and least understood of the four. While a number of recent books have been written about successful church founders, very little is actually known about the decisions that led them to strike out on their own to build a church. There are likely any number of ways one goes from being a minister within an established church to becoming the leader of a newly formed congregation. In denominations where church planting is the norm, ministers may be launched from a congregation, with the originating congregation donating financial support and, sometimes, a portion of its membership as a seed for that launch. Sometimes churches start as para-church ministries—e.g., Bible studies or street ministries—that grow organically into a church. And, of course, some ministers simply find a community of people willing to follow and finance their vision and a church is born.

Bivocational Pastors

While many churches these days are struggling to find pastoral leadership, many pastors are working two jobs to support themselves in other parts of the Protestant religious community. These bivocational pastors supplement their part-time service to the church with a secular job or some other parachurch ministerial position. Bivocationalism is not an unusual path for ministers to take. According to Jackson Carroll, 18 percent of clergy in mainline denominations and 29 percent in the more conservative evangelical denominations work two jobs. In historically Black churches, the percentage of dual-career pastors can climb to as high as 40 percent.[7]

Studies suggest that bivocational clergy claim a number of motivations for choosing this approach to ministry. In one study of mainline bivocational pastors, researchers discovered that nearly 70 percent of those they studied considered bivocationalism a choice rather than a necessity.[8] In many cases, ministers pointed to a second-career calling as key to their decision. They were working full-time in secular careers when the call to ministry came. Instead of quitting their secular jobs, they continued in them while helping to build, usually small, churches. Some described having talents in more than one area, and they worried they could not be fully utilized if they worked in a full-time pastoral appointment. In most cases where pastors can do bivocational ministry for long periods of time, the churches they serve are usually small enough that the plethora of tasks that take up full-time pastors' time—everything from pastoral care to church administration—were easily managed in as little as eight hours a week.

When they pastored larger churches, they could find theological, practical, and even ministerial rationales for retaining their secular jobs. The theological reasons often pointed to biblical persons, such as the apostle Paul, who many believe continued to work as a tentmaker to support himself as a minister. Practical reasons included everything from the friendships that can be comfortably formed at the second job to the independence they have by being financially independent of their congregation. Their ministry-based rationales took two main forms. First, secular colleagues and clients were also outlets for ministry, a kind of second pastorate. Second, by being part-time pastors, they created opportunities for lay-members to take on some of the more routine church ministry.

The bivocational trend is both bane and boon for many mainline denominations whose churches cannot support full-time pastorates. On one hand, it leaves many without any pastors at all. On the other, having a cohort of religious workers who prefer to do ministry as their second, rather than first, commitment is beneficial because it takes pressure off of congregations to pay them.

Lay-Pastors and Lay-Ministers

Another growing trend is the assignment of professional lay-ministers to positions of religious authority in churches. These lay-ministers are not ordained but serve full-time as part of a church's ministerial staff. In some cases, lay-ministers actually take on the role of pastor (usually in very small congregations), and have special dispensation to administer the sacraments in the absence of an ordained leader. These positions are more common in some of the Protestant denominations that need to fill the gaps in church leadership left by the coupling of a shrinking clergy pool with an influx of immigrant congregants. The more common use of lay-ministers, particularly in Roman Catholic parishes and Protestant megachurches, is not as leaders of congregations but as leaders of subdivisions or departments within a congregation.

Defining these religious laborers is a difficult task. The social scientific emphasis on understanding religious laborers as only those who are ordained leaders of congregations is partially at fault here. The closest description of a professional lay-minister can be found in a study commissioned by the Roman Catholic Church in 1983.[9] In that study, this particular category of professional religious laborers included people with master's degrees in theology or a related field, with considerable experience in teaching or administration, who served as salaried members of the local parish or church. Considered "pastoral associates," they serve in a number of capacities but mostly as directors of religious education, youth or family life ministry, outreach, and music. They may carry the title "minister," but are not likely to carry the title "pastor" or "associate pastor" because of their unordained status.

With the exception of sacramental tasks, the tasks engaged in by lay-ministers tend to overlap those considered essential parts of pastoral labor.[10] Lay-ministers are just as likely as their ordained colleagues to talk about feeling called to the ministry they perform, but all the trappings of the ordination process are absent. Their talents are put to use in churches the same way a church/parish might hire a choir director or an administrative secretary. Fox argues that the way they receive their positions (i.e. being "hired for" it instead of "assigned to" it) is one of the major differences between lay-ministry and ordained ministry. Ordained people cannot be "fired" because they don't actually work for the church; as ordinands, they work for God. Lay-ministers, on the other hand, work for the church, are hired by the church, and can be fired from the church.

Lay ecclesial ministers were formally recognized in 1999 by the Roman Catholic Church; much of our understanding of lay-ministers comes from their studies.[11] Lay-ministers also serve in Protestant denominations if budgets allow. In a recent study on Protestant megachurches, churches averaged twenty full-time, paid, ministerial staff persons and another twenty-two full-time, paid, program staff persons.[12] Some portion—not detailed in the studies—of these ministerial positions are held by unordained lay-ministers. Protestant lay-ministers (again, not lay-pastors) are more likely to be found in megachurches because, by definition, they are employed by the church and the ability to hire professional staff is made possible by congregational size.

Structural Obstacles

While these three approaches to clerical employment—full-time, bivocational, and lay-pastors—exist, holding such positions is not the norm among the thousands of men and women who make up the COGIC ministerial pool. Again, of the eighty-five licensed clergy interviewed, five were serving in some full-time capacity as either pastors or hospital chaplains.[13] None was employed as a pastor or lay-minister. While this imbalance is certainly a function of my sampling method, it accurately represents the degree to which secular, rather than religious, employment is the norm for COGIC clergy. In one of the jurisdictions, only 12 percent of the licensed clergy— Licensed Ministers, Elders, Deaconesses, and Evangelists—are serving as full-time or bivocational heads of religious communities. The remainder, all of whom are licensed and operating as clergy, would be overlooked entirely if we studied only those employed as "religious laborers." They all work or are retired from secular occupations. Before detailing the reasons my respondents gave for this kind of pattern, it is important to describe the kinds of structural obstacles that might make seeking religious employment difficult. Just as the process of ordination is gendered, some of these obstacles are gendered as well.

One of the handicaps for men seeking pastorates in the Church of God in Christ is the denomination's limited occupational labor market. There is very little opportunity for mobility between churches because the denomination, at little more than one hundred years old, is quite young compared to most of its peer denominations.[14] Unlike other episcopal-polity churches, COGIC pastors are not itinerant ministers appointed to congregations by a central body. And even though they have the autonomy of congregational-ist churches, the hiring decisions at COGIC churches are not usually made by congregations or groups of elders. COGIC pastors often serve until they retire, sometimes for sixty or seventy years. In fact, most U. S. COGIC congregations are led by their founding pastors or, recently, that founder's designated successor. As that successor is usually a relative, often a son, son-in-law, and occasionally the founding pastor's widow, opportunities for newly ordained Elders to take those positions are reduced considerably. The denomination can no longer be considered a church-planting sect. Jurisdictional Bishops are less likely than in the past to strategize about church growth and actively assign Evangelists and seasoned Elders into communities to start new congregations. Instead, most ministers must approach their calls as entrepreneurs, seceding from their home churches, and starting their own congregations. Occasionally, one may be approached to assume leadership of a dead or dying congregation, but this is becoming even rarer because of the aforementioned trends.

Of course, starting a church is more easily said than done, especially if the Elder hopes to be fully supported by his congregation. Estimates of church financing show that a church needs about two hundred members to afford a full-time pastor: otherwise he should be prepared to continue to work in some other occupation until his church can fully support him and itself. The average COGIC church has 150 members, and many of their pastors are bivocational. A smaller church has an additional problem. Even in a small congregation of 150 adults, some proportion of those men and women are going to claim a call to ministry. While the average seems to be 10 percent of any COGIC church's adult membership believe themselves called to the ministry, even a smaller number would present considerable difficulties if they demanded payment for their services. If a 150-member church can barely support their pastor full-time, being able to support even one additional associate minister is unlikely. As a result, even if an Elder remains at his home church, assisting the pastor as an associate minister, the congregation is not likely to be supporting him in any meaningful way.

One might ask: Why stay in the Church of God in Christ? Why don't these men enter other denominational labor markets once they've been ordained by COGIC? One barrier continues to be the issue that prompted the church's creation: the dual doctrines of sanctification and speaking in tongues. Not surprisingly, some male ministers spoke of the possibility that a Black Baptist church might call them to assume the pastorate of that congregation. In every instance, these men paused to assure me that they would take their understanding of the Holy Ghost, including his roles in exuberant worship and glossolalia, with them to their new church. The Baptist and Methodist denominations that make up the core of the Black Church diaspora still reject—less vehemently than before—both doctrines as scripturally unsound. For example, while the fairly new, ecumenical Full Gospel Baptist Fellowship fully embraces free expression of the Spirit's gifts (including tongues), they do not accept COGIC's belief in tongues as required evidence for the infilling of the Holy Ghost. The candidacy of a COGIC minister who intends to retain all of the traditions and doctrines of the COGIC is likely to be viewed unfavorably by other denominations.

Another challenge for his candidacy would be the higher educational bar that the other denominations have for leadership of congregations. Most COGIC Elders would be deemed unqualified for positions in the two largest Black Methodist organizations—the AME and the CME—because so few of them have seminary training, a requirement for ordination by both the AME and CME bishopric. Conversely, Black Baptist congregations are totally autonomous and have full control over both ordination and hiring of their pastoral leadership. Yet, as the lay-leadership that oversees hiring decisions has become disproportionately well educated, they are beginning to demand intellectual, as well as spiritual, leadership from their clergy. This has resulted in a growing preference for educated, seminary-trained pastors. The low educational bar for COGIC ordination leaves many ordained Elders unqualified to seek these opportunities if they become available. With half of the Licensed Ministers and Elders in my sample having less than an associate's degree, they would be considered woefully unprepared to lead a church where many of the congregants have advanced degrees.

Women in this denomination are far more constrained in their ability to pursue ministry full time. If full-time ministry means leading a congregation, women are incapable of doing that without being ordained by the church. But there are possibilities mentioned by some and modeled by others, for example, institutional chaplaincy or professional spiritual counseling. In order to qualify for chaplaincy in the church, a position that carries the full ecclesiastical endorsement of the church to conduct worship services, religious rites, and pastoral counseling, an aspirant must have a bachelor's degree and, at least, a master's of divinity from an accredited theological seminary.

Similarly, to receive the requisite licensing as pastoral counselors, aspirants for these positions must have bachelor's degrees and considerable additional training. With such a license, women could operate an independent ministry affiliated with her home and other area churches. Lay counseling certificates are available but are primarily useful as an enhancement for one's role as a small group or cell group leader. Usually a license is required to engage in paid clinical or Christian counseling. Many of the women spoke of calls to the areas of ministry that therapeutic licenses address: marriage and family issues, adolescent development, and crisis and abuse. Only three of the female respondents have pursued chaplain's or therapist's credentials.

Another option, observed in the callings narratives, would be to serve as full-time foreign missionaries. While women are not able to pastor a COGIC church, they are given full authority as Evangelists to found new churches in the United States and abroad. This role does not require anything other than the ecclesiastical endorsement that comes with attaining the Evangelist license. In 1925 the church formed a Department of Home and Foreign Missions charged with the spiritual development of missions in underdeveloped areas. The department describes its mission: "To the believer, missions means carrying the gospel message to those who have not heard it and trying to win them to Christ especially through a group of selected workers called missionaries, both men and women, and establishing the Church where it has not been established. In simple terms, Missions mean 'reaching the unreached with the Gospel.'"[15]

While the titles of Deaconess-Missionary and Evangelist-Missionary aren't intended to denote actual church responsibilities, most women informed me that they were called to evangelize the lost and, regardless of COGIC rules, "preach the gospel." Both men and women spoke of dreams and visions of ministering in foreign lands. It stands to reason that anyone claiming such a call would consider the mission field an appealing possibility.

The Missions Department is fairly active. It offers a ministry for young people to visit the mission field for two weeks each summer, ministries that financially support foreign students and children in the United States, and a corps of nurses who occasionally offer their skills on mission trips. Yet, given the thousands of men and women carrying credentials (and, in their minds, callings) to evangelize and preach, the department reports having only three full-time missionaries currently representing the denomination in foreign mission fields. The work of these missionaries is supported by donations to the department. While the church has thirty-five international jurisdictions in more than fifty countries, most of those are overseen by male Jurisdictional Bishops and female Supervisors of Women's Work who reside in the United States and only periodically visit the foreign territories they oversee.[16] Serving full time as a foreign missionary seems like an opportunity ripe for someone claiming a call to missions. Natalie describes being "for-tunate enough to go overseas and [has] a desire to continue to go overseas, wherever God would lead." She says she's called to both local and foreign missions, but at the time of the interview, she had only gone on one short missions trip, to nearby Jamaica, during a vacation from her full-time job in finance.

The final possibility is to operate either part- or full-time as a working evangelist. This role, like missionary, requires only the endorsement of one's pastor and, if female, the Jurisdictional Supervisor of Women. Because most men are groomed to pastor churches, the charge of the missionary/ evangelist—"to evangelize the work of the churches" and "to travel and con-duct revival meetings"—is specifically given to credentialed women in the COGIC manual. The expectation that women would have non-local min-istries is evident in the reminder that "all missionaries are subject to their Pastors and must be a supporter of their local church *before venturing into the gospel field.*"[17] Just as there are few full-time missionaries, there are few women in full-time ministry as COGIC evangelists. One of the best known of these, Dr. Rita Womack, currently serves as the female leader ("Elect-Lady") of the church's Department of Evangelism. Womack has been in full-time ministry as an Evangelist for more than twenty-five years, speaking at and conducting revival meetings, hosting conferences, and even founding her own para-church ministries. Some other women have pursued similar opportunities. Four of them now run successful para-church ministries that grew from lunch-hour Bible studies, personal ministries to grieving families, and involvement in church theater productions.

Resources and Reality Checks

While there are clear structural obstacles that might handicap both men and women's opportunities, it stands to reason that someone with the com-pulsions and abilities ministers described having would make efforts to put these talents into practice. Some men and women in other denominations receive calls that are nothing like the blitzkrieg callings these ministers describe, yet they willingly disrupt their lives to pursue a career in minis-try. A similar expectation informed one of the most difficult questions of my interviews. Usually the last question asked, it was one of the most informa-tive. Sitting across from more than one hundred people who were called to the ministry yet were still working in full-time secular positions—in some cases, years after receiving their call—I asked, simply, "Once you accepted your call to the ministry, why didn't you leave your secular occupation to pursue this religious one? Why not quit your day job?"

For many ministers, the answer was an obvious, if not always comfortable one: they simply did not have the financial wherewithal to pursue ministry as a full-time occupation. Some, like Gary, were quite blunt about this, quoting an edict by the apostle Paul: "If anyone will not work, neither shall he eat" (2 Thess. 3:10). Like-minded ministers at all stages spoke about needing to work in order to support themselves or their families.

Men, whether married or single, tended to argue that their need to support their families was the primary reason they did not pursue full-time ministry. They framed their role as head of household as intrinsically tied to their identity as minister, arguing that working a stable job was a twenty-first-century imperative, particularly if that minister was head of a household. Many spoke of this role—head of household—as a calling in itself. For example, Dwayne claimed that his responsibility to meet his family's needs superseded the call to ministry: "My first calling is to my family. One cannot support their family just on faith. Men must take care of home first. The first institution God created was family and you never put the church above them." If Dwayne, an unmarried Licensed Minister with no children, considers himself responsible to support his extended family, that responsibility is heightened for the 85 percent of my male interviewees who have spouses.

Joel also spoke of family as a calling, stating, "My first ministry is to my family. I can't be effective outside if I'm not effective at home." Likewise, Jeff (whose wife is also a credentialed minister) spoke at length about the difficulty of trying to be consistent in ministry with the responsibilities he has as a husband, "I get phone calls all the time saying, 'Brother, can you go to the prison?' My heart says yes, I want to do it, but at the same token, as a man of God my first ministry is here to make sure that my wife is provided for. If my home is in shambles, God is not going to bless my ministry out there in the streets, so I have to keep a balance."

Ironically, these men associate the success of their ministry to the very thing that hinders their ability to pursue it wholeheartedly: their marriages. Understanding this, Curtis pointed to a different suggestion from Paul (see 1 Cor. 7:32–33) as a warning to singles who might be considering a call to ministry: "Paul said it would be better for people who choose to minister the Word of God to stay single so that they could do whatever the Lord called them to do, but once a man or woman becomes married, then their first obligation is to their family."

You'll note Curtis's equal opportunity approach to the role of provider. Married women also spoke of having to work in order to maintain the lifestyle they had prior to receiving the call. Mona, an Evangelist, spoke of her role in her dual-earner household, "My husband would not have bought the fact that I was going to say to him, 'Oh, God called me to ministry, so I'm quitting my job.' Because when we got our mortgage, we didn't get a mortgage with one salary, we got our mortgage with two salaries." While women mentioned having to support their families, their accounts did not include the idea that, by supporting their families, they were doing ministry. Instead, they spoke of working as a consequence of sharing a home.

In my sample of ministers, most of the women were single; only 41 percent had spouses. In most cases, then, female clergy are their sole providers. Sharon spoke to this, saying "I have to work because I have to eat. I'm a single lady and I don't have a husband to cover me." The challenges were amplified for those women who were single but raising children. Dana stated, "I think the only answer I can give for why I didn't leave my job to go into ministry is because I really need the money. I am our sole supporter."

Just as they would countenance no excuses for not working themselves, ministers were even harder on others who were serving in ministry and not actively seeking secular work that could fully support them. Curtis complained that

> there are some brothers who are up in the pulpit who are dressed to kill and their mortgages aren't paid and their lights aren't paid and they are asking the church for help and food. The Bible emphatically states that a man who cannot support his home is less than an infidel and there is no position that he should hold in the church in leadership until he is able to take care of his own family.

While many of my respondents claimed a call to preach as evangelists (in essence, itinerant ministers), they seemed to ridicule these traveling ministers for depending on congregations they visited for their subsistence. Maria explained that nonpastoral work should not be considered one's main source of income: "When we're evangelizing, we're not doing this as a paid job. We're doing this for the kingdom. A lot of people leave their jobs and end up losing their homes and everything. We even got evangelists losing their house, coming to the church preaching to us to get the money."

Many respondents point to their secular jobs as enabling them to support their families, while others point to their jobs as giving them resources to better support either their current or their future ministries. For example, they argued that their jobs gave them the resources to buy supplies (food, equipment) for their street ministry or to save money for the moment God has them step out into their calling. They, more than others who spoke of a need to work, saw their job as something God had directed them to. Debra claimed her job was an answer to prayer:

> God doesn't want you to be the tail, always on the begging end. God wants you to be on the giving end. I told God I wanted to give him more tithes, so I said if he gives me a better paying job, then I can give him more money. And He blessed me with a better job. God gave me this job, so I assume that's what he wanted for me.

Like Debra, many ministers seemed to have considerable faith in God to give people favor in the secular job market. Indeed, in responses to earlier questions about pursuing their secular occupations, some indicated that these jobs were a result of answered prayer. They also spoke of having prayed for congregants who were struggling to find jobs or pay their bills, reporting miraculous events where people received, in the words of one Licensed Minister, "unexpected money from unexpected places."

For some ministers, however, their explanations for continued secular employment did not have this same air of confidence in their own supernatural abilities or in God's. Some, like Natalie, joked that "it's nice to say that God takes care of you, but we live in the real world where it takes money." Others seemed even more skeptical that going into ministry full time would be a wise decision. Bryant said, "I got faith in God, but I ain't got faith like that. Some of that faith stuff is crazy. You got folks that say, 'I'm quitting my job today 'cause the Lord says I'm called to be in full-time ministry.' Some people got that kind of faith, but it ain't for me." Jeff, a minister who believes that God called him to the ministry in numerous supernatural (and twice, nearly fatal) ways, suggested he would quit his job, if only God would tell him to do so: "It's easy to say, 'Well, Lord, I'm going to quit my job. I'm going to go full time in the ministry because I know you're more than able to provide.' I would be a fool to do that. I would be a fool. I'm not going to do nothing without me hearing God say do it."

In many respects, these ministers engage in the kind of rational behavior any professional person might engage in if given an opportunity to switch employers. They enter into a costs-benefits analysis, weighing the costs of leaving the old job against the benefits of taking the new one. For these ministers, the promises of their new employer—God—seem to be found wanting. For many ministers, this calculus doesn't seem as dramatic as the Pauline dictum "no working, no eating" would suggest. After all, among my respondents, most men and a third of the women have working spouses who might support them financially. It is more likely that ministers aren't comfortable with the lifestyle changes that many who *do* pursue ministry (even part-time) accept as a cost of agreeing to the call. Victor describes this tension pragmatically:

> I understand we have a new employer but there's a lack of faith. You have to ask will God supply your needs according to the style to which you are accustomed. Maybe I like wearing my three-piece suits and my gators and driving my Chrysler 300. If I stop working and do more ministry that's going to hurt. Selfish but true, blunt but it's honest. Nobody really wants to give up anything.

Elaine McDuff and Charles Mueller again provide a context for this kind of economic rationality. They argue that there is a difference between decisions clergy make about their profession (ministry) and decisions they make about their employer (ostensibly, a church).[18] While a calling may be a critical component in a minister's decision to leave the profession, their decisions to leave one employer for another are based more on economic rationality. The COGIC ministers are not being forced to decide if they should leave one low-paying religious employer for a higher-paying one. Instead, they're having to decide if they should leave their high-paying secular employer for the economic risks inherent to itinerant ministry or a founding pastorate.

While some ministers are resigned to working outside of the church to support themselves (at whatever level), there is considerable anger directed at both local pastors and jurisdictional leaders for the position these men and women find themselves in. Essentially, they argue that their home churches should pay them for the ministry they do. Bryant angrily blames his pastor for the time he spends working as a carpenter, "I'm forced to give man all those hours and stuff when I could be giving those hours to God's people. I don't want to spend all my years giving to the man. Those forty hours a week could be given to people. We should have some full-time ministers in the ministry and pay them their worth."

Few COGIC churches can afford to hire full-time staff beyond some administrative support. Even when they can afford to hire some of their ministers to full-time positions, the pay is not likely to be competitive with what those ministers might make—given their other training and skills—in secular employment. This was the case for Chris, an ordained Elder who left his position at his church to pursue other opportunities:

> It's all because of income. The church wasn't able to afford what I needed to sustain my living expenses: two children, wife, a home, car, insurance. At the end of the day, I could either live below my means really working hard here at the church or get a full-time job and have my needs met so I can give and do the things I want to do.

Ultimately, Chris's choice left him much less time to do ministry. After the forty to fifty hours he devotes to his job and the additional time he commits to helping his wife raise his family, he is reduced to doing no more than four hours of active ministry in any given week.

A major point of contention for these ministers is the group of "ministers" they believe *are* paid their worth: church musicians. They argue that in their churches, musicians are often put on the payroll. While no one seems to argue that these are well-paid positions, they do feel that having a steady income from the church is better than having nothing. In fact, some complain that musicians are paid salaries, while they (ministers) are often not even given an honorarium on occasions when they speak. Ashley's scripture-laced comments serve as an example of this criticism: "[The Bible] says muzzle not the ox, but a lot of times we preach at six o'clock service and we don't get a nickel. The bottom line is people should never preach and no one take an offering for them, especially when [the pastor] makes sure they take an offering for him every Sunday."

Ministers in this denomination want to be treated, at least, like musicians, who are on the church payroll for two reasons. First, they are paid to reward them for their services to the church. Second, they are paid as a disincentive to take their talents to some other church or to a secular outlet. On behalf of Ashley and other clergy, Curtis argues for treating ministers and musicians the same:

> The Church of God in Christ is the only organization I know that don't pay. That boy at [COGIC'S Presiding] Bishop Blake's church gets like $75,000 a year to run his music ministry. His organist and all those guys are paid anywhere from $35,000 to $55,000 a year, but is he paying all his ministers and missionaries like that? You see, if you don't pay your people as professionals, they won't be professionals. You get what you pay for in life.

Of course, this comparison to musicians is not a fair one. In any given COGIC church, at least 10 percent of the adult population claims a call to ministry. Churches do not grant credentials based on demand for their services; they grant them based on the supply of people who claim a call. Unfortunately for these ministers, COGIC clergy are actually in surplus in many congregations. In contrast, rarely does any congregation find itself with more musicians than the music ministry requires. The law of supply and demand asserts itself as expected.

Another major difference between ministers and musicians is the thing that all ministers claim makes them distinctive: their call to do ministry. Consider, again, Jimmy's statement describing the imperative of the call to ministry:

> I was already very committed to my work as a deacon. When [my pastor] called me to be a deacon, I felt like I was serving him. Sometimes I would slack off because I knew that if I wasn't available, the other brothers would pitch in. But when God called me to preach? Slacking went out the window because you get a higher level of accountability. God picked me specifically for a job no one can do but me.

Deacons, musicians, and other lay-ministers are thought to require different incentives to keep them committed to church work. They're free agents who can, indeed, take their talents elsewhere. Not so with the ministers who, in claiming a call to ministry, can be counted on to protect that claim. It is more difficult to refuse to do religious tasks without compensation when one has announced that God has commanded them to do those things. James Gustafson, in his discussion of secular professions as "callings," warns that defining one's labor as "calling" makes that worker vulnerable to exploitation by his employer. He described blacksmiths who once felt such a profound sense of duty and obligation to their employers that even a pension was seen as a gift they were not entitled to. This is the dynamic at work within the Church of God in Christ: if one is called to labor, he or she should expect "payment" from the one who called them: God.

According to my respondents, this reasoning is used by their pastors, but the respondents reject those rationales. For example, Dwayne argues that "Everything is talked about in terms of 'your calling should lead you to do without pay.' I think they should step up and pay people. Other churches are . . . hiring people and they're willing to pay them." Debra concurs, comparing her church to others, "White churches put people on salary. If you expect people to be here 9 to 5 doing God's work, you need to pay them. People have to work to pay bills. What we want people to do is volunteer and I have a problem with that. We don't ask the pastor to volunteer. He gets paid for what he does."

Shadow Occupations

In 2004's *Kill Bill 2*, the titular antagonist of the film explained the difference between two comic superheroes, Spider-Man and Superman:

> Now, a staple of the superhero mythology is, there's the superhero and there's the *alter ego*. Spider-Man is actually Peter Parker. When that character wakes up in the morning, he's Peter Parker. He has to put on a costume to become Spider-Man. And it is in that characteristic Superman stands alone. Superman didn't become Superman. Superman was born Superman. When Superman wakes up in the morning, he's Superman. His *alter ego* is Clark Kent. His outfit with the big red "S"? Those are his clothes. What Kent wears—the glasses, the business suit—that's the costume.[19]

The Superman alter-ego metaphor is apt in understanding how a few of the men and many of the women seem to understand their identities as ministers. When these ministers wake up in the morning, they are ministers. Like the stockbroker who pores over newspaper market reports at breakfast, ministers have their own morning rituals, e.g., reading the Bible, which they consider preparation for their day at work, even if that work is as the stockbroker's secretary. Even riding to their jobs listening to tapes of sermons can all be an expression of their primary identity as Christians and ministers. It is upon their arrival at the office, hospital, or in one case, the prison, that they transform into their alter ego. Paul, an Elder and a corrections officer, told me, "This probably isn't the right word to use as a minister, but you could say that my uniform is drag. I might be dressed up, you know, and look like a corrections officer, but in my heart I'm walking in there as a man of God."

For these ministers, their called identity operates very much like their Christian identity. Just, as they consider themselves Christians outside of the boundaries of Sunday morning worship, they likewise consider themselves ministers beyond the walls of their church. This is not just a statement about working in a prison ministry or a nursing home; these men and women argue that they may be called on to minister on their way to their secular jobs. Angela describes that possibility: "I could be standing on the corner waiting for a bus and people sometimes just stop and start talking to me. It's something about me, they just start talking, and who knows what God is going to have me share with them. So ministry can be 24/7, every day."

Other professionals—physicians, firefighters, elementary school teachers—describe this same dynamic. They know that even when off duty, they may be called upon to use their unique set of skills or aptitudes to solve problems, be it a medical emergency or arranging a play-date. The possibility that the call "is there a doctor in the house?" might interrupt a physician's dinner plans must always reside in the back of her mind. In the same way, COGIC ministers argue that they too are on call *all* the time, never knowing when an opportunity for ministry might present itself. Of course it is unlikely that an opportunity to preach is going to be afforded one of these men and women while they're waiting for a bus. Nevertheless, they believe that God may use them to do ministry at any time because, like a shadow, their sense of themselves as ministers follows them from situation to situation. This begs the question "what kind of ministry are we talking about?"

The sociologist Muriel Mellow suggests that there is considerable ambiguity in the ministry as a form of labor. While formally, the minister's responsibilities seem limited to ritual leadership and preaching, in truth "the work of clergy is often situated in settings or activities that do not appear work-like by conventional standards, happens at unexpected times, and may merge or overlap with community and domestic responsibilities."[20] Mellow points to the way informal interactions at community events continued to be "work" for rural ministers who considered nurturing relationships with their parishioners central to their work. Having to delineate between church work and volunteer work, or attending birthday parties as pastor and attending them as a family friend, is reflective of the way the boundaries between ministers' public and private lives can become blurry as a result of task ambiguity for religious laborers.

This is especially the case for COGIC ministers as few of them spend much of their time at all—even on a Sunday morning—participating in ministry's formal tasks. They're not preaching on Sunday mornings since many of them continue to serve as associate ministers within a lead pastor's church. In most COGIC churches, the sacraments of baptism and communion may only be offered once a month and, even then, women cannot participate in administering these sacraments. While most aspirants approach their church leadership with a call to preach, the ministry most of them do on any given Sunday is likely to be far removed from that particular task. As a result, the meaning of clerical ministry has expanded considerably.

In addition to occasionally being able to preach, ministers find fulfillment in any number of tasks that they consider part of their calling. Some of these may be as prosaic as praying for the spiritual well-being of others or offering words of encouragement to people struggling with problems. Then there are the ministries that seem to be explicitly supernatural in nature, such as healing the sick, prophesying, or giving "words of knowledge," that is, a revelation of God's will for a person with details about him or her that the speaker isn't otherwise privy to. Between these poles are a host of fairly ambiguous tasks—organizing, leading, teaching, serving and helping, facilitating worship, counseling, and developing leaders—which, taken together would account for more than half of any full-time pastor's responsibilities. Since few pastors can find time to manage all these tasks efficiently, having associate ministers claim calls to these specific functions enables them to meet the growing needs of contemporary congregations through delegation. The impact of this expansion of the called ministry is a concomitant reconceptualization of the word "ministry" itself.

Women and "Full-Time" Ministry

This reconceptualization is evident in the way ministers continue to perceive of themselves as legitimate ministers in spite of the seeming imbalance between their full-time secular labor and their barely part-time religious labor. Like Angela, who is a full-time auditor, many of my interviewees argue that ministry *is* their full-time job; they're ministers 24/7. The ministers claim that the ministerial identity, their alter ego, manifests itself in the same way we might think of race or gender operating: it isn't tied to particular people, particular contexts, or even particular environments. People respond to them as ministers even when the circumstance might be inappropriate to do so. They suggest that even when they're not trying to act upon their ministerial identity—they're in their office with their Clark Kent glasses and tie on—people are able to see through the disguise and call on them for ministry. Angela argues this point by saying,

> God didn't call me to quit my job because in my job, people knew I was saved, and they would come to my booth. Do you know how many people you can minister to sitting right there in your office? Some people just needed to talk. Some people wanted me to pray with them. So even though it's an office, ministry was still going on and even witnessing. Sometimes that job's your area or sphere where God wants you to minister.

Alesha, an Evangelist, has similar experiences. Even as a full-time middle-school teacher, she's recognized as an Evangelist even without the costuming that might mark her as one:

> God can anoint you on your lunch hour. I read my Bible and people find me. I don't have to seek nobody out. Do I walk around with a big cross on my chest? No. Do I walk around with a big license that says Evangelist? No. It's that I carry myself in such a way that people respect me and become curious about what is it about me. That gives me a chance to share. I evangelize on my job—very discreetly but not ashamedly. I don't have to broadcast that I'm an Evangelist.

Ultimately, ministers like Alesha argue that they have not taken an untraditional path for ministry. For them, their full-time secular employment isn't inconsistent with their ministerial identities. In fact, many were surprised by the suggestion that by retaining their secular jobs, they weren't living out their call.

Often those working in certain secular occupations, such as nursing or social services, explicitly defended their occupational choices as fully consistent with their ministerial ambitions. These ministers—almost all women—explained that they didn't need to quit their jobs to do ministry because their jobs were outlets for their ministry. If called to the ministry of healing, the nursing career gave them opportunities to operate in that ministry. If called to exhort, their jobs as social workers put them in the position to encourage and offer support to their clients. Of all the professions where ministers spoke of secular jobs serving as ministry locations, teachers tended to have the most sophisticated explanation for how their callings—to teach, pray, exhort—are manifested in their daily encounters with students and those students' parents. Consider the following interview excerpts:

> I have had to spend a lot of time in prayer for these children, and I can see that when I come into their presence they're totally different. The love that the anointing gives off, I think it draws them. Before they were like, "oh, I hate you," this kind of thing. And now it's just "I love you." They just, they have changed immensely. (Raquel, an Evangelist)

> Well, I'm over there with the children, right there with them. Of course we can't speak [of] Jesus, but I'm right there. I may not be able to say anything but I can anoint these hands and pray for them as I'm touching them, as I'm lining them up. When the parents come to pick them up or a mom

may come up and say, "I'm having a bad day today," that door can open where I can minister to that parent. (Mylisha, an Evangelist)

Because a lot of the things I do as a teacher, I do for the Lord. I don't have to do the things I do, like hug the children. That's not my job as a teacher; not that I've seen. I get a chance sometimes to feed my students. I get a chance to give them clothing or their parents clothing. I open up my phone to my parents and when school is out I say, "I'm praying for you and with you" but we have to use wisdom. (Paula, an Evangelist)

In all three cases, these Evangelists describe doing what they consider calling-related ministry. Raquel and Mylisha both pray for their students. Mylisha and Paula encourage and minister to their parents. Paula pointedly explained that she's not doing these things as a teacher. For her, hugging the children isn't part of the job description of the teacher; it's part of the job description of the Evangelist. In this way, their Evangelist position operates as a kind of "shadow occupation," with its own skills requirements, work values, and work activities. And as such, the Evangelist's rules for conduct are given credit for behaviors that might otherwise be considered the expected behavior of an elementary or middle-school teaching professional.

Other professionals also treated ministry as a "shadow occupation," crediting their ministry and calling for their ability to serve the clients. Sharon, a Deaconess who works as a parole officer, says she operates in the gift of exhortation in her job:

My job is my ministry. I work in social services with a lot of people with issues. Everything I say to them leads somehow back to the things of Christ. I can't say Jesus or anything, but they understand where I'm coming from. They see the cross. They see me reading the Bible. So they recognize me as a Christian. I have to operate differently in the capacity of that job because I have a responsibility to operate in the job description. It would be a conflict to minister in that manner but that doesn't mean that I can't minister to other areas of their character. It's my role at this time to affect these people, because if I'm not in this position, who else will touch them.

Certainly, this approach to ministry has its difficulties. In the excerpts from Sharon's and the teachers' interviews, there is a challenge implicit with working in secular occupations and claiming the responsibility to do the work of a "shadow occupation" like ministry. Sharon's statement "I can't say Jesus or anything" makes truly manifesting her evangelizing call difficult to do. After all, how does one "share the gospel of Jesus" in an environment where you're barred from saying anything about Jesus?

Similarly, both Mylisha and Paula speak of having to be careful in the manner in which they approach students and parents. Not being able to "speak Jesus" or actually pray with the children (rather than say they're praying for them) seems to handicap their ability to fully do the ministry they believe they're called to. Some ministers reject this approach to ministry, arguing that the ways their peers understand the call to ministry reflects a lack of understanding of the responsibilities of all believers. "I think if you're called, you would go beyond your normal," says Kelly, an Evangelist who is seeking chaplaincy credentials in another denomination. "I believe we're all called to do some things ministers do. For example, we're all supposed to share our faith. But I believe that a person who has a legitimate call is called to do more than that. You don't need nothing supernatural from God to tell you to be a light at work."

Men and "Part-Time" Ministry

Women, more than men, were able to describe ways that their secular jobs served as the location for ministry or facilitated doing ministry. Men, at all levels, were much less likely to speak of their jobs as ministry locations in the sophisticated manner the women did. Aspiring Ministers, in particular, tended to resort to the kinds of defense of their secular jobs that Kelly and others reject. In response to a question about how much time in any given week he will be able to do ministry if he retains his full-time job, Bob, an Aspiring Minister, responded,

> When I talk to people about what I believe then I'm ministering. My everyday experience is a ministry. When I go to the market I'm walking in the mind of ministry. In my silence or not speaking the energy that I project is ministry to somebody. My smile is ministering. The Lord showed me that it can elevate you to another level of ministry. Because it's not just in the pulpit and it's not just in the classroom. It's in your everyday experience.

Given Bob's aspirant status, it is not surprising that he would have a relatively unsophisticated understanding of what clerical ministry might entail. In fact, this kind of response was common among Aspiring Ministers. In answer to a similar question, Victor, who works as a chef, said, "I can't quantify what I give God. If I'm driving down the road and I see someone's broke down, do you drive by or do you ask if they need some help or do you just call with a cell phone or God forbid you take off your jacket and you help him change his flat tire. That's ministry."

On the other end of the spectrum, ordained Elders, surprisingly, also describe their ministry in terms of noninstitutionalized or organized religious practice. In spite of the fact that many of them were involved in some form of street or prison evangelism—usually leading a service one or two days each month—they did not point to these acts of ministry to argue that they were living out their calling. It is especially revealing that none of the men mentioned activities explicitly associated with ordination—praying for parishioners, administering the Eucharist—as ministry. When challenged to consider if and when they do ministry in spite of their commitments to secular employment, they often drew on extra-church (e.g., coaching community sports teams) activities as examples of their commitment to ministry. Bryant and Chris, both Elders with considerable church responsibilities defended their choices. Bryant replied, "I work with young people every day. I coach basketball and football. I'm outside of the church walls pouring into people's lives. I don't just teach them the sport, but I interject God in there and teach about Christ. Sometimes people don't see it, but I'm out there working ministry . . . teaching kids about life and about God."

Descriptions of the occasional interplay between the sacred call and their secular vocations (or avocations) notwithstanding, few male ministers would argue that they have consistent opportunities to do ministry. There simply aren't enough "spiritual emergencies" in any one day or week to truly consider oneself fully operating as clergy. When directly asked, most indicated some dissatisfaction with the status of their ministry and a sense that they're not fulfilling their understanding of what God truly wants out of their ministry. This was especially the case for men, who indicated less satisfaction with ministry than did their female compatriots, even though the men were allowed to be ordained.

The most likely explanation for men's difficulty in seeing their secular jobs as either facilitating ministry or serving as a mission field is the interaction between the types of jobs many of them have and the kind of ministry they believe themselves called to. Nearly two-thirds of the men in my sample who are not serving as full-time pastors or chaplains work in one of the following occupations: protective services, motor vehicle operations, food processing, construction or maintenance, or business and financial operations. Given their claims to a preaching (or, ultimately, pastoral) ministry, they would find it difficult to craft a narrative that plausibly conflates their work as, say, a bus or truck driver, with a calling to preach.

Unfolders and Tentmakers

For some respondents, full-time ministry was not something to be pursued as a career option. They balk at the idea that upon receiving the call to ministry, they should begin a process of finding full-time ministerial opportunities. Instead, they see their work in ministry as unfolding in stages and would be considered "unfolders" rather than "pursuers." At each stage, particularly the most radical one of resigning from their secular jobs, they wait for God to give them instruction. In fact, some of them describe themselves as anxious to begin ministry, but yet they feel held back because God has not directed them to move forward in the ministry he called them to. "I would love to have him call me off my job," remarks Natalie who describes herself as being called to foreign missions, "I would love that. If I could do missions and all the things I love to do for a living, I would. But God hasn't called me to quit my job yet." Men too seem excited about the prospect of doing foreign missions but are waiting for specific instructions from God before pursuing opportunities to do so. For example, Joel excitedly reports, "I say, 'Lord, I would love to do ministry full time and if you say to do that, I will do it.' If God says go to Africa, I'm out, whether my wife wants to go or she don't."

Again and again, ministers assured me that the only thing hindering them from pursuing full-time ministry was God's lack of specificity in their calling. Evangelist Nichole had a particularly long pathway into ministry. She stated that she didn't want to go into ministry at all, but when she received a prophecy stating that "all would be revealed," she took that to mean that God was going to reveal some secret sin to the church. Upon consulting with friends and other ministers, she came to recognize the statement as directing her into ministry. She began the credentialing process and found herself satisfied with the Deaconess license. From her perspective, if God wanted her to do something in ministry—even "speaking His word"—the opportunity would unfold before her. She recalled the experience that led her to pursue the Evangelist credential:

> I was raised to believe that your gift will make room for you. So I stayed a Deaconess for many [nearly six] years because I wasn't one of those who were gung-ho to become an Evangelist. Then one year we were having all-night prayer during Lenten season and the Lord spoke very clearly to me. He said, "It's move up time," and it dropped in my spirit like crazy. I got right up in the middle of the prayer, walked around that platform, and told Mother the Lord just spoke to me and said it's move up time.

The level of specificity that Nichole received to go into the ministry and then to "move up" to the terminal license informed her sense that any further steps would come just as unexpectedly. When asked why she didn't pursue full-time ministry upon receiving her Evangelist license, her answer was an easy one: "Because first of all I feel that the Lord didn't tell me to give up my job. If I felt the Lord had told me to go on to full-time ministry, I would've done it. He never told me that. That's all it would've taken for me: a specific word."

The conviction that it is not right to move forward without a specific direction from God is grounded in the belief that God speaks to them and would give them direction if it were His will to do so. Becca, an Aspiring Missionary, explicitly characterized moving into ministry *before* God instructed her to as "foolish" and "on dangerous ground," suggesting that ministers should not move "too far behind God, but you definitely can't be running too far ahead of Him." For some, that danger was not simply the usual concerns about financial provision. Jeff, for example, worried that moving into ministry would be unproductive:

It's easy to say, "Well lord, I'm going to quit my job. I'm going to go full-time in the ministry because I know you're more than able to provide." But I would be a fool to do that. Why? Because I'm not going to do nothing without me hearing God say do it. If I go out there on my own accord, even if I go believing that God will provide . . . if God didn't okay it, then it's not going to work. It's not going to be effective.

Bryant makes a similar point by alluding to one of the three temptations of Christ before he started his ministry:

You got a lot of folks who be out there in error. Yes, God said you would be in full-time ministry. Well, God also said if you jump off a cliff, the angels will pick you up lest you dash your foot on the stone. So now you want to put God to the test? God doesn't tempt you and so don't tempt him. Even though I know the angels will bear me up, I'm not going to jump off the cliff. That's tempting God. Same thing with my job. Yes, the Lord told me I'll be full-time in ministry. Yes, the Lord told me I'd be a pastor. But there is a season for everything and I'm earnestly seeking God on that. I'm saying, "Come on Lord. Open up some doors."

Again, Bryant seems anxious for God to open "some doors"—ministerial opportunities—for him, but in the meantime he seems satisfied that the timing is wrong.

This language of "seasons" was repeated by three other ministers, all women and all still licensed only as Deaconesses. Kathryn uses the term, anticipating a moment yet to come when God will free her to pursue ministry full-time. She says, "I believe this is my season in God, but not my time. When my time comes, everything that God is going to have me to do, I'll do and just trust in the Lord. It has to be 100 percent. God has not given me my time. It's coming, but it's not now." Ashley, too, spoke of seasons and her patient waiting for doors to open: "I'm not on a full-time ministry because I do not feel as though it is my time to be on it. I feel as though what God does for you is when He wants you to go full time, He opens that opportunity for you. He leads the way."

For some of the interviewees, timing had to play a part: they were, after all, only *aspiring* ministers. They considered their secular jobs to be training camps for skills that they believed they would need once they were licensed to do ministry. Kathleen, an Aspiring Missionary who works as a financial sales associate, explains:

> My ministry is not always at church. When I talk to people on the phone, even when I'm giving them customer service, it is still service; it is still ministry. Most of the people that God uses He always puts them in some kind of menial service type job to get them ready. David was in the sheepfold. Moses was a shepherd. Most of the people God chose to be ministers, they got some kind of position where they had to learn how to take it on the jaw a little bit.

Aspiring Ministers also spoke of their jobs as giving them the resources to pay for additional training or, occasionally, to be able to afford the infrastructure they'd need once licensed and/or ordained.

While aspirants spoke of needing to work to pave the way for future ministry, Licensed Ministers and Elders predicted that they would need to work, at least at part-time jobs, even if they found themselves serving as "full-time" ministers. The Elders, who were now fully authorized to found churches, found legitimacy for their continued secular employment following the examples of other COGIC leadership. Many of my respondents, both male and female, look to their own church leadership as role models. "The pastor was not always doing full-time ministry," Ronnie, an electrician, explained, "There was a time when he was the pastor, when I first met him, and he was still working at the barbershop because he was waiting for God to open that up, open a door to just be a pastor." Langston, a sixth-year Elder and full-time maintenance worker, offers even more detail about his pastor in his defense of his own continued secular employment:

> I don't have to look far for a model. I've got Bishop. He was a mailman when he started his church and he left from work, came to the church and mopped the floors, and he did his thing on Sundays. He maintained a job until the church grew in such a way it was able to support him. Then he devoted himself full-time to the church. Everybody [who wants to be a minister] should be looking to him to mirror him.

The irony for these men, and other Elders who claimed to model themselves after their pastors, is that they all continue to serve as unpaid associate ministers at their churches. Not one was actively working on starting his own congregation. Instead they all continue to serve in roles in their local churches that are only a step above the kind of ministry lay-leaders are serving in.

The pastors these aspirants described worked in secular positions while starting their churches. The two pastors tell of working all week in blue-collar occupations, and then pastoring and building their churches at night and on weekends. They pointed to biblical examples to explain why, originally, they too did not leave their secular jobs. They argued that Jesus continued as a carpenter, that Matthew continued his work as a tax collector, and that Paul continued to make tents. The example of Paul, from Acts 18:1–4, was also used by other men and women at all three stages of credentialing, arguing that they are today's equivalent of "tentmakers." By identifying with Paul as bivocational, they are able to find legitimacy in their decisions to continue to work in secular occupations. Yet, unlike bivocational clergy, including the pastors they claim as role models, none of the ordained Elders work in any measurable way toward a goal of pastoring their own congregations. They are biding their time until their own pastors recognize their value and add them to the church payroll; most have been waiting for years for this to come to pass.

Some of the men who argued that their churches should pay them also asserted that continuing in their secular jobs was endorsed by the tent-making Paul. As it turns out, some of Paul's statements would make him a poor witness for their argument that the church should pay them. Paul made a point of saying, "I have coveted no one's silver or gold or apparel. You yourselves know that these hands of mine have provided for my necessities, and for those who were with me" (Acts 20:33–34) Similarly, in the verses surrounding the oft-quoted "if a man will not work, he shall not eat," Paul also said, "Nor did we eat anyone's bread free of charge, but worked with labor and toil night and day, that we might not be a burden to any of you, not because we do not have authority, but to make ourselves an example of how you should follow us" (2 Thess. 3:8–9). Following Paul's example as a tent-maker would require these men to work just enough to sustain them, or as Eric, an Aspiring Minister, described, "no more than to have my simple needs met, to pay for my overhead." Certainly none of them could claim that they have attained the balance of "tentmaking" and ministry that their role model, Paul, might boast of.[21]

The Role of Rhetoric In Redefining Religious Labor

While conducting these interviews, I visited a church where the sanctuary is a converted gym. The basketball hoops and the scoreboard still hang from the rafters of the worship space. When the church has teen lock-ins, or banquets, or church-league sporting events, the carpet is taken up and the basketball hoops are released for use. With just those subtle changes, the sanctuary transforms into an ordinary community center gym; the sacred becomes the secular for those two or three hours.

Almost all COGIC ministers argue that they're no different than that sanctuary. They're still Deaconesses or Elders when they're sitting at their desks taking calls or driving their city buses. In their mind, their calling travels with them to work, transforming their cubicles, vehicles, and classrooms into sacred spaces. In the same way, for some of them, their calling also transforms secular tasks—caring for patients, counseling abused women, or working as a hairstylist—into opportunities to perform sacred labor. There is a kind of vocational syncretism that makes religious shadow-occupations work. The blurring of the lines between the sacred and the secular is facilitated by an expansion of what the sacred duties of ministers might include. From pastoral care and counseling to the kind of soft-sell evangelism taught in "seeker" churches, the work that contemporary ministers do can easily find purchase in secular work environments.

The sociologist Richard Lloyd's *Neo-Bohemia* states that "artists take service-sector jobs on the premise that these jobs will support their 'real' work as cultural producers."[22] For example, artists claim to work as bartenders because the part-time night work leaves their days free to produce art. The artist is their true "shadow" identity; the bartender is an alter ego. The problem, as Lloyd describes it, is that the demands of even part-time labor "proves extremely draining, and thus may be incompatible with the diligent pursuit of other interests."[23] They find it difficult, if not impossible, to find the time and energy to produce art once they've gotten "stuck in the hustle-bustle of the job."

My respondents, like Lloyd's artists, voice some disappointment that the demands of their secular labor (and for most, the additional responsibilities of family) leave very little time to do the kind of ministry they thought God had called them to. It therefore seems problematic that they use these rhetorical flourishes to negotiate the seeming mismatch between the urgency of the call to ministry and their active pursuit of professional or paraprofessional opportunities after accepting that call. Indeed, some of the same men and women who told me that they had to work in order to support themselves had earlier shared blitzkrieg calls where God caused them to lose their jobs because they were slow at accepting a call to ministry (see chap. 2).

In his book, Lloyd describes the perspective of Tom, a Chicago painter. Tom says, "I have something I do that is very important to me—making art—and I'm prepared to forgo other comforts for that. It's going to be a long time, if ever, before I own a new car—I never have. But that doesn't really enter into my consciousness."[24] As we've read in earlier sections of this book, the call to minister is claimed as an imperative. One might argue that the desire to pursue a ministerial calling should be as compulsory as some artists' arguments that, like Tom, they *must* make art even if it means they must abandon more lucrative opportunities. These men and women do describe ministry as a compulsion, as something they are hungry for and feel obligated to do. Yet, very few of them have taken any steps toward pursuing their calling in any, seemingly, meaningful way.

In larger churches, some ministers are actually doing *less* ministry than they were doing prior to becoming part of the ministerial staff. Now they do street evangelism or prison ministry only on the days their teams are assigned to. They abandon more time-consuming ministries (e.g., music) to coordinate two-hour monthly auxiliary meetings as leaders of those auxiliaries. Even the men, who are capable of pastoring churches, seem somewhat satisfied having less responsibility than other denominations' unordained and uncalled deacons and trustees.

The pastors I interviewed were clearly disappointed with the status of some of the men and women they've licensed and ordained. They recognize that it is the rare licentiate or even ordinand who fully takes advantage of the credentials they've been given. They decry the fact that few ministers are willing to sacrifice anything for the calling they claim to have. Walter, who pastors a church where some of my respondents serve, says:

Everyone who is saved has an obligation to do something in the church. But when you feel a divine calling, that means you feel obligated to God to put your time and energy into something. You make sacrifices for your own calling even if you're sitting up under someone else's ministry. Lots of times these ministers haven't gotten obsessed with it. They're obsessed with the call, but they're not obsessed with the work of the call. Nobody can motivate you to work this thing. You've got to be obsessed with it. If it were me, the prison ministry would be my church until God gives me one. I'm going to work that thing like I'm crazy. I'm waiting on one of these brothers to come to me and say "Make me a Sunday school superintendent and let me tell you what I'm going to do with this. Instead they go through the process and all they want to do is the bare minimum we ask them to do. Makes no sense.

While pastors like Walter are disappointed that these licensed men and women aren't doing more, they weren't particularly enthusiastic about pushing them out of the nest. Notice that Walter speaks more about ways male ministers can serve in *his* congregation than ways he would equip them to start their own. In smaller churches, a too-successful youth director or religious education instructor may indeed be problematic. Pastors and some ministers intimated that some of their peers actually slow down the ordination process, keeping their male ministers in the liminal status of licensed ministry, because they fear that once ordained, these men will take members with them as they launch their new churches.

My evidence shows that these fears may be unwarranted. The costs—time, money, human resources—of starting a church on one's own are too prohibitive for those who already consider even slight reductions in their paid labor to be untenable sacrifices for the work they do as associate ministers. Their determination that "one's family is his primary ministry" puts them at a perpetual disadvantage given the blue-collar jobs many of them have. Certainly, the often-repeated phrasing "if a man doesn't work, a man doesn't eat" isn't reflective of their situations: their secular jobs are *not* barely meeting their needs for sustenance. But in order to obey the dreams and voices that some say will lead to a fulfilling ministry, they're going to have to make a considerable investment in the future. Unlike Tom, the painter, they seem unwilling to "forego other comforts" in order to make those investments. The rhetorical redefining of their secular responsibilities as sacred duties, ultimately, renders those kinds of investments unnecessary for both men and for women.

Another important component of this can be found in the answers men give when asked what their calling is, each and every man said "preach." While further questioning led some to say they were hoping to pastor, they understood themselves as preachers first. Even for those men who preferred to do other things in ministry, like Joel who was satisfied with running a ministry that fed the homeless at night, preaching was the ministry they felt God pushing them toward. On the surface, the difference between "preaching" and "pastoring" may appear to be merely one of semantics. But in reality, preaching and pastoring have a quasi-syllogistic relationship in the Church of God in Christ: all pastors preach, but not all preachers pastor.

In addition to worship/sacramental leadership, the Black pastor's work week includes but is not limited to the following: pastoral counseling, visiting members, administering congregation work, attending congregational meetings, and maintaining their involvement in both denominational and civic affairs.[25] Of these tasks, preparing and presenting a sermon accounts for only 20 percent (ten hours) of the work they do. None of my male respondents describes a calling to do the day-to-day work of a pastor. In fact, neither dreams nor visions included administering the sacraments, probably the task most associated with ordained clergy. Contrary to Walter's suspicions, these men *are* obsessed about their calls to preach. Their aversion to investing too much in the pursuit of ministry as we understand it comes from a related, but different, source. While the idea of delivering sermons to a congregation seems to be an appealing aspect of men's call to ministry, they do not express much interest at all in what separates preaching from pastoring, and that is actually having to *lead* a congregation once the worship service ends.

COGIC ministers are not unique in this regard. There is considerable evidence showing that young seminarians in a host of religious traditions are reporting a call to ministry but do not feel a call to pastor churches.[26] Even among those clergy serving congregations as pastor, there is considerable dissatisfaction with the role. They suffer the twin challenges of role strain and role conflict, which overwhelm them with responsibilities that are complex and, often, contradictory.[27] Many pastoring clergy regret that so much of their time is taken up with tasks related to church meetings and administration, leaving much less time to do what they value most in ministry: preaching, teaching, and leading worship.

Today, many young seminarians are declaring, upon entry, that they are not interested in pursuing full-time employment as the leader of a religious community. Certainly, the pastorate is not appealing to them for the expected reason: low salaries that cannot keep up with rising costs of living and the increasing financial investment seminary training requires. But they also are not interested in the other challenges that come along with the life-style of the pastor, including the loss of privacy, having to be "on" at all times, and managing multiple administrative tasks. Aspirants can indeed operate in their calling by preaching or leading a worship service and feel no further compulsion to pursue full-time employment as a pastor. What leads to the low level of satisfaction with the state of their ministry is that, as associate ministers serving senior pastors, the opportunities to preach and lead are few and far between.

"Chew the Meat and Spit Out the Bones"

Negotiating Women's Clerical Identity

Let a woman learn in silence with all submission. I do not permit a woman to teach or to have authority over a man, but to be
in silence.

1 Timothy 2:11–12

My attitude about some of this is you have to chew the meat and
spit out the bones. These rules about women can do this but
can't do that, it doesn't get in the way of what God's called me to
do, so I'm not bothered by it.

Debra, Evangelist

In seeking to understand "religious professionals" or "clergy," social
scientists have had to agree on a definition of the occupational category that
would enable them to compare their findings across denominations. Many
denominations do not require external credentials (e.g., seminary degrees,
master's and doctoral degrees in divinity, etc.) and not all religious professionals work in full-time positions as congregational heads. Regardless of
their training or employment, the one thing most clergy are expected to have
is the denominational credential called ordination. Ordained ministers are
presumed to have what Zikmund and her colleagues call "full ministry," that
is, they have "the most complete and unrestricted set of functions relating to
the ministry of the Gospel, administering the Word and Sacrament or carrying out the office of pastor or priest of the church."[1]

In many cases, scholars do not offer a definition of clergy; they take for
granted that we know what they're referring to. Certainly there are important distinctions among ordained clergy—some, for example do not have full
standing in denominational decision-making processes—but in most cases,

when scholars speak of religious professionals, they refer to ordained clergy. In the Church of God in Christ, women are still banned from this category: they are not allowed to be ordained. Given the explicit and long-standing constraints on women's opportunities to pursue ordination, how do these women (and the men who labor alongside them) make sense of their call to religious labor?

Gender Discrimination and Religious Credentialing

The ordination of women has been one of the most contested doctrinal issues in modern-day Christianity. Only half of the Christian denominations in the United States ordain women. This list includes liberal denominations like the Episcopal, Methodist, and Presbyterian churches and more conservative ones like the Assemblies of God and the Church of the Nazarene. Of these denominations, the Pentecostal Assemblies of God has the greatest number of ordained women—nearly four thousand—a number that dwarfs that of some mainline denominations.[2] For example, the United Church of Christ, the first U.S. denomination to ordain women, has half as many ordained women. While it is difficult to get an accurate count of how many of the nation's ordained clergy are women, only 17 percent of employed clergy are women.[3]

In each of these ordaining denominations, women (like men) must give some explanation of a call to ministry. Whether that call is something as dramatic as the kinds of blitzkrieg calls described earlier or something as uneventful as leaving a summer-camp experience feeling that she should do more for God, these women express and pursue this call to vocational ministry. If these calls are, in fact, a product of a vertical interaction with God and not just a horizontal interaction with a religious community, the experience of a call to ministry should also be occurring in those religions that do not ordain.

In spite of the claims—and in some cases, realities—of clergy shortages, the Roman Catholic Church (the largest religious body in the United States), the Southern Baptist Convention (the largest Protestant denomination in the United States), and the Church of God in Christ (the largest Black and the largest Pentecostal denomination in the United States) do not ordain women. That is, they do not accept women's beliefs that they are called to "priestly" office and the duties designated for those offices. As their peers were reconsidering their stances against ordaining women, these three denominations and some others resisted, further defending and concretizing their prohibitions against the trend. In some cases, internecine political battles prompted some religious organizations to further assert the importance of patriarchal leadership, an assertion not always rejected by female lay-members of these denominations. Ultimately, the arguments against ordaining women are motivated by two different, but related, rationales: biblical inerrancy and liturgical sacramentalism.

The biblical inerrantists point to New Testament scriptures that explicitly forbid women from taking on roles in which they had authority over men. They argue that verses such as 1 Timothy 2:12–14 or 1 Corinthians 14:34–35 are unambiguous in their presentation of limitations on women's roles in religious settings. In addition, inerrantists point to biblical descriptions of particular church positions, namely deacons and elders in Titus 1:5–7 and 1 Timothy 3:1–13, as further evidence of a divine gendering of the clergy. In an effort to maintain what they consider a biblical standard for authority, these churches allow women to serve in supportive roles but, ultimately, priestly leadership roles are reserved for men. Leaders of liturgically sacramental denominations point more to the tradition of men, from the Levitical priest Aaron to Jesus and his disciples, serving as the sole biblical exemplars of religious leadership, specifically as relates to the administration of the sacraments or leading people in worship. Because these denominations consider priests and pastors to operate as representations (*in persona Christi*) of Jesus, an ideal representation would necessarily have to be male.

Sometimes these prohibitions against female religious authority extend beyond the pulpit and begin to affect women's opportunities in nonsacramental roles where female participation might otherwise be acceptable and even preferred. The sociologist John Bartkowski's book *Remaking the Godly Marriage* describes an evangelical church where women cannot serve as pastors, cannot sit on the elders council, and do not teach Sunday school classes.[4] On this latter point, there was no formal rule barring women from positions as Sunday school teachers. Instead, the system had evolved over time because of the numbers of men available to teach those classes. Yet, when the system was questioned, discussions about the system centered on Paul's statements forbidding women from exercising authority over men. The major question became "what age can males be in a Sunday school class taught by a woman?" While women exercise spiritual authority over their own sons, when are women no longer free to exercise that authority over other male children in their churches?

When confronted with arguments about the leadership of Deborah, the Old Testament judge, both inerrantists and sacramentalists argue that Paul's injunctions against women's leadership did not extend to political roles. They also characterize prominent women in the New Testament—Timothy's mother and grandmother, Eunice and Lois; Aquila's wife Priscilla; and the prophetic daughters of Philip—as operating in an appropriate capacity as trainers of children or supplementing the male leadership of their fathers or husbands. None of these roles contradicts the doctrinal or traditional defenses of exclusively male religious authority.

These arguments against women's ordination are neither new nor unique to those denominations that continue to bar women from priestly, pastoral, or even "preaching" ministries. At some point in their histories, many of the female-ordaining denominations also used one or both of these arguments before adopting new stances toward female clergy. In many denominations, women were already serving alongside their husbands as missionaries, helping to build churches in locales both near and far. Some of the most famous of these, like the three consecutive wives of Baptist missionary Adoniram Judson, lost their lives will serving as missionaries in locations as "exotic" as India and China.[5] In fact, serving as missionaries was the major entry point into ministry for women in the late eighteenth and early nineteenth centuries. According to Zikmund and her colleagues, by the end of the nineteenth century, more than half of the overseas missionaries from Protestant denominations were women.[6] Many of these missionaries were supported by fundraising organizations run by women in the states or abroad.

Just as women experienced calls to minister overseas, other women felt the compulsion to pursue similar missionary paths at home. Even though women were not authorized to pastor, some took advantage of the phenomena of itinerant preaching that was becoming a norm in early nineteenth-century America. The White revivalists Abigail Roberts, Sharon Brown, Salome Lincoln Mowry, Harriet Livermore, and Phoebe Palmer were increasing the demands on churches to ordain women. Often facing considerable opposition, these women met claims of heresy and charges of witchcraft in order to pursue the preaching ministries they felt called to.[7] In Black communities too, female revivalists like Julia A. J. Foote and Jarena Lee were preaching long before their denominations formally began ordaining women to do so.[8]

In 1853 the Unitarian/Congregationalists, the precursors to the United Church of Christ, became the first of the burgeoning mainline churches to begin ordaining women. Even in their case, the decision to ordain was not a top-down decision; ordination began among the Congregationalists when a congregation voted to do so. At the same time that long-standing denominations were beginning to ordain women, new, more conservative, sects like the

Salvation Army, the Church of God, and the National Baptist Convention, Inc., began to ordain them as well. In some cases, the restrictions against ordaining women, or giving them full rights of clergy, prompted female religious entrepreneurs like Aimee Semple McPherson to break away from their denominations and start new sects.[9]

Pentecostal and Holiness churches were on the leading edges of the trend toward ordaining women primarily because of their experimental nature and the value they place on the prophetic preaching voice.[10] While most denominations who now ordain women were doing so by 1960, there was a dramatic surge in ordinations in the late 1970s and early 1980s. Much of this growth was a result of some of the largest mainline denominations—Lutherans, Methodists, Presbyterians, and Episcopalians—ordaining women or doing so in greater numbers.[11] The changes in practice coincided with changes outside of the churches as women's movement activists sought to promote change in multiple institutions, from the workforce to the family. Institutional isomorphism, the tendency for organizations to begin looking like others in their organizational grouping, further promoted these changes as the mainline denominations endeavored to appear legitimate. The ecumenical relationship blossoming between denominations promoted that process.

Another trend that prompted an increase in ordinations and changes in denominational rules was the entry of women into seminaries in large numbers. Even if their denomination had not changed its stance on ordination, many women entered seminaries in anticipation of such changes. In some cases, their training gave them a stronger argument for their ordination. Seminaries became fertile ground for challenges to religious patriarchy. Women's knowledge of the Bible and the means to interpret it successfully gave them the tools to argue for their own liberation from patriarchal attitudes in the home, the workplace, and, ultimately, their churches.

While women (and their male advocates) were successful at opening the doors to ordination, many newly ordained women were finding church doors closed to them. Churches were ordaining women in large numbers, but hiring committees and congregants often remained resistant to the idea of women clerics. In some cases, the resistance was projected on other parties. Hiring committees imagined their congregants opposed women ministers and that such hires would create tensions in what may have already been a fracturing laity. Lay-members suspected the leadership of similar resistance. However, Chaves suggests that many members of both bodies were ambivalent, or even positive, about the prospect of having female ministers.[12]

When women could find a pastoral placement, they tended to be hired by smaller, lower-paying congregations. Even for some early denominational adoptees of women's ordination, transitions from sect to church, from a prophetic focus on message to a priestly focus on methods, prompted subtle changes in the treatment of women. Women began to steadily lose their influence over decision-making and also lost their autonomy, more often finding themselves relegated to supervised and "nurturing" supportive positions.[13] According to the sociologist Frederick Schmidt, women report feeling marginalized and like "outsiders."[14] They have earned the credential, but for many it is a hollow victory. One of Barbara Zikmund's respondents quipped, "God calls and the church stalls."[15] Women encounter what has come to be known as the stained-glass ceiling, a metaphorical barrier similar to the secular glass ceiling in which women's advancements to leadership positions seem possible but are ultimately hampered by structural or outright discriminatory barriers.[16]

COGIC Gendered Pathways to Ministry

The stained-glass ceiling phenomena is precisely what women in the Church of God in Christ encounter. They have limitless access to middle-management roles but are constrained from gaining any real access to upper-management positions as leaders of congregations, jurisdictions, or of the denomination itself. A special section of the COGIC manual describes the church's stance on "Women In The Ministry," which starts with the statement, "The Church of God in Christ recognizes that there are thousands of talented, Spirit-filled, dedicated and well-informed devout women capable of conducting affairs of a church, both administratively and spiritually."[17] The statement continues speaking very favorably of the many ways women served within the early church. They make room for women in ministry to contribute through "prayer and fasting, visiting the sick, instruction of women, preparing women for baptism, assisting in the administration of both the baptismal and communion ordinances, teaching, and even have charge of a church in absence of its Pastor, if the Pastor so wishes."[18] Yet, the manual stops short of stating a case for women to be ordained as preachers and, by extension, pastors. Instead, women who claim a call to ministry must pursue, first, a local license as Deaconess and then the national/jurisdictional license as an Evangelist.[19]

In addition to the aforementioned contributions that women are allowed to make to COGIC ministry, the specific duties ascribed to Deaconesses and Evangelists are as follows: (1) to evangelize the work of the churches as much as lies within her power; (2) to travel and conduct revival meetings; (3) to carry a gospel of comfort and deliverance to the hospitals, jails, convalescent homes and the like; and (4) to visit the sick and give physical assistance when there is a need. Women, like male aspirants, have to meet the basic qualifications of having a convincing call to ministry (but not to preach), be active in their local church, be tithers, and complete a course of study approved by their jurisdiction. Evangelists are licensed by Jurisdictional Bishops at the same ceremony as the ordained Elders. As the women are not being ordained, they are formally recommended for licensing by the very powerful Jurisdictional Women's Department, a recommendation that, ironically, follows testing administered by the Jurisdiction's Ordination Committee.

Both the Deaconess and Evangelist licenses, like those held by Ministers and Elders, create a boundary between women and the laity. While the women are not ordained, they exist in these congregations as more than lay-leaders; they serve congregations as clergy, performing the same tasks (except preaching) as the Licensed Ministers. When Missionaries become Evangelists, they are seen as "speaking" rather than "preaching" even when doing so from the pulpit. In practically all cases, this is a symbolic distinction as few congregants (and, per my interviews, ministers) recognize any real difference between the two actions. In fact, most of my respondents suggest that, beyond recognizing the special role of Pastor, congregants are not cognizant of any of the distinctions the church makes between male and female clergy.

Asia, a very visible and influential Evangelist in both her church and jurisdiction, explained the confusion promoted by the bifurcated licensing processes:

What I found interesting was that if you were an Evangelist moving on, the men and women were taking the same classes. We took the same exam, but under the COGIC heading, it stopped right there. Even the ceremony was the same. In some other faiths, I would be known as Elder. Even when I told people I was moving to the next level, I had people coming to me wanting to get married and they said, "Well can you perform a marriage? Don't you have a license?" I'd have to say, well, I have my license but under the Church of God in Christ I cannot marry you. And they didn't understand that.

She went on to voice a common complaint among female ministers:

> Most of the time the women that go through are much more educated. They've gone to college and they've gotten a degree. And I know some of my other classmen in the training didn't have that basic credential. And I know some of them, I'm sorry to say, could not conduct a service because they didn't know the basic setup. It's a chauvinist thing. I'm just going to come right out and say it, that that's what it comes down to. But as we know it's a man's world.

The view that these values are based in male chauvinism was repeated again and again, but most women would only go so far at suggesting that the behavior was outright sexism. Women declared that "The Church of God in Christ is a man's church" (Alesha, an Evangelist) or that the constraints were merely "a man thing" (Sarah, an Evangelist), but they seem to understand, and ultimately accept, the constraints on women's roles in ministry.

Eve, a well-educated young Deaconess raised in the denomination, argued that the treatment is understandable: "I think society is set up in a way where leaders just get comfortable with what they know. That doesn't mean tradition is always correct, but it also doesn't make promotion of a man before a woman sexist. Some people would tell you this is a sexist system. I don't know that it is. I haven't experienced sexism in the system."

The church's justification for barring women from ordination is similar to that used by other conservative denominations:

> The Church of God in Christ recognizes the scriptural importance of women in the Christian Ministry . . . but nowhere can we find a mandate to ordain women to be an Elder, Bishop or Pastor. Paul styled the women who labored with him as servants or helpers, not Elders, Bishops or Pastors. Therefore the Church of God in Christ cannot accept the following scriptures as a mandate to ordain women preachers: Joel 2:28; Gal 3:28–29; Matt 28:9–11. The qualification for an Elder, Bishop, or Pastor are found in I Tim. 3:2–7 and Titus 1:7–9. We exhort all to take heed.[20]

Nevertheless, the scriptures listed as unacceptable were used by both men and women in my interviews to support their positions that women are both called and worthy of ordination, especially the quotation from Joel 2:28–29 ("I will pour out My Spirit on all flesh; your sons and your daughters shall prophesy . . . and also on My menservants and on My maidservants I will pour out My Spirit in those days."). The New Testament belief that women would be empowered to prophesy and that God no more distinguishes between male and female than he does slaves and free persons (Gal. 3:28), leave many women thinking that the constraints on them are more sociological than theological. They argue that these scriptures in particular point to what God has intended for the contemporary church and that the denomination is bound by antiquated and traditional approaches to ministry.[21] Some women were especially frustrated that a denomination whose founding and very nature was untraditional would retain such a conventional stance on women in ministry. Angela, a longtime Evangelist, argues:

> They know that without the women, the Church of God in Christ would not be what it is today. They are so afraid of change, but sooner or later, they're going to have to address that issue. Some people can be steeped in tradition. I mean, steeped in it, and the sad thing is, when [Bishop C. H.] Mason broke away, him and his group of people broke away because of difference in doctrine. He believed in the baptism of the Holy Ghost, but you know the Bible says the Holy Ghost would open the door for sons *and daughters* to prophecy. But he only brought in one part of that verse. It's just a man thing. People don't want to change tradition. Some traditions are good, but if it's hindering your church from going to the place where God wants it to go, you need to let that go.

If ordination is indeed like other professional credentials, it should make clear the lines between the professional and the paraprofessional. Because women cannot be ordained as Elders in the Church of God in Christ, they are automatically fated to serve only in paraprofessional positions in the church. While social scientists use ordination as an important boundary marker for clergy, ordination is almost always just a symbolic marker for the men and women ministers in the Church of God in Christ. None of the women see their role as *assisting* their male counterparts, pastors excepted, as subordinates. While they are subordinate to their pastors, any Elder who serves in that pastor's church is similarly subordinate to and serves at his direction.

In most congregations in COGIC, the only distinction between men's and women's ministry is the formal label for the people and some of the tasks they perform. With the exception of ministries specifically and exclusively aimed at men or boys, women can be found in practically any ministerial role made available to their male peers. In fact, it would not be unusual to find a church where the majority of ministerial positions—in music, education, outreach, youth, and "helps" ministries—are held by women. Like their male peers, women conduct worship services, visit jails and hospitals, do street evangelism, teach in any number of instructional situations, and expound on religious themes in sermons and other messages.

Only men "preach," but as the sociologists Mark Chaves and Cheryl Gilkes illustrate, this is a difference without distinction. While COGIC formally considers women's sermons "teaching" or "speaking," the behavior (if not always the context) is the same. While women often referred to a "double pulpit," where only male ministers were allowed to speak from the primary podium and women spoke from some other location on the pulpit, the women did so in retrospect. They often offered examples of women who speak—"preach"—from the same podium their pastor preaches from, with the caveat that they were certain this was not the case at other churches.

Gilkes states that "since the women's 'teaching' is indistinguishable from the men's 'preaching' there are no tasks of ministry that are the monopoly of elders."[22] While this is true about most tasks, there is one task in which ordination is a real requirement. It is not merely terminology that bars women from officiating at a wedding. Evangelists in the Church of God in Christ cannot sign marriage certificates and thus are incapable of truly legally solemnizing a marriage. This remains the only ministerial task women—unless endorsed as Chaplains or serving as Shepherdess in a congregation—cannot perform.

There are other tasks that women would not be allowed to perform within the context of their local church, but that they might perform, often in an unauthorized capacity, as ministers in other contexts. While COGIC protocol bars women from officiating at funerals, this role is a purely symbolic one that involves eulogizing the deceased and "committing them to the ground." Ultimately, the state requires the actual burial process to be overseen by a licensed funeral director; anyone can perform these other tasks. Both unordained Licensed Ministers and Evangelists informed me that they had officiated at funerals outside of their church. Often this is done without permission but still accepted by the families who invited them to officiate. In the absence of an Elder, both Licensed Ministers and Evangelists have administered communion in hospitals and congregants' homes. Other symbolic acts, such as christening children or blessing homes, are also formally reserved for Elders, but if the parents or homeowners approbate the female minister's clerical bona fides, even a Deaconess may be asked to administer these rites.

Women's Responses to These Differences

Other than the special case of wedding-officiation, most of the distinctions between male and female clergy in the Church of God in Christ appear to be rhetorical. Much of the ambiguity that I observed can be traced to the autonomy that leaders at every level—jurisdictional, divisional, congregational, and even by congregational ministry—have over the men and women they are responsible for. Pastors, especially, play a significant role in shaping the meanings of the call for men and women who become ministers under their guidance. Their ambivalence about ecclesiastical rules of order, a state that leads to often conflicting and ambiguous applications of these values, was most responsible for women's sometimes muddled defenses of their ministerial identities. In the sections that follow, their responses reflect a complex differentiation between a "call to be" and a "call to do." Regardless of the restriction or circumstance, they recognize a call to be ministers. On the other hand, what they do in that capacity is shaped by other dynamics, including both the call itself and the authority they are willing to grant to culture, doctrine, and the leadership in their churches.

Callings and Gender

For those women raised in the Church of God in Christ or in some other denomination where women are not ordained, the first challenge they faced in making sense of a call to ministry was their own belief that such a thing—ordination of women— wasn't possible. They had internalized the sexist ideology, an action that rendered their calling inauthentic to them. Angela spoke of the impact her father's beliefs had on her, "My father didn't believe in women preachers, and I feel that was a factor in why I stayed back so long before I stepped out. He'd say, 'No, God ain't called women to preach.' He had a great influence on me."

Women who spoke of these preconceived notions about the call to ministry all reported some kind of blitzkrieg calling. It was the nature of the call, the strength of the voices and dreams, that ultimately prompted them to move. As described in chapter 2, women were less likely than men to describe an "urging" into ministry. Women raised in the church report either drifting into ministry or having clear calls into ministry that didn't always have the kind of specificity that might lead them to fully reject it.

For most of these women, though, the ambiguous nature of their call lent itself to some experimentation with ministry. For Monique, her call to the title of Evangelist did not have any clear meaning. She said, "I heard God say to me, 'I have called you to be an Evangelist.' Not understanding what an Evangelist was at that time, I replied back, 'But you know I don't believe in women preachers.'" Eventually she came to accept the call because the work she ultimately did as a minister—lead prayer services—did not contradict her belief that women do not preach. While she is now occasionally asked to preach in her capacity as an Evangelist, not finding preaching among her core ministerial tasks enables her to remain comfortable with her calling. Her own successes as a preacher have tempered her belief that women cannot preach. Since operating in her call for many years, she has encountered (and trained) many women who are also very successful preachers; she now advocates for them.

The most difficult calling a woman in the Church of God in Christ might experience would be a call to pastor. There is considerable blurring around the edges of "preaching" ministries and thus serving the sacraments, but there tends to be only one route to a female pastorate in the church: the woman's pastoring husband must die and leave her as custodian of the ministry. While some women suggested that God might eventually call them to pastor, only a few described having a clear call to the position. Justine somberly relayed the following account:

> I have a call that the only way I can fulfill it is if my husband died. COGIC doctrine is depressing. When I heard my call—and it wasn't to pastor at that point—I felt a sense of joy. But in seminary, I came to realize there was a pattern. Whenever they'd talk about pastors, I would break down. That year, I heard the voice of the Lord say "pastor." I began to talk to my professors. My pastoral care professor told me that my personality assessment says, "yes, you have a pastor's heart and you're going to have a period of rebellion against that system"—the man was prophesying—"because eventually you're going to want to come forward and you're going to find this to be a problem. Either you're going to be a trailblazer in your church or you will have to leave your church."

The pastoral care professor was right. She did an internship in a non-COGIC church and now serves as an associate minister at a Baptist church.

No Limits

On the surface, the codes of conduct that create rhetorical boundary lines around women and men, the "only-licensed" and the "ordained," seem meaningless. Each of these women has overcome any apprehensions they might have had about whether God calls women to the ministry. They each claim an understanding of the scope of ministry they feel God has called them to perform in this particular denomination. Nichole, an Evangelist, responds this way when asked if she feels limited by the church protocol:

> See, for me, it's not that important. I don't care if I'm not allowed to pastor. I don't care if I'm not allowed to [makes quotes with fingers] "preach." As long as I can speak the Word, I just feel like it's the same thing. Some women are very, very hung up on the fact that we don't have women pastors, but there are a lot of women pastors around here. Sure the Bishop will just call them Shepherdess, but who cares about the title? They're still doing the same thing. They're burying. They're marrying. They're having church. The title does not concern me. I just see it as words, the male version and the female version, labels for the same works. I had a speaking engagement at a church on Sunday at 11 o'clock service. I was the main speaker. Whether they saw it as speaking or preaching or whatever, I saw it as preaching because that's what I'm called to do.

Women described it as rare for them to be interested in doing something in ministry and having their pastors deny them the opportunity. In contrast to what we might imagine, many of the women in the denomination seem quite satisfied with the status afforded them. This may not be as unusual as one might assume. In 1982, the social psychologist Jane Crosby introduced what has come to be known as the "paradox of the contented female worker."[23] She observed a similar dynamic: some women are surprisingly satisfied with jobs that don't afford them the same pay, status, autonomy, or work conditions as their male counterparts. That is not to say that they don't recognize the differences as injustices; they do. Crosby believes there is another phenomena—a denial of personal disadvantage—at work here. She argues that these women can perceive that an injustice affects members of their reference group, but they believe that they are personally exempt from those injustices. This is the case here. As Nichole argues in the passage above, she recognizes the injustice as real, yet she doesn't feel limited by it. She feels unconstrained in the pursuit of the ministry she believes herself called to do.

There is a great deal of consensus on this issue. Most women believe that on any given day, they are fully empowered to operate in the capacities they feel called to. The least discomfited responses to questions about limitations came from women in either the early stages of their credential process or those fully satisfied with their Deaconess' license. "I've come a long way spiritually," says Anna, a longtime Deaconess. "Some of the stuff with the doctrine, you have to eat the meat and spit out the bones. It doesn't get in the way. I personally don't believe that COGIC or any other doctrine can block what God has for me and my life. What God has for me, it is for me." These sentiments were echoed by Amy, who was raised Roman Catholic and only recently received her Deaconess license:

> I would say over the past several years, I don't feel limitations. I feel fortunate because I feel I've come in at a time where there's been a big transition as far as women are concerned. I don't feel hindered mainly because I don't have the desire to sit on the pulpit. It's not a big deal to me. Sure, I could never be called pastor, but I don't feel called to be pastor . . . not right now anyway.

In both of these cases, women recognize the potential limits but argue that the injunctions against pastoring or administering the sacraments are irrelevant; they haven't felt a particular call to the pastoral role or the sacramental responsibilities.[24] As a result, they find it possible to remain satisfied in a denomination that, on paper, is inequitable and discriminatory.

When asked about her use of the often-repeated phrase "eat (or chew) the meat and spit out the bones," Tiffany, a Deaconess, explained that the Bible "tells us to check out everything, but then we have to hold fast to what's good." (see 1 Thess. 5:21). I think there's a lot of good in what COGIC is doing and I'm not going to let go just because it has some things I might not agree with. These titles don't define me. God defines me." Being licensed rather than ordained, like the contrast between "preaching" and "speaking," becomes just another abstract distinction that is overshadowed by the concrete practices of ministry in these churches.

Doctrinal Limitations

Women are more likely than men to describe a calling to teach and evangelize. In an effort to understand just how unlimited they believe they are to live out religious mandates related to those tasks, I asked each of the women about the last few verses of Matthew 28. These verses, colloquially referred to as "The Great Commission," represent the last major directive made by Jesus to his disciples first and, ultimately, to all of his followers. Without exception, the women agreed that the tasks listed in the directive are to be followed by all believers, not just those in ministry. The verses read: "Go therefore and make disciples of all the nations, baptizing them in the name of the Father and of the Son and of the Holy Spirit, teaching them to observe all things that I have commanded you." In each interview, I point to the four commands in the verses: to go, to make disciples (i.e., to evangelize), to baptize, and to teach. I then ask a question based on a biblical account of the deacon Philip's encounter with an Ethiopian eunuch. The eunuch was having difficulty understanding a prophecy in the Bible that pointed to the coming Messiah. Philip explained the scripture to the man and the man agreed to convert to Christianity. When their chariot came to a body of water, the eunuch exclaimed, "See, here is water. What hinders me from being baptized." Philip responded, "If you believe in your heart, you may" and, stopping the chariot, baptized the eunuch there on the side of the road (Acts 8:26–40).

After describing the story to each woman, pointing to the ways Philip played out each of the commands in the Matthew 28 directive, I asked them if they would have baptized the eunuch given the rules against it for women in COGIC ministry. Their answers revealed some of the inconsistencies in their steadfast admissions that they're unlimited by church doctrine. While many agreed that even I, a layperson, might be free to baptize the young man, most hesitated to give a definite yes in response to my query. They indicated that they had no concerns about going to the eunuch, sharing the gospel, and helping him become a disciple. The final stage—baptizing him—yielded three possible responses from the women. Twenty-four percent gave an unqualified yes, another 20 percent said they would do so if the Lord gave them specific instructions to baptize him, and the remaining 56 percent said they would not baptize him.

The women who would have baptized him, without any additional directives from God, were also more likely than others to directly state that the rules governing women's roles in the church were sexist. In fact, two women pointed out that any one of Philip's four daughters, who are mentioned as prophetesses in Acts 21:8, might have baptized the eunuch if they have happened upon him. "I would baptize him," declared Dana sheepishly, "If it's being done outside of the church and the young man asked me to do it, I would. I guess I would have to be disobedient to the church authority." While all of the seminary-trained women did not agree to baptizing the man, most of the women who had spent considerable time being trained in either a non-COGIC Bible school or seminary did agree. Anitra points to her training as a source for understanding what she should do in that circumstance: "I know that I'm a woman of God and I have to do things that God requires me to do. If I felt that this young man wanted to be baptized right then, I would say, 'Come on.' In the school I came from, you can do this in a bathtub if you're there and that's what is necessary."

Some of the female ministers put the onus on God for their decision. They would move only if God gave them an additional command to do so. Certainly the women who said no and the women who said yes *may* have sought further instructions from God before making their final decision, but only these women (20 percent) specifically brought God into the equation. Kathryn was clear about the role that doctrine and God's will would play in her ultimate decision,

> As far as doctrine goes, no, I can't baptize anybody, but if God told me right then and there that this is what He wanted me to do, I would do what He told me to do. God has shown me many different ways that going along to get along is not how He operates with me. I'm going to have to do it even if it makes me disobedient to Pastor or COGIC doctrine. God's word supersedes COGIC doctrine, especially since my ministry isn't just here at the church, but it's out on the streets.

Ultimately, these women's first impulse was to be governed by church doctrine. Kathleen, an Aspiring Missionary, would try to remain within the confines of the denomination's rules, but also described God as "working outside the box." She went on to say, "if there came a moment like that when I was outside the box and couldn't find any other solution and I felt like it wouldn't offend God or violate what He wanted me to do at that moment, my allegiance would have to be to the Lord. But I still could not be rebellious to the [church] manual."

The remaining 56 percent indicated they would not baptize the young man. In most cases, they argued they were bound by the church's authority over them and, in spite of their admission that this might put them at odds with the scripture, they needed to obey that authority. Abigail's argument is representative of this perspective:

> If that ever were a situation I faced, I wouldn't be permitted to baptize him. I wouldn't do it. I would tell him that we can set a time aside for some Elders to do it. We are under certain rules in this church and we know what we're not supposed to do; we're not free to do that. Because being in the Church of God in Christ there are certain rules, and if you're going to be a part of the church, you need to obey that authority.

Most of the women described their pastors as "lenient" and even "liberal" in their dealings with women in ministry, but they also felt that disobeying denominational rules governing women's abilities to administer ordinances would put them at odds with these men. "The Bible says obey those that have rule and govern over you," argued Linda, a young Aspiring Missionary, "I'm under a head and you have to respect what your head says. That's scriptural. If I believe I'm called to be at that church, I have to be under the authority of that. If that person really wants to be baptized, he can wait and do it. I wouldn't overstep those boundaries." Doctrine may have informed the work of her call, but not her understanding of herself as called.

Biblical Limitations

Again, the boundaries that COGIC's leadership has erected around the ordained clergy find their origins in the Bible itself. When discussing the kind of character the ministry requires, both men and women pointed to verses in the book of 1 Timothy. They cited verses from the first chapter of the book, arguing that the "insubordinate," and especially "fornicators, sodomites, and liars" were not fit to serve as ministers. Some also quoted similar verses from 1 Corinthians 6 and Galatians 5 to underscore their belief that engaging in any of these behaviors put a ministers' anointing at risk and, if unrepentant, should disqualify a minister from moving forward with his or her credential. These charges were aimed at male clergy (both specifically and generally) more often than at female clergy and the charges were more often made by women.

Women, in particular, also complained that men were being promoted whose character did not line up with the qualifications for the position of Bishop, Elder, and Deacon listed in 1 Timothy 3. In those verses, which are also used to argue against women's ordination, Elders and Deacons "must be blameless, the husband of one wife, temperate, sober-minded, of good behavior, hospitable, able to teach, not given to wine, not violent, not greedy for money, but gentle, not quarrelsome, not covetous, one who rules his own house well, having his children in submission with all reverence . . . , [and] not a novice" (1 Tim. 3:1–7). Church leaders point to the second of these qualifications—"the husband of one wife"—as their primary evidence that female leaders are unscriptural because only men can be husbands. Of course, this qualification is not absolute; 15 percent of the male ministers in my sample were unmarried.[25]

As women pointed to these verses, with particular emphasis on certain components of it (i.e., "blameless," "able to teach," "rules his own house well"), only one alluded to the "husband of one wife" portion of the passage, paraphrasing it as "not divorced." Generally, women were much more critical of their fellow ministers than were the men, and these chapters from 1 Timothy more than others seemed ripe with examples of what made one's calling questionable. The irony of the choice of qualifications from this biblical book is that sandwiched between chapters 1 and 3 are two verses often used by opponents of women in ministry: "Let a woman learn in silence with all submission. I do not permit a woman to teach or to have authority over a man, but to be in silence" (1 Tim. 2:11–12). While almost all of the women were familiar with these verses, none of them considered these verses to hold much value in understanding women's roles in ministry.

When asked directly if they felt these verses placed limitations on their call to ministry or the ministry they did, even those who felt constrained by COGIC rules on baptism argued that these verses did not constrain them in any way. There were three approaches they took in explaining this stance. Most argued that these verses (and Paul's gendered descriptions of Elders and Deacons) should be viewed in their historical context. Other women pointed to inconsistencies between this scripture's limitations on women and other scriptures that detailed the works of women in ministry. Some pointed to Timothy's grandmother Lois as an example; others pointed to Priscilla, the wife of Aquila who joined Paul in tentmaking. Along these same lines, Linda argued:

> That can't be God's all the time plan if Mary Magdalene was the first evangelist. God used Deborah as a judge and all the other women in the Bible, how can that be? He's not a schizophrenic. The Bible says in the last days your sons and daughters will be anointed to go out in ministry. Now we can take 1 Timothy, but it doesn't throw out the rest of the Bible and all the rest of the scriptures where women were used by God.

Some women rejected the verses entirely as instances of Paul's own culturally induced sexism, not directives from God. As a result, they believe the COGIC interpretations of the verses are contrary to God's actual will for contemporary women. "If you come into an organization, there are always going to be things that don't line up with the word," remarked Kenya, one of the women who would have baptized the eunuch, "If you were to sit down and really follow some of the things we teach, you would never get to do what you're called to do. I'm in COGIC and there are things that we're supposed to think that doesn't line up. It doesn't. If this isn't what God wants us to do, we're all out of order."

While many women hinted at the sexism in these injunctions, only a few were comfortable saying it directly. Adrienne said, "I think people have made it sexist. I believe sexism's creeped into the church. There are some women who preach as strongly and as anointed as any man, so I don't see why she shouldn't be made an Elder. Just because she's a female?" Most women saw these scriptures as irrelevant in their call. The verses were framed, narrowly, as a guideline that was necessary for the particular set of women Paul was dealing with. Ashley summed up the argument this way:

> That was a specific thing Paul was talking to those specific women. It's a guideline so you won't go too far to the left or too far to the right. Yes, sometimes women are too bossy. Yes, most women ministers are alright, but some go too far. You have to meet out the Word of God where it's necessary. Me, I just chew the meat and spit out the bones. This doesn't apply to me.

Even though Ashley argues that Paul's statements were aimed at a particular set of women, she does betray a sensibility that was voiced by some women. While most women lifted other women up as role models for ministry, some argued that there may be some lessons to be learned in Paul's admonitions.

Abigail, a woman who decided to remain a Deaconess instead of pursuing the Evangelist license, was critical of women who were demanding ordination: "Some women I know are very dogmatic, very pushy. They're going to have their way or no way. I believe that an anointed woman of God would be led by God. Her ministry can be blessed by God because of her obedience to those God's put in place. Let God fight those other battles."

This critique of female leadership was especially harsh when aimed at women who were leading congregations as "pastors." Again, the denomination does not formally recognize women as Pastor because that title is reserved for those (men) who have been ordained as Elders. While some women assume the role of Pastor (formally Shepherdess sans portfolio) of COGIC churches by inheriting the congregation from a deceased spouse, other women are ordained as Pastors in other denomination and then merge their congregations with the Church of God in Christ.[26] These mergers present jurisdictions with an interesting problem because the denomination's bureaucratic structure is so gendered. It is customary for Pastors, who are all Elders (and therefore men), to report to the male leadership. Because female pastors are, nominally, "Evangelists," they are expected to answer to the jurisdiction's female leadership. Not surprisingly, this dynamic brings female pastors into conflict with the female leadership, because some reject their authority, demanding to be treated like any other congregational head.

Women who were privy to these conflicts expressed deep ambivalence and, in some cases, outright hostility to women's calls to the pastorate. They argued that Paul, and by extension the denomination, was right to limit women's opportunities. Dawne, an Evangelist, said:

> I wouldn't go too far with this—and don't put my name next to it in your book either—but God may have known what He was doing when He said that. Women then probably weren't no different from some women now, bossy, controlling, and probably need to be sat down somewhere. Maybe it's not in our nature to be submissive and this was just another way God was trying to teach women to be more submissive .[27]

Pastoral Limitations

In order to allow the mergers described above, Jurisdictional Bishops and Pastors have operated in the wide gaps in episcopal accountability prevalent in the denomination; gaps that, in the end, enable women to essentially ignore the doctrinal injunctions against their assuming real clerical status. Ashley, the Evangelist quoted earlier, went on to say, "A lot of these brothers who are pastors realize they can't hold the women down. Pastors know they have preaching women. They know that, so they don't bother to fight it and just let it go."

Many COGIC Pastors simply turn a blind eye to the church's gendering of clerical labels and terminology. Women, for the most part, referred to their Pastors as "lenient" and even "liberal" in terms of their approach to their ministry. In the historian Daphne Wiggins's *Righteous Content: Black Women's Perspectives of Church and Faith*, she reports that laywomen, too, perceive their pastors to be more supportive of women in ministry than COGIC church protocol might suggest.[28] While women don't always extend this sense of leniency to other male jurisdictional leaders, the jurisdictions they serve in all have women in leadership positions. Certainly COGIC values allow for women to lead other women, but women also serve as jurisdictional treasurers, convocation coordinators, directors of education, and music ministries, and as heads of congregations. These roles and others place women in authority over men, sometimes even making them supervisors for male clergy and lay-leaders.

In describing an opportunity Courtney, an Evangelist, had to teach her church's deacons, she explains why pastors may resort to using women in ways that seem to contradict church protocol,

> They had me teach the deacons and I actually said to [the female head of the church's education program] "But I'm a woman, are they going to accept my teaching?" And the answer was "they don't have anybody else." Pulpit full of men, but no one else to teach these deacons? The key is I was qualified to do it. The anointing destroys the yoke, the chains, the mentality that says as a woman I can't have anything to offer the men. Men might not respect the fact that I'm in a position, but ultimately they have to yield to the anointing because that makes the difference.

Some women specifically talked about the paucity of available men in their churches. In many smaller churches, there may be no Ministers or Elders other than the Pastor. In one jurisdiction, churches had, on average, eight credentialed clergy including the pastor.[29] In churches with fewer than eight ministers, 58 percent of the ministers were female. In churches larger than that, that number rose to 62 percent, even in very large churches led by District Supervisors or Bishops. Even when there was numerical parity between men and women in all stages of credentialing, female Evangelists outnumbered male Elders by a two-to-one margin. So, the issue of pastors *needing* women to do ministry is an important part of the calculus many make in determining how strongly they heed denominational protocols hindering women's work.

Women sometimes described themselves as "rocks," alluding to a scripture where Jesus told some critics that if he told his disciples to stop praising him, the stones would cry out in their stead (Lk. 19:40). The female ministers argue that they are "rocks" doing the work of the men who either aren't accepting their calls to ministry or will only do ministry that gives them an opportunity to preach. "At the time Paul wrote that, men were serious about ministry, but it's a new day," Paula, an Evangelist, argued, "It's a new day and everybody's not stepping up to the plate. And before He allows His word to return void, He's going to use whoever's available. If I got to be a rock, I'm comfortable with that." Justine went further, comparing herself and other women to five sisters in Joshua 17:3–4:

> I see it like this. We're like the daughters of Zelophehad. We might not have been due to inherit the ministries and callings that God's granted us, but since there aren't any male heirs as it were, we're petitioning God to

give us our due. And He's doing just that. Isaiah said when God called, there was no man to answer. Women are answering.

Of course a "lenient" or "liberal" pastor who referred to women as "preachers" in spite of COGIC protocols or who allowed women to teach men in spite of biblical injunctions might be considered insubordinate to the authority he himself is under. Women were asked to consider how they would respond if their pastors, in being obedient to church protocol, decided to curtail some of the liberties they believe they had been granted. Because many women were currently involved in teaching mixed-sex classes, working with men in prison and homeless ministries, and overseeing mixed-sex ministry teams, a shift of this kind would affect them in relevant ways.

The most common response was to remain obedient to their pastor's authority and restrict their ministry to women and/or children. "I gotta be obedient to God," declared Kathleen, an Aspiring Missionary, "but that doesn't give me carte blanche to be rebellious to the authority that I've submitted myself to. If I'm rebellious to that authority—sexist, nonsexist, whatever—the leader that God appointed for me, then by being rebellious to him, I risk being rebellious to God." This language connecting obedience to pastoral authority with obedience to God was repeated by other women, for example, Davita, a longtime Evangelist, who said:

> I would obey because I wouldn't want to be beat up by God later. Even if I felt strongly that he was not correct, I would tell God, "you go deal with him," and I would sit down. I believe that if God didn't want it that way, he would deal with him, but God has led me here. Since he's given him authority over this flock, then I as a sheep in that pasture need to be obedient.

Of course, as with a pastoral rejection of a calling itself, women also emphasized the role prayer would play in their decision to accept pastoral authority over their calling. While their immediate response would be to accept it, like Davita, most say they would consult God's will directly. If women felt their ability to do ministry too constrained by their pastor's edicts, they would seek out a new pastor who would be more supportive. Natalie argued:

> No man can stop anyone from doing what they're called to do. It's up to that individual. If they're really called to do something, it's up to them. If

they feel they're being stifled, then they have a decision to make. Do I stay here or do I go where I feel I can do what God has called me to do? If I was prevented from doing what God has called me to do, I would have to leave.

Men's Responses to These Differences

In discussing his experience in the Sunday school class of one of his church's "most dynamic woman Evangelists we have around here," Aaron, a newly Licensed Minister, argued, "The powerful teaching we got from this sister just goes to show you that when God calls you He doesn't call the gender. He calls the spirit. These women have the same anointing, the same calling, and maybe more degrees." Positive experiences with successful female ministers left many of my male respondents confused about the role of women in COGIC ministry. Like Aaron, most of them have had significant experiences with very effective female clergy.

Nevertheless, the contradiction between these experiences and doctrinal arguments against women's capabilities makes some men uneasy. Mark, an Aspiring Minister, exemplifies this uncertainty:

> I know what the Bible says and I see what my church does and I ask, "What's going on here?" Am I breaking a commandment by sitting in Evangelist McAdam's Sunday school class? I know she's anointed to teach, but teach who? Should she teach just because she's effective? Con artists might have the gift of persuasion, but is that God's will for that gift even if they're effective at it?

The inconsistencies are especially problematic given the eventual responsibility of these men to enforce the church's rules within their own congregations.

In spite of this confusion, most men were positively predisposed to having women join them in ministry. They agreed that women could be called to do ministry and should be given opportunities to operate in those ministries. No one seemed to support a doctrinal position that would require women to "be silent in church" or forbid them from teaching or even "preaching." That said, there were some distinctions to be found in how far men were willing to go toward giving women full access to the roles (i.e., Elder/Pastor) and the freedoms that came with ordination.

The degree to which men believe women should be ordained as Elders is strongly correlated with whether they have a spouse or other female relative (usually a mother) operating in one of the clerical roles available to them.

Most (85 percent) of the men I interviewed are married, and of that group, nearly 40 percent have wives who are Aspiring Missionaries, Deaconesses, or Evangelists. Nearly half of the interviewees have a wife or a mother serving in one of those positions in the Church of God in Christ or some parallel position in another denomination.

These men were more likely than even their female counterparts to consider the constraints on women to be sexist. "I think these rules are just man hindering women's calling," argued Bryant, an Elder, whose wife is a recently credentialed Missionary:

> God uses women all the time. I find it amazing that the first people that went to the tomb to witness the resurrection was women; the men all ran. I think most of the Church of God in Christ stuff *is* sexist. We have some of these bishops who can get married two and three times and then try to put women in a box because of scripture. If we gonna march Bible, then let's march all the Bible.

While ministers' husbands argued vehemently that women should have equal access in ministry, they still came short of stating that women should have equal status to men. Their statements in support of women serving as heads of churches often came with two revealing caveats.

Bryant's full-throated defense of women ministers included this common refrain: "Now I *do* believe God said man is head of the house. That's not sexism; that's God. But as far as ministry-wise, I don't have a problem with women pastors. I don't know if *I* could sit under a woman pastor though." Both these men and those who rejected women's ordination agree that men's position as head of household is a reflection of divine order. Men who were not married to ministers rejected the idea that this order was relevant only within the home. Langston, an Elder whose wife was not a minister, argued that in the apostle Paul's (1 Tim. 2) prohibitions against women's authority, he "isn't just talking about husbands and wives like sisters want to argue. He was talking about authority in the church too. Just like God told Adam not to touch the tree and his job was to teach God's word to Eve, the word is given to man first and then that word is given to women. That's God's order."

While ministers' husbands rejected Langston's ultimate conclusion that God's order also bars women from teaching men, they still voiced the opinion that they would have a difficult time serving under the pastoral authority of a woman. When pressed to explain his general support for female pastors but his aversion to being under the authority of one, Adam, an ordained Elder, said:

Personally, I would never sit under a woman pastor. Not because of her, but because it would be a reflection on me. If I'm a male and I'm called to ministry, she shouldn't have to be standing in that role. If a man's available, God's called the man to be out front. I'd have a hard time—and this is crazy because I've had female bosses on the job—but I'd have a hard time, as a man, being led by a woman at church.

Adam went on to suggest that he'd have no problems co-pastoring a church with his wife and would want her to have the full authority to administer the sacraments that any Elder at his church might have. Other ministers' husbands voiced similar desires for their wives, arguing that she would need that authority in order to be a true partner in their future ministries.

In sharp contrast to men whose wives were ministers, other men echoed the denominational perspective, explaining that the church's prohibitions against ordaining women and allowing them to serve in the priestly role are, as Langston argued, "God's order." Joel, an Aspiring Minister, drew on an incident from 1 Samuel 13:1–23 to make the case that sometimes God decides that only certain people are approved to do certain rituals:

When they went out to battle, they were supposed to wait for the priest to come and do the sacrifice. Saul took it on himself to do the ritual sacrifice. After all, he *was* the king, right? He knew all the practices. But God had not granted him the authority—the anointing if you want to call it that—to do the sacrifice. Only the Levitical priests were who God had ordained to do that. I see that happening now with women wanting to step out of their place just because they can. Women are ordained to do a lot of things in the church, but some things God has reserved for men.

These men were more likely than their peers to point to the usual slate of scriptures (e.g., 1 Tim. 2–3; Titus 1) to defend their beliefs about women's roles in the church. Not only did they believe women should not be in full authority over men (i.e., as pastor), but they also rejected women's demands to be allowed to administer the sacraments.

They argue that contemporary women misread the prohibitions as a means of stigmatizing them. "Paul wasn't trying to put women down," says Donald:

He was trying to deal with confusion. I believe that women who really understand their call would rather have a man doing it. The Bible says humility will bring her more honor than fighting authority and writing letters and whatnot. Because really when women are up there fighting and demanding their rights in the middle of the national meetings, they're just playing out exactly what Paul was talking about.

These men, joking that they're accused of being legalistic on these points, eventually settle on an argument that even some women who feel unconstrained by the doctrine use against women who want more freedoms. Jeremy, an Elder, stated, "If you're in a particular body, the Bible says obey those that have rule over you. Being in it doesn't mean you agree with it, but when you're under great leaders, you got to take it easy and let God deal with it. If you can't agree, don't be disagreeable. Just find you a place that agrees with you."

Zones of Ambiguity: Women Making a Way

In a foreword to the newest edition of the COGIC manual, the then Presiding Bishop J. O. Patterson described the manual as "an earnest attempt to transcribe in contemporary terms the doctrine and discipline of [the] Church and hopefully it will counteract the malicious and seditious doctrines flourishing again in this age of insecurity." Its aim was to "exhort men to consult their heart instead of their heads." This statement is similar to one later put forth by Southern Baptists in a 1984 resolution: "Therefore, be it Resolved, That we not decide concerns of Christian doctrine and practice by modern cultural, sociological, and ecclesiastical trends or by emotional factors; that we remind ourselves of the dearly bought Baptist principle of the final authority of Scripture in matters of faith and conduct." The Southern Baptists' resolution was written, specifically, in response to challenges of their doctrine barring women from becoming clergy. While the COGIC manual's description was likely intended to be more general, the sentiment inscribed within it could just as easily be applied to the issues of women's roles in that church as well. They, like the Southern Baptists, would argue that cultural and sociological trends regarding gender equality in professions are irrelevant; scripture forbids female leadership of churches.

COGIC struggles with a kind of organizational schizophrenia, where leaders at the top of the organizational hierarchy pass ecclesiastical edicts that are ignored or "liberalized" in the practically autonomous churches that make up the denomination. There are a number of occasions where we can observe clear contradictions between the doctrinal and organizational demands of the denomination and the ways either jurisdictional or congregational leadership circumvent them in order to create an opening for individuals' service to their religious communities. These contradictions are especially visible in this gendered arena. It is in the interstices between denominational and congregational environments—these zones of ambiguity—where women find opportunities to develop their own understanding of themselves as ministers.

Daphne Wiggins's description of Black women in Pentecostal and Baptist churches points to the phenomenon described here. She says that "more Pentecostal women than Baptists have been exposed to women clergy. Among the COGIC, the office of Evangelist and Missionary are highly recognized and provide women the opportunity to preach."[30] It is simply the case that COGIC women, because they perform practically every role in any given congregation that the men do, are perceived as and operate as clergy even without ordination. They do so with the same conviction because, like men, they also claim calls to the ministry.

The calling stories and experiences, while different in some minor ways, were no less powerful for the women than for the men who were speaking them. It is true that women were somewhat less likely to report blitzkrieg calls, although this seems to be a function of their situation *when* God called them. No thunderbolts and visions were necessary to draw women's attention to the "harvest"; in most cases, they were already laboring in the field. It was not uncommon for many of these women to be already serving in the exact ministry or some related one that they serve in now as licensed clergy. It is a fairly short step from being a member of the street evangelism team (as laity) to pursuing a call to be an Evangelist leading that team. The work didn't change; the position did. But if God calls you to "preach" or "pastor," as COGIC assumes happens exclusively to men, neither of those ministerial tasks can be done outside of the boundary line of ordained ministry.[31] Even teaching, which in COGIC (as in other denominations) is listed as one of the major fivefold ministries, is done in many churches by unordained and unlicensed lay-members. Thus, when a woman declares that God has called her to "expound the Scriptures," a phrase directly pulled from the Evangelist license, she's already been doing that as a Sunday school teacher for many years.

Another important issue to address is that of "power envy," that is, the assumption that all women want the same power men in these denominations have. Much of the feminist critique of churches that deny women ordination focuses on the access to the levers of power denied to the unordained. This is an important and valid critique, but while COGIC women cannot administer the sacraments or become Elders, they argue that that is not where the action is in ministry. Instead they say that the symbolic authority men gain in the ordained priestly position pales in comparison to the real power they have gained in their unordained "prophetic" ones. This is particularly the case in COGIC where so many ordained men sit, stagnant, waiting for opportunities to "preach" while their unordained female counterparts run practically every auxiliary in their churches.

Other than their senior pastors, no other men were mentioned as either inspirations or mentors by men and women in my sample. In every case where they mentioned someone who taught them something in ministry, that person was either the male Pastor or a female Sunday school, Young People Willing Workers (YPWW), or other auxiliary leader. Other than the Pastor, the charismatic, prophetic authority in these churches is held by female Deaconesses and Evangelists. This, then, is not just another form of symbolic traditionalism where women settle for gender inequality under the rhetorical guise of "gender complementarity." COGIC women are *not* just performing the "duties associated with the domestic sphere within the life of the congregational 'family.'"[32] As detailed in other texts about women in Black churches, and the Church of God in Christ in particular, if it were not for the women, many of the men leading churches would still be sitting in the pews.[33]

In her study of ordained female clergy, Zikmund and her colleagues posit that the limited career opportunities they face do indeed lead to women "creatively claiming new ways to 'be clergy.'"[34] This same dynamic is at work in the Church of God in Christ. While seemingly constrained by not being able to claim a "call to preach," their boundaryless claim to a "call to the ministry" gives them the same "incredible freedom to push the edges of ministry beyond historical habits" that their ordained female counterparts are having in other denominations.[35] Whether "speaking" the gospel or *only* "expounding the Scriptures," women are doing as much, and likely substantially more, ministry in any given week as their ordained male counterparts. This reality is not lost on some of these men. Jeff, a newly ordained Elder, spoke eloquently about the pattern he has observed where men are constrained by a "call to preach" while women are liberated by a broader "call to the ministry":

It is problematic. Women do more than men do in our calling. We come in together, but it seems like the women go into their calling faster than the men. And for some men, that's a problem. They understand that they're *called* and I know quite a few men here and if they can't preach, they ain't doing nothing. That's too confined. You're not called just to preach. You're called to be on the front lines and do whatever needs to be done. Sometimes the men need to look at how these women around here [are] working. Men try to limit God [saying]. "If I can't preach, man, I ain't doing nothing." That's not what being called is all about. There's so many other things that need to be done . . . and the women are out there doing it.

Conclusion

7 ────

Legitimating New Understandings
of Ministry and the Clergy

Let us hear the conclusion of the whole matter.

Ecclesiastes 12:13

If you're answering the call on your life, you're now being led to
be a part of God's called out, God's chosen, God's anointed, and
God's appointed to minister to the body of Christ as well as to
the world.

Monique, Evangelist

The sociologist Richard Christopherson makes the observation that
"the work of physicians, social workers, attorneys, scholars, professionals
and semi-professionals of all sorts has usurped much of the territory that
formerly belonged to the church, and these developments have often left the
clergy scurrying about looking for something to do—and not incidentally,
someone to be."[1] This ongoing expansion of the boundaries of the cleric's
vocational identity has made the attributes that might mark the clergy as
a profession more ambiguous. There was already evidence to support the
fact that many clergy are not seminary trained, that many are either bivocational or not serving as congregational leaders, and that there are women
(and men) doing ministry at very high levels who are not ordained. The findings offered in this book further demonstrate these facts in one of the largest
religious organizations in the country. Yet, many who study religion from a
social-scientific viewpoint suffer a kind of myopia when it comes to clergy.
As we have seen, studies of clergy are still drawn almost exclusively from
three places: seminary rolls, lists of congregational heads, and denominational ordinand listings. By continuing to overlook the hundreds of clergy
who are not likely to be found in these places, researchers are unlikely to
achieve a full appreciation of the subtle ways in which cultural conceptions
of the ministerial role are produced, reproduced, and understood.

| 213

Religious Training:
Seminaries Aren't the Only "School of the Prophets"

In one COGIC jurisdiction, the Ordination Committee requires each pastor to submit an evaluation of candidates for ordination. With a range of "very good" to "unsatisfactory," the evaluation asks the recommending pastor to evaluate the candidate on ten items: his spiritual behavior as a minister, his moral character, his ability to orally read correctly the Bible, his understanding of the Bible, how well he gets along with others, how well he supports the church with tithes and offerings, his leadership ability, his physical appearance, his self-control under pressure, and his love for his family. The pastor is then asked to rate the person as a candidate for ordination, indicating if the ordinand has met the jurisdiction's requirement of two years of service as a Licensed Minister. Rarely does someone come to the Ordination Commissioner with both a pastor's recommendation and unsatisfactory, or even satisfactory, marks on this evaluation. In fact, Ordination Commissioners often have to challenge recommending pastors to be more discerning; they give candidates all "very good" marks on each point in the evaluation.

That leaders of congregations so strongly support men who have been serving them for two to three years is not a surprise. If candidates have reached the point of receiving the recommendation, it would be more surprising if the support wasn't this strong. After all, this process is not the same as that for the 150 students I teach each year who might ask for a recommendation letter; pastors know these men well, and their success signals the pastor's strengths as both leader and mentor.

What *is* surprising is the list of ten points they are asked to evaluate. Setting aside the almost laughable "requirement" that aspirants be able to read the Bible orally, the only criterion that might require some professional religious training is "understanding of the Bible." The measurement of this understanding, like the measurement of "his physical appearance," is likely to be subjective. After all, how much does one need to know in order to preach a thirty-minute sermon or visit elderly parishioners in the hospital? During one presentation of my findings, a sociologist in the audience asked an important question, "If the church doesn't require them to go to seminary in order to receive their licenses, why should we care?" Like many of my respondents, this scholar argued that the work of ministry may *not* require the kind of "special competence in esoteric knowledge" that Magali Larson's professionals stake claims to.[2] Confirming this possibility in the accounts of COGIC ministers allows us to reconsider the clerical professional's claims to special knowledge.

The evidence, in my sample and beyond it, is overwhelming. Clergy can easily consider themselves a success with only a rudimentary level of training as religious professionals. Again, the majority of COGIC ministers are not seminary trained. The bulk of their religious knowledge is gained sitting in the same Sunday school classrooms as the lay-members they claim a call to lead. My interviews with these clergy suggest that many have only as much biblical literacy as any other actively engaged member of their churches. Given the range of tasks any one of them might be assigned to in their local congregation, the need for high levels of biblical literacy or mastery of ecclesiological concepts varies considerably. My own analysis of most of these tasks—which range from comforting convalescents to much more "priestly" tasks like administering the Eucharist—affirms my sense that most religious labor can be done competently without much religious training at all.

Possessing a "sound understanding of the things of God" is the extent of the denomination's educational requirement for licensing as a minister in the Church of God in Christ. How this "understanding" is measured is left to jurisdictional leaders and, for men and women who minister as Aspiring or Licensed Missionaries and Ministers, their pastors. Even when there is a seemingly concrete standard for biblical literacy, the abstraction implicit in any final determination of clerical competence can make even a written test of biblical literacy a poor measure of one's qualifications. Members of ordination committees intimated that it is not uncommon that an ordination candidate fail the catechism-like multiple-choice examination administered as the main jurisdictional test of competence.[3] In some cases, they say, candidates fail the test multiple times and yet are ordained because their pastors argue that even this basic test of biblical literacy does not adequately measure clerical competence. In one example, the aspiring Elder had been preaching successfully for years. According to members of the ordination committee, his Pastor argued that "two or three points don't change your anointing" and, ultimately, the young man was ordained without their recommendation.

Because COGIC does not require educational credentials for advancement to the terminal stages of religious credentialing, COGIC ministers—particularly the ordained men—problematize the usual typology of professional priest and charismatic prophet. COGIC clergy, like clergy in any Christian denomination, are church leaders. Max Weber points out that priests can have charisma, but it is their professional status that gives them authority over a body of believers. Leading religious organizations is their job, a position gained either by choice or by succession. Ministers operate in a number of quasi-professional roles in their churches, sometimes as leaders of them and sometimes not. To a great degree, the status and authority they receive comes from their clerical positions as Licensed Ministers, Missionaries, Elders, and Evangelists. Even if only serving as a member of the church's hospitality ministry, these titles bring with them the status that might be given to any professional priest.

But unlike their seminary-trained priestly peers, they cannot claim legitimacy or status based on (in Weber's terms) any "professional equipment of special knowledge, fixed doctrine, and vocational qualifications."[4] Instead, their primary claim to religious leadership in their churches is their call to that role and the anointing that follows such a call. They serve as priests but are licensed and ordained as prophets. Competence continues to be important, but is not necessarily associated with any training they might have. Instead, they believe their competence—even when they have been well trained to perform these tasks—is a function of their possession of supernatural powers that are manifested in revelation rather than reasoning.

Religious Labor: No Boundaries between the Sacred and the Secular

Emile Durkheim argues that among religious communities, there is a distinct separation between the sacred and the profane. He describes sacred artifacts, places, and even people as "par excellence that which the profane should not touch, and cannot touch with impunity."[5] In Durkheim's descriptions, both the sacred *and* the profane could be mundane and ordinary objects, people, or actions; it is the meaning given to them that makes them distinctively different. In addition, it is the setting of one against the other that gives each their distinctive meaning.

In the past, the primary work of the priest—mediating the relationship between God and man—was a sacred duty. As the work was sacred, so was the position assigned to that work: the priesthood was considered a sacred office in the church. Even the prophet, with his sacred revelation brought from God to man earned himself a place in the oft-quoted list of sacred church offices: "some apostles, some prophets, some evangelists, and some pastors and teachers" (Eph. 4:11). The priest's works and the prophet's words were sacred because both work and word were limited to those who had a particular sacralizing relationship with the divine.

Over time, the routinization of charisma, the loss of sacramentalism as a core component of congregational worship, and the Protestant doctrine of universal priesthood or "priesthood of all believers" have dramatically decreased the sacredness of church work and, by default, church workers.[6] Now it seems that anyone can do ministry. As we have established, most of the COGIC aspirants did not receive their calls as pew-sitters. They received their calls while doing some form of ministry in prisons, on street corners, in homeless shelters, as well as in church classrooms, choir lofts, and auxiliary offices. As credentialed clergy, they continue to serve alongside and are often even led by people engaged in the work of the church without any kind of sacralizing call. In their churches, "ordinary" people are doing extraordinary things.

In the same way, churches have expanded the definition of ministry to include everything from overseeing the church nursery to managing the church bookstore, from organizing church potlucks to ensuring the safety of cars in the church parking lot. Once mundane and ordinary organizational tasks now take place in clergy-led church ministries where members point to scores on "spiritual gifts inventories" as evidence that even these tasks require them to have supernaturally granted talents and abilities.

The bright line creating a boundary between sacred work and non-sacred workers, between the secular and the sacred has been erased. Following this latter trend, Pentecostal ministers argue that their sacred labor (and laboring) has no boundaries. If an Evangelist believes herself called to a ministry of exhortation, responsible to encourage people and make their lives better, she argues that she can operate in her call whether she's praying for someone at an altar or counseling them as a social worker. More importantly, she might argue that it would be a waste of her calling to restrict her religious labor to so-called "church work." As Monica reminds us:

> I'd rather work outside these walls. Some people ain't going to darken the doors of this church. Look at Jesus. He didn't operate out of a church; he was out there in the world. Just riding the subway to work every day, I run into people who need what I got more than people in these pews who already got it. They're here already. I'm trying to help those who ain't.

When asked "why didn't you quit your job to pursue ministry," some portion of ministers explain their job as either a location for, or a facilitator of, ministry opportunities. If asked "why didn't you go into ministry full-time," a much larger contingent responds with "I *am* in ministry full-time." In making this statement, they aren't simply talking about tasks they perform; a day may come and go without their doing something they might consider ministerial. Instead, they're referring to a vocational identity, *minister*, that they carry with them from situation to situation. They then argue that this alter ego is activated often enough that they can claim its influence in any number of seemingly secular situations. In fact, many men even conflate their family's provider role with their priestly one. Whether operating as provider-priest at home or principal-prophet at the local middle school, there is no separation of the sacred and the secular: they inhabit the same vocational space.

The sociologist Lynn Smith-Lovin argues that many of today's institutional settings segregate us into single-identity environments.[7] When we go to work, we're not expected to perform our jobs as "parents" or "Protestants" or "Republicans." In the same way, once we leave work, our social networks—for example, our children—expect us to leave the physicist or prison guard identities there at our place of employment. Smith-Lovin observes that there are few situations which elicit multiple identities, especially if those identities are different in meaningful ways.

One vocation that may well exemplify the kind of rare situation Smith-Lovin points to is the "job" of homeschooling children. Certainly in most industrialized societies, education and the family inhabit different spheres. For homeschooling parents—usually mothers—these spheres are collapsed upon each other. She is, at once, mother and teacher, caregiver and disciplinarian. Research indicates that many homeschooling mothers find it difficult to adjust to the teacher role and experience burnout trying to meet the demands they feel both roles, mother and teacher, place on them.[8]

The parents who successfully reconcile these demands find similarities between the tasks required in each role and then are able to integrate the two. They don't start the teaching day taking off the mother-identity and putting on the teacher one. They combine their understanding of the two roles, treating one as an extension of the other. Instead of seeing themselves as "teachers" who want learning to be structured and measurable, they see themselves as "facilitators," a role that resembles the way they parent. Once teaching their children to read is treated like teaching them to walk or feed themselves, they find it less stressful and have more success.

Clergy experience their dual vocations the same way. They don't use the dominant definition of clergy that narrowly defines their work as something done in particular environments (e.g., churches), with particular people, and using particular language or behavior. They don't compartmentalize. Instead, they sacralize their secular labor, making it an extension of their sacred labor. In their minds, their primary vocation—ministry—gives them the tools to be more effective in their secondary vocation as teachers, parole officers, and bus drivers. The clerical "shadow occupation" supports the secular one.

Religious Credentials: Making Visible the Invisible "Clergy Women"

The tendency to find ministry wherever one finds it becomes especially important when we consider the situation of women in COGIC and other denominations. There has been considerable scholarly interest in the organizational circumstances that either contribute to or work against the ordination of women. Because more women are now taking their place alongside men in ordained ministry, the focus is shifting away from describing organizational barriers to ministry to describing the lives, professional orientations, and contributions of the women who have broken through those barriers.

While there is great value in understanding women who are ordained, this focus renders invisible a multitude of unordained women who continue to seek opportunities to operate in ministry. Church of God in Christ women are missing from these studies because COGIC, like a number of denominations, continues to bar women from ordained ministry. The COGIC manual section on "The Call to Ministry" includes a description of only the Elder's ordination, a credential exclusively held by men. Not only does this render illegitimate women's claims to a call to preach, but it calls into question women's claims that God has placed a call on them at all.

Certainly, the biggest interdenominational point of conflict in the Church of God in Christ is the role of women. It is no accident that the number of women in my sample is more than double the number of men. Just as women outnumber men as members of these churches, they often outnumber them in "called" ministry positions. In one of the jurisdictions whose ministers I interviewed, more than 60 percent of the credentialed ministers are women. This imbalance is a reflection of one of the central ironies of the COGIC credentialing process: there are more women than men serving in the "called" positions of ministry in a denomination that explicitly privileges maleness. From its inception, COGIC has been structured in ways that inadvertently enabled women to challenge the symbolic limitations placed on them by a sexist and patriarchal religious hierarchy. In many ways, the women are often more "qualified" for ministry than the men, having more religious education, experience, and a more rigorous multistage process for credentialing. That said, the pursuit of women's callings is complicated by the legitimacy female ministers (and sympathetic male associates and leaders) still give to constraints on women's practice of their calling, constraints that they recognize as sexist but nevertheless are content to operate within.

This contentment is sustained and promoted because, for most COGIC women, the constraints are only rhetorical; they're just words and labels.

These women operate in their religious communities as full-fledged ministers, performing practically all of the tasks their male counterparts perform, but without the credential—ordination—that would attract scholarly attention to their existence or their labor. Methodologically, this is problematic.

While social scientists studying clergy continue to apply a fairly strict definition to this "professional" class—that they all be ordained and have full rights of congregational leadership—the definition of clergy in religious communities like the Church of God in Christ is not nearly as precise. Even the legal definition of a "minister" has evolved over time. For example, just having the title "minister of education" does not qualify someone to be a legally recognized minister. In *Lawrence v. Commissioner*, Bob Lawrence served as his Baptist congregation's "minister of education," a position that gave him extensive responsibilities in his church.[9] He supervised the church's religious education programs, visited the sick and provided counseling, and even assisted at and, occasionally, preached at worship services. In that case, the court decided that Lawrence's lack of ordination—he was only "commissioned" by his church—and his inability to officiate over baptisms and communion disqualified him from receiving the minister's housing allowance.

A 1989 Tax Court case, *Knight v. Commissioner*, is often seen as clarifying the legal definition of minister, at least for tax purposes.[10] Using what was referred to as the "Wingo" test, four factors were deemed necessary to consider when determining someone's status: (1) does the person administer sacraments, (2) does the person conduct worship services, (3) does the person perform services in the control, conduct, and maintenance of a religious organization, and (4) is the person ordained, commissioned, or licensed.[11] At the time, the Wingo test was considered a fairly high bar requiring the aspirant to perform each of the first three activities and have the last attribute. In defining a minister, the government focused on two factors: whether the person performs ministerial duties and whether that person holds a ministerial credential; position in the religious organization was irrelevant.

In making their decision in *Knight v. Commissioner*, the court stated the following: "Congress used the phrase 'ordained, commissioned, or licensed' perhaps to allow for differences in methods and terminology among various religious groups in investing their religious leaders with ministerial or priestly authority. Some groups describe this investiture as 'ordination,' others as 'commissioning,' and others as 'licensing.' Applying the statute narrowly could have had the salutary effect of avoiding an inquiry in every case into the nature of a 'minister's' duties to decide whether religious offices were equivalent among differing religions."

In this statement, the court argues that of all four factors, only the fourth—that the person be ordained, commissioned, or licensed—is required.[12] They further stated that "in weighing the importance of petitioner's ministerial limitations, it appears that petitioner's incapacity to perform the Lord's Supper, baptism, marriage, or otherwise participate in church government did not diminish the ministry that petitioner did perform. Petitioner preached, conducted worship, visited the sick, performed funerals, and ministered to the needy in the exercise of his ministry." This argument that the work of ministry may be as important as credentials one might hold added a fifth question to the Wingo test: Is the person considered to be a spiritual leader by his or her religious body?

Like the petitioner in this case, who ironically was endeavoring to be seen as a "non-minister" in order to be exempted from self-employment taxes, COGIC's Deaconesses and Evangelists meet three of the five Wingo/Knight factors. They conduct worship services, they are licensed, and they are considered to be spiritual leaders in their congregations. In many cases, they also meet aspects of a fourth factor: performing services in the control, conduct, and maintenance of a religious organization. Some of these female licentiates serve as local church trustees; retain titles such as Minister of Music, Youth Minister, and Minister of Christian Education; and hold major leadership positions in both local jurisdictions and the international governing assembly. For example, the denomination's five major Auxiliaries in Ministry (AIM) are currently led by a licensed Evangelist (e.g., music) or by a team composed of an ordained Elder as president and a licensed Evangelist as either an Elect Lady (Evangelism), an International Field Representative (Sunday school), or an International Chairlady (Youth). Even the first of the four Wingo factors—administering the sacraments of communion and baptism—may be done by licentiates in the Church of God in Christ. While officiating over these ceremonies is usually a duty reserved for the senior Pastor or an ordained Elder. In the absence of either, a licensed minister can fulfill this role. In fact, administering the sacraments to parishioners in hospitals, prisons, and convalescent homes is often a duty assigned to "licensed" Deacons, Licensed Ministers, and in some congregations, even licensed Evangelists.

Women in the Church of God in Christ do not use the Wingo factors to argue for their legitimacy; they haven't had to. Instead, these factors serve as further evidence of the naive distinctions we continue to draw between those who are formally ordained and those who, in lieu of that particular credential, are still invested with considerable authority to perform religious labor on behalf of their religious community. The distinctions between the relevant terms for religious work (e.g., "preaching" vs. "speaking"), religious workers (e.g., "Pastor" vs. "Shepherdess"), and religious credentials (e.g., "ordination" vs. "license") become irrelevant in practice. This decoupling of church rule and church practice is more than an interesting footnote in our understanding of organizational resistance to ordaining women. Instead, these findings underscore the importance of this zone of ambiguity as fundamental to women's understanding of themselves as clergy in the absence of a scholarly, legally, or religiously recognized credential of such a status.

Making Things Up or Making Things Work?

Jerome Bruner describes an important tension in storytelling: "The only requirement imposed by having to *tell* a life story (even when only invited to do so by a psychologist) is that one tell something 'interesting'—which is to say a story that is at once recognizably canonical and recognizably non-canonical."[13] The calling stories recounted in my interviews reflect some of what Bruner describes. The calling experience and the narrative that follows must be recognizably canonical, but they are interesting because they aren't a normal experience for the callee. Canonical experiences are those that are "culturally comprehensible" inasmuch as the religious culture the callee is imbedded in gives her imagery, icons, or other symbols that she recognizes as components of a religious message. Doves are canonical; pigeons are not. A dream about fishing is canonical; dreams about playing baseball are not.

On the other hand, an interesting experience is one that catches the callee's attention because, for him, it doesn't fit his expectations or his understanding of what is common or normal. Cultural context plays as much a role here as it does when we differentiate between a wink and a blink. An otherwise ignorable blink becomes a noticeable wink because of related cues that accompany it. For example, in Moses's call, a bush burning in the desert was interesting only because it wasn't consumed. A dream about a fishing excursion for a callee who goes fishing all the time might not be interesting enough to suggest a calling. But as described in the chapter on vertical calls, a fishing enthusiast having a dream where he catches fish "that you see on those wildlife shows" becomes an interesting experience.

"Interesting" and "canonical" are schema that callees use to give meaning to events that might otherwise be ignored as meaningless, particularly in terms of a calling experience. Culture (or more narrowly, church culture) gives these men and women a framework on which to hang these experiences. Many of them say that there were signs of a calling that went unrecognized as they were growing up or unaffiliated with a religious tradition of some kind. Once affiliated, sermons, Sunday school lessons, religious talk with friends and family, and their own reading of the Bible gave them a set of interpretive tools that informs their understanding of feelings, voices, dreams, and otherwise insignificant coincidences as important components of a calling narrative.[14] They might then experience a dream, or remember a *past* dream, as part of a call to ministry that may not, in reality, be there.

It may also be the case that the cultural milieu that surrounds these men and women gives them a requirement to insert a dove or an audible voice into the calling narrative in order to give that account power. The meaning of a dove or the description of a powerful outside-of-self voice is shared by the pastors, religious peers, and religious family members they might first approach with the calling story. In a not-insubstantial number of these narratives, the person(s) first told actually become part of the narrative, being remembered as witnesses to the calling by their ready confirmation of either the experience or, more likely, the interpretation of the experience.

What makes this confirmation both possible and powerful is the fact that the symbols described in these interesting accounts are shared by members of the callees' religious community. Not only are the symbols shared but the meaning of those symbols as canonical elements of a "true" calling story is also shared by the community. At this point, the story doesn't have to be interesting (although being interesting helps), but it *must* be canonical.

As a kind of cultural codebook for these narratives, the canon may be different across religious traditions but is likely to be fairly consistent within one. Conventional calls may be more canonical in some traditions (e.g., Roman Catholicism, Anglicanism), and the kinds of blitzkrieg calls described by many of my respondents would be disbelieved at best and considered heretical at worst. In other traditions, like Pentecostalism, such calls would be acceptable, but there might be additional requirements of commitment or competence that must support them. It is clear from my interviews with both licentiates and those who license them that, in the Church of God in Christ, a blitzkrieg call is the more powerful of the two types. Simply saying "I want to do more for God" is not enough. In fact, pastors stated that they sometimes pressed aspirants for canonical elements of the call when they were absent from the narrative. They didn't demand specific imagery, but they did request more evidence of an *experience* with God when they didn't feel aspirants had volunteered it. That said, they also suggested that they did not have to press often; aspirants usually came in prepared with enough canonical components to make a call sound reasonable. Again, while pastors claim that they only acknowledge the story (as interesting or possible), the very fact that they do not turn the aspirant away confirms, for the aspirant and others, that the call is canonical and real.

In the end, this confirmation of a vertical calling story as canonical has a pronounced effect on aspirants. It was clear in interviews of those still in the Aspiring Minister or Missionary stage that they were quite convinced that they were ministers—already—mainly because their pastors have confirmed their account of the vertical call. Aspirants believe that these leaders have the power and authority to tell them that they are or are not ministers. This power and authority is not just invested in them as leaders of an organization; the aspirants trust that these leaders hear from, and can speak on behalf of, God. If they go to their pastor, believing he has some supernatural means of discerning one's calling, and the pastor responds with "I knew it," the aspirants' beliefs that they've been called have been fully confirmed by God, "in person" in the vertical call and now, by proxy, with His human spokesperson. This sanctioning of their call gives them a license to announce to others that they've truly been called to the ministry; the pastor's confirmation backs them up. Family members, co-workers, and other members of the church also assume that a religious leader would have some ability or authority to disconfirm a call if it were not present. His or her sanction, even if unintended, is an implicit sign that other people can now start treating the aspirant as "The Called" as well.

For these men and women, this moment of confirmation—not just the moment(s) of a call itself—is the genesis of what appears to be a "master identity" for them. That term has been used to describe the way particular ascribed characteristics—usually gender, but sometimes race, class, and sexual orientation—come to shape our behaviors in most social interactions. Where role-identities operate in specific situations based on the relationships with and responsibilities to the other people we're interacting with, the master identity applies across situations. The attitudes and actions related to the master identity are not evoked only by specific institutional contexts but are instead likely to be elicited by any number of contexts.

My respondents tend to describe their called-identity this way. The respondents are men and women who consider themselves as "anointed, "Evangelists," and "The Called" whether they're in the mall looking for a parking space, in the schoolyard monitoring children's activities, or serving as provider for their families. The "thickness" of the "Called" master-identity—the extent of its reach across different contexts—is not only similar to characteristics callees are born with but also takes on the characteristic of the "Christian" master identity that my respondents might argue they are "born-again" with.[15] They certainly suggest that their Christianity, like their race or gender, is not the kind of identity that is limited to a religious context. Similarly, the Called identity, their understanding of themselves as ministers, is (at least rhetorically) operating at all times, in all environments, and with all audiences.

Whether clergy are truly called in an interaction with God or not, a relationship with a religious community is an important element of that interaction's transcendence from experience to action and, ultimately, to identity. Like the family of origin for a child, the congregation-of-origin plays an important socializing role for these aspiring clergy. It is these congregations, not the ones that eventually hire them, that inform, confirm, and affirm the future cleric's belief that he or she has had a meaningful encounter with the divine that, from their perspective, affects who they are and what they are to do.

There is an ongoing debate among social scientists that takes the form of a kind of chicken-or-egg argument: Which is really operating here—social structure or individual agency? It would be easy to suggest that the entirety of the call—from incident to interpretation, from affirmation to accomplishment—is a function of environmental influences. I certainly would not argue that the complex matrix of cultural, organizational, and theological forces acting upon these men and women plays no role in setting boundary markers for the calling. Even the symbolism that makes the calling experience noticeable is born out of a relationship with a religious community. These clerical aspirants have learned what a call to Protestant—and particularly, Pentecostal—ministry looks like. It is clear that they recognize that the calling has a particular set of cultural markers. They mobilize cultural tools in a way that gets them over the important hurdle of convincing church leaders and other parishioners that they are "the real deal." The church has expectations of both a calling narrative and a called individual. Whether God or man, the originator of the impulse to pursue a call to ministry uses those expectations to create the *interesting* and *canonical* components of a recognizable narrative description.

Unfortunately, many men and women also find themselves in the not-so-unique position of being constrained by a set of structural circumstances that make it difficult to bring *all* of the usual markers to bear in that definition. In a perfect world, COGIC's clerical aspirants might do what many of their peers in other denominations do: seek opportunities for advanced training in the profession they claim a call to. Yet, while all of the jurisdictions my respondents are affiliated with have well-known seminaries, it is unlikely that they would be considered as options because of prohibitive costs (even for part-time students) or the admissions requirement of a bachelor's degree. In a different denomination, the men who are called to preach may find themselves in an ordered labor market where they could apply for pastoral positions in centuries-old congregations or even paid associate positions in wealthy ten-year-old ones.

The women, with their abundant talents and experience, could make the choice to lead a congregation and not, merely, serve within one. But these options aren't available to COGIC women. Do they throw up their hands in frustration and abandon the identity? Apparently not. These constraints instead put them in a position to renegotiate the meaning of "ministry" or "calling" in order to neutralize the disconfirming evidence against their legitimacy. Their commitment to the identity—strengthened in ways described in chapters 2 and 3—requires them to construct new meanings. It is clear that they don't simply make up brand-new meanings out of whole cloth. They cannot radically reinvent what it means to be "called," ignoring all of the conventional understandings of the term and trying to operate as a category of one. An outright rejection of all of the conventions would be done at one's peril. Outside of *any* social conventions, we are inclined to assume one's embrace of a godly call is a sign of delusion, not divine choice.

Rather, these COGIC women become what the anthropologist Mary Douglas might call "category polluters," people who can stake a strong claim to the category in *some* conventional ways, but "dirty it up" by not being able to fully embrace *all* of its conventions. The ambiguity already present in religion as an institution and the multiple zones of ambiguity present in the Church of God in Christ create ample room for women clergy to shape the calling to fit their particular circumstances. Instead of rejecting all of the markers of "ministry" or "calling" simultaneously, they select among them, disregarding (and even denigrating) those that are unavailable to them. They then harness other social resources—symbols, language, scriptures, and even experiences—from within that same environment to interpret their callings in not completely conventional, but ultimately satisfactory, ways. The availability of these tools in that same cultural toolbox further affirms their sense that, within this cultural milieu, they aren't making anything up but are actually just making things work.

The power of ministers' reconstruction of what it means to be the Called was especially evident when challenged by questions in the interviews. In each instance, whether discussing training, employment, or licensing, the calling became a strong card that was used to counter any seeming credibility gaps.

In terms of understanding how they can do ministry with very little train-ing in what other religious traditions might consider important professional knowledge, COGIC ministers argue that their calling—or more accurately, the one who called them—gives them the supernatural ability to do min-istry. This ability, the anointing described in chapter 3, operates in lieu of education, endowing them with whatever knowledge or abilities they need to do ministry. Conceptually, the anointing is so important that ministers who have secular training in some of the tasks they might do as a minister claim an inability to do those tasks effectively without it. They do not reject secular education as important; they just find that it pales in utility when compared to the anointing that flows from their being the Called.

Similarly, being the Called enables them to claim a clerical identity even when they have no clerical occupation. They argue that the god of the call-ing puts them to work where, when, and how He sees fit: if He's satisfied with them working as banker, carpenter, teacher or chef, then they're satis-fied with these occupations. This perspective is affirmed in a religious com-munity where both scriptural and contemporary examples modeled "extra-church" or "tent-making" approaches to ministry. They argue that Jesus was most effective because he made his living as carpenter and not as priest. Their own pastors and other ministers they respect had and have full-time secular jobs, doing ministry as a kind of "second-shift" occupation. While it is clear that most of these ministers would prefer full-time employment in a religious setting, where that's not possible, they still consider themselves credible religious laborers because the sacred shadow occupation overlaps the secular tangible one.

Finally, being the Called in a denomination that denies women the right to ordination, but still offers them ample opportunities to do the ministry they feel called to, makes their claims to the identity credible. Even when challenged by questions about the authority of COGIC doctrine, the Bible, and COGIC leaders over the work of ministry, women rely on the simple fact that they are still doing ministry in COGIC environments, and doing so more fervently than those who are ordained. This affirms the sense that their calling supersedes any limitations that doctrinal values or even scrip-tures might place on them. The churches they attend are so good at affirm-ing women's abilities to operate as the Called that a significant number of women had never even struggled with scriptural injunctions against their ministry. Those who had struggled had ready-made, culturally informed responses to charges that they were less credible without the ordination credential.[16]

This book argues that those interested in understanding how people make sense of themselves—professionally, religiously, racially, etc.—must think more critically about which cultural markers informing that understanding are most negotiable. Clearly, education, full-time employment, and ordination are not the salient markers of a calling for the COGIC ministers we have met. Instead, they argue that a dependence on God's power, purpose, and passion is the indispensible evidence of a call to the ministry. Social scientists should be careful, when choosing markers of particular identities, to determine which markers matter more, which matter most, and which are more amenable to negotiation and selective mobilization. Understanding which markers are sine qua non, sitting at the core of any understanding of the category rather than the periphery of it, will not only affect our sampling but will ultimately impact our science.

Appendix

TABLE I
Selected Demographic Information For Respondents

Name	Denominational Upbringing	Gender	Clerical Credential	Age Bracket	Occupational Category	Marital Status	Education BA or Higher
Aaron	Baptist	Male	Elder	50's	Professional	Married	No
Abigail	Baptist	Female	Missionary	60's	Service Occupations	Married	No
Adam	Baptist	Male	Elder	40's	Construction Trades	Married	No
Adrienne	None	Female	Deaconess	40's	Management	Single	No
Alan	Catholic	Male	Aspiring Minister	50's	Service Occupations	Married	No
Alesha	Baptist	Female	Evangelist	40's	Professional	Single	Yes
Alesheia	Baptist	Female	Evangelist	40's	Service Occupations	Single	No
Alexandria	Methodist	Female	Deaconess	40's	Management	Single	No
Allen	None	Male	Elder	30's	Transportation	Married	No
Amanda	Baptist	Female	Deaconess	60's	Management	Single	No
Amelia	Baptist	Female	Missionary	50's	Service Occupations	Single	No
Amy	Catholic	Female	Deaconess	40's	Management	Single	No
Andrew	Baptist	Male	Aspiring Minister	40's	Service Occupations	Married	No
Angela	Baptist	Female	Evangelist	50's	Management	Married	No
Angelo	Baptist	Male	Elder	20's	Professional	Married	No
Anitra	Pentecostal	Female	Evangelist	50's	Management	Single	No
Anna	Baptist	Female	Missionary	70's or Higher	Service Occupations	Single	No
Ashley	Holiness	Female	Evangelist	60's	Professional	Single	No
Asia	Pentecostal	Female	Evangelist	60's	Service Occupations	Married	No
Becca	Baptist	Female	Missionary	30's	Professional	Married	Yes
Bill	None	Male	Elder	30's	Service Occupations	Married	Yes
Bob	Baptist	Male	Aspiring Minister	30's	Professional	Single	No
Bryant	Church of God	Male	Elder	30's	Construction Trades	Married	No
Chris	Methodist	Male	Elder	30's	Management	Married	Yes

Name	Denominational Upbringing	Gender	Clerical Credential	Age Bracket	Occupational Category	Marital Status	Education BA or Higher
Courtney	COGIC	Female	Evangelist	50's	Professional	Single	Yes
Curtis	Baptist	Male	Elder	50's	Management	Married	No
Damian	Methodist	Male	Minister	30's	Professional	Married	Yes
Dana	Baptist	Female	Aspiring Missionary	60's	Professional	Single	No
Darrin	None	Male	Elder	40's	Professional	Married	No
Davita	Baptist	Female	Evangelist	50's	Service Occupations	Married	No
Dawne	Baptist	Female	Evangelist	40's	Professional	Married	Yes
Deana	Baptist	Female	Missionary	40's	Professional	Single	Yes
Debra	Baptist	Female	Evangelist	60's	Production	Married	No
Diane	Baptist	Female	Evangelist	70's or Higher	None	Single	No
Donald	Baptist	Male	Minister	40's	Construction Trades	Married	No
Dwayne	Catholic	Male	Minister	30's	Professional	Single	Yes
Eric	Baptist	Male	Aspiring Minister	50's	Management	Single	No
Erica	Baptist	Female	Aspiring Missionary	30's	Management	Single	No
Erika	Methodist	Female	Aspiring Missionary	30's	Management	Single	Yes
Eve	Church of God	Female	Aspiring Missionary	50's	Service Occupations	Married	Yes
Francine	Baptist	Female	Aspiring Missionary	50's	Management	Single	No
Francis	Methodist	Male	Elder	50's	Professional	Married	Yes
Gabrielle	Baptist	Female	Deaconess	30's	Management	Single	No
Gail	Episcopalian	Female	Evangelist	70's or Higher	Professional	Single	No
Gary	None	Male	Minister	50's	Construction Trades	Married	No
George	Episcopalian	Male	Elder	60's	Professional	Married	Yes
Gwen	COGIC	Female	Missionary	40's	Professional	Single	Yes
Jeff	Baptist	Male	Aspiring Minister	50's	Management	Married	No
Jeffrey	None	Male	Aspiring Minister	40's	Production	Married	No
Jeremy	Church of God	Male	Elder	50's	Management	Married	Yes
Jermaine	Baptist	Male	Elder	30's	Professional	Married	Yes
Jimmy	Baptist	Male	Minister	40's	Service Occupations	Married	No
Joel	None	Male	Minister	40's	Professional	Single	Yes
Joi	Baptist	Female	Deaconess	20's	Management	Single	Yes
Jonell	Baptist	Female	Aspiring Missionary	30's	Office and Administrative Support	Married	No
Jordan	Baptist	Female	Aspiring Missionary	50's	Service Occupations	Single	No
Juanita	Baptist	Female	Evangelist	50's	Production	Single	No

Name	Denominational Upbringing	Gender	Clerical Credential	Age Bracket	Occupational Category	Marital Status	Education BA or Higher
Judi	Baptist	Female	Missionary	50's	None	Married	Yes
Julian	Baptist	Male	Elder	40's	Management	Married	Yes
Justine	Baptist	Female	Deaconess	30's	None	Single	Yes
Kasim	Baptist	Male	Elder	60's	Management	Married	Yes
Katherine	Baptist	Female	Evangelist	40's	Management	Married	Yes
Kathleen	Holiness	Female	Aspiring Missionary	30's	Management	Single	Yes
Kathryn	Methodist	Female	Deaconess	50's	Management	Married	Yes
Kelli	Baptist	Female	Deaconess	30's	Management	Single	Yes
Kelly	Baptist	Female	Evangelist	50's	Management	Married	Yes
Kenya	Church of God	Female	Missionary	40's	Management	Single	Yes
Kortnea	Baptist	Female	Aspiring Missionary	50's	Professional	Single	No
Ladasha	None	Female	Aspiring Missionary	30's	Professional	Single	No
Langston	Episcopalian	Male	Elder	40's	Installation	Married	Yes
Linda	Baptist	Female	Aspiring Missionary	30's	Service Occupations	Single	No
Luke	Baptist	Male	Elder	60's	Service Occupations	Married	No
Marcus	None	Male	Aspiring Minister	40's	Management	Single	Yes
Mark	Church of God	Male	Aspiring Minister	40's	Professional	Married	No
Michelle	COGIC	Female	Evangelist	40's	Management	Married	Yes
Misty	COGIC	Female	Deaconess	20's	Professional	Single	Yes
Mona	COGIC	Female	Evangelist	50's	Management	Married	Yes
Monica	COGIC	Female	Aspiring Missionary	50's	Management	Married	Yes
Monique	COGIC	Female	Evangelist	50's	Office and Administrative Support	Married	No
Mylisha	Methodist	Female	Evangelist	40's	Professional	Married	No
Natalie	COGIC	Female	Missionary	40's	Management	Single	Yes
Nichole	Holiness	Female	Evangelist	50's	Management	Single	Yes
Octavia	Baptist	Female	Missionary	50's	Management	Married	No
Owen	Baptist	Male	Minister	30's	Professional	Married	No
Pam	COGIC	Female	Aspiring Missionary	40's	Management	Single	No
Paul	Baptist	Male	Aspiring Minister	30's	Service Occupations	Married	No
Paula	None	Female	Missionary	50's	Professional	Single	No
Paulette	Catholic	Female	Deaconess	30's	Office and Administrative Support	Single	No
Penny	Catholic	Female	Missionary	40's	Service Occupations	Married	No
Rachael	Methodist	Female	Evangelist	70's or Higher	Professional	Married	No
Rachel	Baptist	Female	Missionary	30's	Professional	Married	No

Name	Denominational Upbringing	Gender	Clerical Credential	Age Bracket	Occupational Category	Marital Status	Education BA or Higher
Ramona	COGIC	Female	Evangelist	50's	Management	Married	Yes
Raquel	Baptist	Female	Missionary	50's	Professional	Single	Yes
Regina	Church of God	Female	Aspiring Missionary	30's	Office and Administrative Support	Single	No
Ronnie	Baptist	Male	Elder	60's	Construction Trades	Married	No
Sarah	COGIC	Female	Evangelist	50's	Professional	Single	Yes
Seth	COGIC	Male	Elder	20's	Professional	Single	Yes
Shana	Baptist	Female	Missionary	40's	Service Occupations	Single	No
Sharnise	Baptist	Female	Missionary	40's	Professional	Married	No
Sharon	COGIC	Female	Aspiring Missionary	30's	Professional	Single	Yes
Shaunda	COGIC	Female	Evangelist	30's	Management	Single	Yes
Shawn	COGIC	Female	Chaplain	50's	Management	Married	Yes
Sheba	Baptist	Female	Aspiring Missionary	30's	Management	Single	Yes
Sheila	COGIC	Female	Evangelist	60's	Professional	Married	Yes
Stephanie	Baptist	Female	Evangelist	50's	Professional	Married	Yes
Tanya	Baptist	Female	Missionary	20's	Office and Administrative Support	Single	Yes
Tasha	COGIC	Female	Missionary	50's	Management	Married	Yes
Tequia	Baptist	Female	Missionary	40's	Service Occupations	Married	No
Tiffany	Baptist	Female	Missionary	30's	Professional	Married	Yes
Tyson	None	Male	Aspiring Minister	40's	Transportation	Married	No
Vance	None	Male	Minister	40's	Service Occupations	Married	No
Victor	Catholic	Male	Aspiring Minister	40's	Production	Married	No
Walter	COGIC	Male	Elder	70's or Higher	Professional	Married	Yes
Wanda	Baptist	Female	Evangelist	60's	Professional	Married	No
Yvonne	COGIC	Female	Evangelist	60's	Service Occupations	Single	No

TABLE 2
Means Table For Relevant Clergy Characteristics

	Men	Women
Age (in years)	46	49
Years Of Education	14.58	14.53
No College	41%	34%
Bachelors or more	38%	46%
Some seminary training	26%	16%
Married	85%	38%
Denominational Upbringing		
Baptist	44%	51%
Church Of God In Christ	5%	19%
Other (includes Church of God, Episcopalian, and Methodist)	51%	28%
Ministry Credentials		
None (Men: Aspiring Ministers / Women: Aspiring Missionaries)	28%	21%
Local (Men: Ministers / Women: Deaconess)	21%	41%
Jurisdictional (Men: Elders / Women: Evangelists & Chaplains)	51%	38%
Satisfaction With Status Of Ministry (By Credential)		
None (Men: Aspiring Ministers / Women: Aspiring Missionaries)	3.00	3.48
Local (Men: Ministers / Women: Deaconess-Missionary)	3.11	3.17
Jurisdictional (Men: Elders / Women: Evangelists & Chaplains)	2.87	3.24
Influences On The Call To Ministry		
A private time in prayer or discernment	4.0	4.5
Thru scripture reading, study, inquiry, and conversation	3.7	4.1
An audible voice from God	3.2	3.4
I came to it over a long period of time	3.8	3.1
Something was missing in my life	3.5	2.6
I had a "spiritual awakening" regarding my occupation	2.2	2.4
The "call" came after I entered seminary or Bible school	1.5	1.8
Someone whom I admired said I should be a minister	1.8	1.6
Occupational Category		
Construction and Installation	15%	0%
Management and Business Operations	21%	38%
Office and Administrative Support	0%	7%

	Men	Women
Production	5%	3%
Professions	36%	32%
Community and Social Service (e.g., clergy, parole officers)	18%	5%
Education (including education administrators)	10%	16%
Others (e.g., engineers, nurses, scientists)	8%	11%
Service	18%	17%
Trades	5%	0%
Not Applicable (e.g., homemaker, student)	0%	4%
Reasons To Remain Employed		
Money	71%	44%
Have to work to pay bills	48%	39%
Have to support my family	43%	11%
Timing	35%	72%
God hasn't told me to leave my job	40%	56%
God is still preparing me (e.g., seminary, other training)	20%	28%
Lifestyle	38%	50%
My secular job facilitates my ministry	24%	31%
My secular job is my ministry	0%	25%
I minister through my lifestyle	20%	25%

Notes

NOTES TO INTRODUCTION

1. There has been an ongoing debate about the continued inclusion of the ministry as a "profession." This long-standing debate reaches back to Gannon (1971) and has been continued by Christopherson (1994) and others. I attempt to contribute to, but in no way resolve, this debate in this book.

2. Myers 1994:219.

3. See Anderson and Anderson 2005; Dokecki 2005; and Shupe 2007.

4. See Djupe and Gilbert 2003; Schmidt 2005; and Smith and Harris 2005.

5. See Chaves 1999; Dodson 2002; Nesbitt 1997; Purvis 1995; and Zikmund et al. 1998.

6. See Fox 2002; Stillwell 2002; and Wallace 2003.

7. For more definitions of professions, see Abbott 1988; Greenwood 1966; Goldstein 1984; Leicht and Fennell 2008; and Strauss 1963.

8. Niebuhr 1956:64.

9. There is some theological debate about whether this belief that one is called to become clergy as something distinctive from one's call to salvation (or the laity) is supported by a biblical model. When someone is called by God, that calling (*kletos*) is to be a servant of God in the general sense (see Rom. 1:7; 8:28). But Paul used a variation on the word *kletos* when describing his call to be an apostle in Rom. 1:1 and 1 Cor. 1:1. While people understand the word "clergy" to have its origins in the Greek word *kleros*, it is more likely that the words evolved much later and did so, mainly, from Paul's use of the word.

10. Goffman 1983:5.

11. See Basset, Staton-Spicer, and Whitehead 1979; Carr, Lavin, and Davies 2009; Harris et al 1983; and Leathers 1992.

12. Goffman 1959.

13. Ibid., 67.

14. Ibid., 75.

15. I capitalize these labels to differentiate them as titles (e.g., Licensed Minister or Missionary) from similar roles (e.g., minister or missionary), which may not actually represent a credentialed category of church label. The majority of respondents were recruited by contacting each Jurisdictional Bishop or ordination commissioner. Lists of respondents were compiled and then recruited directly with their permission. Additional respondents were recruited via snowball sampling, that is, members of my sample recruited their peers to the study.

16. *USA Today*/Gallup poll, May 1, 2010.

17. Berger 1980.

18. For examples, see Ammerman 1997; Glock 1962; Nelson 1997 and 2005; McRoberts 2004; Poloma and Pendleton 1989, and Smilde 1998. The theologian Rudolf Otto (1962) points to two different kinds of experiences with the divine: the *mysterium tremendum,* which repels, and the *mysterium fascinans,* which compels. Clergy describe both sensations, being both fearful of and attracted by the manifestation of God expressed in their calls.

19. Stark 2003:11–12.

20. Occasionally, I abandoned this effort at the conclusion of some of my interviews (particularly with pastors and ordination committee members) in an effort to offer some policy suggestions regarding the intentional (and inadvertent) role leaders play in this process.

NOTES TO CHAPTER 1

1. Sawyer 2000. The National Baptist Convention USA and the National Baptist Convention of America are mistakenly believed to be interchangeable names for one denomination: the National Baptist Convention. The National Baptist Convention split in 1919 into two separate religious entities, the NBC-USA and the NBC-A.

2. McRoberts 2003:38.

3. Examples of this research include studies of ritual behavior in the church (Boggs 1977; Burns and Smith 1978; Clark 1937; Hinson 2000; Kroll-Smith 1980; and Paris 1982), community and culture (Goldsmith 1989; McDaniel 2004; Williams 1974), and women's roles (Butler 2007; Gilkes 2001; Wiggins 2005).

4. Pointedly in Baer 1992; Baer and Singer 2000; Clemmons 1996; Hollenweger1997; MacRobert 2000; and Synan 1997.

5. Wacker 2001.

6. Hollenwegger 1997; and Synan 1997.

7. Weber 1930.

8. Smith 1893.

9. Daniels 2002.

10. Maxwell 1996.

11. Lincoln and Mamiya 2000:335.

12. See Daniels 2007 for more on this.

13. COGIC webpage (http://www.cogic.com) .

14. Range 1973:58.

15. Range 1973:46.

16. Ibid.

17. Poloma 1989; Wacker 2001.

18. Lundskow 2008:351.

19. It is understandable then that my respondents would believe that the key to their ability to do effective ministry is an experience with the Holy Ghost. What is unique about them as "called ministers" is that there is a distinction between this "Baptism of the Holy Ghost" that all believers should have and the "Anointing of the Holy Ghost" that uniquely equips and empowers them. I will explore this anointing concept further in chap. 5.

20. Hollenwegger 1997; MacRobert 2000.

21. Synan 1997:110.

22. Clemmons 1996:6.

23. Tucker 1975:92.

24. Lincoln and Mamiya 1990; Range 1973.

25. Range 1973.

26. Butler 2007; Range 1973.

27. Butler 2007; Lincoln and Mamiya 1990.

28. Lincoln and Mamiya 2000.

29. Range 1973:132; emphasis mine.

30. Butler 2007:32, 34.

31. Again, I capitalize these labels to differentiate them as titles (e.g., Licensed Minister or Missionary) from similar roles (e.g., minister or missionary), which may not actually represent a credentialed category of church label.

32. Range 1973.

33. Ibid.

34. COGIC webpage (http://cogic.net/cogiccms/military-institution-chaplaincy).

35. While some women do serve as Chaplains, the application process has not changed to incorporate them. The application for admission to the COGIC Chaplain corps still asks if the aspirant's "wife" is involved in ministry.

36. For more on the interracial history of the Church of God in Christ, see Daniels (2002).

37. Clemmons 1996; MacRobert 2000; and Maxwell 1996.

38. Daniels 2002:256.

39. Clemmons 1996; MacRobert 2000.

40. Poloma 1989.

41. Ibid.

42. Assembly of God Constitution (Bradford 2009);

43. Aimee Semple McPherson, probably one of the best-known Assemblies of God ministers, left the denomination in 1927 to found the International Church of the Foursquare Gospel. She is thought to have done this as a response to AOG's refusal to grant full access to ordination to women.

NOTES TO CHAPTER 2

1. Durkheim 1995:419.

2. Weber 1904:80.

3. Christopherson 1994:219.

4. Bellah et al. 1985.

5. Ibid., 66.

6. Serow 1994.

7. Moberg 1962.

8. Ibid., 485.

9. Zikmund, Lummis, and Chang 1998:96.

10. Ibid.

11. Ibid.

12. Ochs 1986:109.

13. Zikmund 1998.

14. Mk. 1:16–18

15. Jn. 1:35–42

16. Cullinan 1999.

17. Kroll 2002:73.

18. Cullinan 1999.

19. Zikmund 1998.

20. Calvin 1843:259.

21. Ibid.

22. Kroll 2002:70.

23. Witham 2005:10.

24. Washington 1901:82.

25. Range 1973:28.

26. Rasor and Chapman 2007.

27. Woolever and Bruce 2004.

28. The sociologist Timothy Nelson (2005) argues that one's beliefs about the causes of particular experiences play an integral role in shaping the meanings of those experiences and, thus, in shaping the experiences themselves. It is attribution and not quality of the experience that makes it religious. Certainly, these conventional calls seem easily explained away as "natural" or "coincidental." That said, I am not inclined to assume that every call these men and women experience has a "natural" explanation, especially since these experiences tend to go far beyond the kinds of everyday issues (e.g., being able to pay bills) that Nelson and some psychologists of religion (Gorsuch and Smith 1983; Lupfer, Brock and DePaola 1992; Spilka 1983; and Spilka, Shaver, Kirkpatrick 1985) tend to point to.

29. Schmidt 2000:77.

30. Cullinan 1999.

31. Myers 1994.

32. Sugden and Wiersbe 1973:9.

33. Zikmund 1998:93.

34. Croft 1999

NOTES TO CHAPTER 3

1. For examples, see the following: Adams 2007; Baum and Pilarczyk 1989; Beraud 2007; Bonifield and Mills 1980; Broholm 1985; Chaves 1991; Fox 2002; Roof and McKinney 1987; and Witham 2005.

2. Parker 2006.

3. Dorsett 1997:401.

4. This is particularly important because of the many nondenominational and congregationalist churches who are not governed by episcopates, bishops, or other episcopal hierarchies.

5. Orwell 1950:12.

6. Goffman 1959.

7. For example, McCall and Simmon 1966; Stryker and Serper 1994.

8. Searle 2001:84.

9. Range 1973:21.

10. Searle 2001:21.

11. Myers 1994:7.

12. Bruner 1990 and 2004; Rosenwald and Ochberg 1992:1.

13. Searle 2001:84.

14. Stryker 1980. Also see Cast, Stets, and Burke (1999) who argue that high-status people can strongly influence our understanding of ourselves, especially if (relative to them in relevant ways) we feel we have lower status than they do. In these scenarios, the spiritual leader is, obviously, both high status generally and higher status (spiritually) relative to any of my respondents.

15. Goffman 1961.

16. Goffman 1959:26.

17. Range 1973:119.

18. Ibid., 108, emphasis mine.

19. Rothman 1999:2–3.

20. Rotté 2000:71.

21. Ibid., 75.

22. Range 1973:132.

23. COGIC Women's Department 1989:6.

24. Miller 1949.

25. Brissett and Edgeley 1990:6.

26. Goffman 1959:202.

27. Ibid., 224.

28. Ibid..

29. Alston 2010.

30. See Anderson 2005; Dokecki 2004; and Shupe 2007.

31. Jenkins 1999.

32. Wessinger 2000:32.

33. Woodward 1977:79.

34. Woodward 1978:72.

35. Shupe 1998.

36. White and Cones 1999:54.

NOTES TO CHAPTER 4

1. Reich 1992.

2. Abbott 1988.

3. Weber 1922.

4. Van Biema 2001.

5. Larson 1977.

6. Brubacher 1997.

7. Ibid., 201.

8. The idea for a "School of the Prophets" is derived from the prophetic guilds that the biblical priest organized (see 1 Sam. 19:20 for an example). Also called the "sons of the prophets," these groups of prophets are believed to have been training grounds for potential religious leaders.

9. Holifield 2007:116.

10. Ibid., 117.

11. Larson 1977:122.

12. Finke and Stark 1992.

13. See Finke and Stark 1992; Fraser 1988; Hall 1994; and Hatch 1989 for more on this history.

14. Finke and Stark 1992.

15. Zikmund 1998.

16. Miller, Donald 2003.

17. Ibid., 20.

18. AME webpage (http://www.ame-church.com) .

19. A group of Congregationalists founded Howard University and its Divinity School.

20. Wilberforce University webpage (http://www.wilberforce.edu).

21. Lincoln and Mamiya 1990.

22. Ibid..

23. Ibid..

24. Mamiya 2006.

25. Lincoln and Mamiya 1990:130.

26. Williams 1974:113.

27. DeVeaux, 2010.:8.

28. Smiley 2003.

29. Ibid.

30.Ibid.

31. Mamiya 2006.

32. Carroll 2006.

33. Tucker-Worgs 2002.

34. Chaves 2004.

35. Smiley 2003.

36. See Range 1973 and Clemmons 1996. In a *Christianity Today* article, Joe Maxwell (1996) quotes Mason: "The Lord showed me that there was no salvation in schools and colleges, for the way that they conducted themselves grieved my soul," Mason recounted later. "I packed my books, arose, and bade them a final farewell to follow Jesus, with the Bible as my sacred guide." According to Daniels (2002), Mason transferred to, and eventually graduated from, the College's Minister's Institute.

37. The Mason Institute (now the Charles H. Mason Theological Seminary) is part of Atlanta's Interdenominational Theological Center (ITC). As part of an ecumenical group of seminaries, the Mason Theological Seminary is joined by the Gammon Seminary (United Methodist), the Morehouse School of Religion (Baptist), the Phillips School of Theology (Christian Methodist Episcopal), the Johnson C. Smith Seminary (Presbyterian), and the Turner Theological Seminary (African Methodist Episcopal).

38. This is much higher than Lincoln and Mamiya's (1990) findings of about 11 percent for COGIC clergy. It is important to realize that their count only includes male pastors and does not include the many more nonpastoring male clergy and unordained women.

39. This number is consistent with Lincoln and Mamiya's (1990) findings of 19 percent..

40. For more on late-career clergy, see Carroll 2006; Weems and Michel 2008; and Witham 2005.

41. Carroll 2006.

42. Ibid.

43. Ibid.

44. Brooks and Hawthorne 2002.

45. In order to maintain the anonymity of the source of this document, its bibliographic information is not being supplied here.

46. Wacker 2001.

47. Weber 1922a:47.

48. Weber 1919:168, 171.

49. Stone 2008.

50. Weber 1930:182.

51. Weber 1922b:425.

52. Ibid., 241.

53. A more refined view from Peter Berger (1963) helps us understand that, in the biblical case, there was no great antipathy between priests and prophets. If anything, the prophets of the Old Testament were an extension of the priest. Some (e.g., Ezekiel, Jeremiah) either served as priests or were born into priestly families. Priests and prophets represented the same God and preached, essentially, the same message. The prophets certainly did not seek to draw the Israelites into some new cult; their message of reform was intended to turn people back to Jehovah.

54. See Bryman 1992; Conger 1998; Conger, Kanungo, and Memon 2000; Gardner and Avolio 1998; Howell and Shamir 2005; Kitay and Wright 2009; Oakes 1997; and Steyrer 1998.

55. Weber 1922b.

56. Ibid., 241, emphasis mine

57. Ibid., 440.

58. Poloma 1982:102.

59. Van Biema 2001.

60. Dessauer 1955.

61. *Economist* 2009.

62. Range 1973:73.

63. Some ministers describe the anointing in a way that is reminiscent of the Force from the *Star Wars* movie series. They speak as if the flesh must be managed because the anointing's power is undifferentiated; it can be used for good or for evil. Both Sharon and Dwayne spoke of it this way. Sharon, who believes she is called to prophetic ministry, suggested that some people were trying to make a living on their anointing to give prophecies or "words of knowledge": "I think you can misuse or abuse the anointing. You can use your anointing inappropriately and it can be taken away." Similarly, Dwayne described scenarios in which God would have to take away someone's anointing because of the damage they might do with it: "He'd have to because maybe the person strayed or was going out on their own, really believing and trusting in their own beliefs instead of God's principles and precepts. And so the calling can be there, but the fact that God is not behind what you're doing can be very impairing and dangerous. God can't leave that kind of power in the hands of someone who can't be trusted with it."

64. Durkheim 1912:38.

65. Wacker 2001:62.

66. Nearly 15 percent of these interviews were carried out in the homes of the respondents.

67. Eckhardt 2007.

68. See Conwill 1991; Fine 2004; Peterson 1997; and Russell 2001 for more on this.

69. Fine 2004:39.

70. Lee and Sinitiere 2009:69–71.

71. Ibid.

72. Ibid., 44.

73. West 1984.

NOTES TO CHAPTER 5

1. Fox 2002.

2. Becker and Carper 1956.

3. McDuff 2002:466.

4. Chaves 1999. One of the biggest challenges for some denominations is finding clergy who are willing to pastor rural congregations and dioceses. For more on this see Carroll 2006, Chaves 2004, Hoge and Wenger 2005, and Lincoln and Mamiya 1990.

5. McDuff and Mueller 2000.

6. For more on clergy labor markets, see Bonifield and Mills 1980; Chang 1997; Christopherson 1994; Mueller and McDuff 2004; and Wildhagen, Mueller, and Wang 2005.

7. Carroll 2006.

8. Brushwyler 1992.

9. Walters 1983.

10. Fox 2002.

11. The most comprehensive of these is Zeni Fox's (2002) book on lay ministry.

12. Thumma and Travis 2007.

13. This number does not include unlicensed Aspiring Ministers and Missionaries.

14. The AME (1794), AME Zion (1801), and National Baptist Convention (1880) had very early foundings. In a number of cities, existing AME and NBC church buildings are older than the entire COGIC denomination.

15. COGIC webpage (http://www.cogic.com).

16. COGIC webpage (http://www.cogic.com); and Daniels 2007.

17. Range 1973:150, emphasis mine

18. McDuff and Mueller 2000.

19. Bender and Tarentino 2004.

20. Mellow 2007:60.

21. Weber also spoke to this expectation that prophets—which Paul could likely be one and whom these men and women claim as role models—do not work for any local religious community; they work for the God who called them and gave them their unique revelation. Weber states that "[w]hat distinguishes the prophet . . . is an economic factor, i.e., that his prophecy is unremunerated. This criterion of gratuitous service also distinguishes the prophet from the priest. The Christian prophet was enjoined to live by the labor of his own hands. These injunctions were repeatedly emphasized in the Pauline epistles. The dictum "whosoever will not work, shall not eat" applied to missionaries, and it constitutes one of the chief mysteries of the success of prophetic propaganda itself. (Weber 1922:47–48).

22. Lloyd 2006:182.

23. Ibid.

24. Ibid., 160.

25. Carroll 2006.

26. Carroll 2006; Nesbitt 1997; Zikmund, Lummis, and Chang 1998.

27. For more on clergy dissatisfaction and role strain, see Hatcher and Underwood 1990; Hoge and Wenger 2005; Kuhne and Donaldson 1995; Malony 1988; Mueller and McDuff 2004; and Zikmund et al. 1998.

NOTES TO CHAPTER 6

1. Zikmund, Lummis, and Chang 1998:3.

2. Few of these women serve as heads of pastoral staffs.

3. United States Census Bureau 2010.

4. Bartkowski 2001.

5. Stuart 1872.

6. Zikmund, Lummis, and Chang 1998.

7. See Lord 1854; Roberts 1858; and Davis 1843 for their autobiographies.

8. Lee, the first female preacher of the African Methodist Episcopal Church of America, was approved (but not ordained) to preach by Bishop Richard Allen and claims that "from the second day of July to the fifteenth day of October, I had preached 138 sermons, and traveled between 27 and 28 hundred miles" (Lee 1849:79).

9. International Church of the Foursquare Gospel.

10. See Baer 1992; Barfoot and Sheppard 1980; Harris 1996; Lehman 1985; Poloma 1989; and Poloma and Pendleton 1989 for more.

11. Chaves 1996.

12. Chaves 1999.

13. See Barfoot and Sheppard 1980; James 1980; Nesbitt 1997; Purvis 1995; Scanzoni and Setta 1986; Stanley 1996 and 2001; and Sullins 2000.

14. Schmidt 1996.

15. Zikmund, Lummis, and Chang 1998:105.

16. Adams 2007.

17. Range 1973.

18. Ibid.

19. In some COGIC churches, there is an intermediate stage between Aspiring Missionary and Missionary called "Missionary." The Missionary license has the potential to add an additional two years to the career ladder for a woman seeking her clerical credentials. There is no similar intermediate stage for male Licensed Ministers.

20. Range 1973.

21. Many women were hopeful that under the leadership of the now-deceased Presiding Bishop Patterson the injunctions against female Elders might crumble. Some, like Asia, pinned their hopes on the outspoken wife of the former bishop, "I know I returned from the national women's convention and the [former] Bishop's wife spoke and she did turn around to the official board and said 'give the women their due' and by her being the national Bishop's wife, she had the authority to say it. You know she got a big cheer since it was the national women's convention and there were thousands of women there." That window closed upon the death of Patterson in 2007.

22. Gilkes 2001:109.

23. See Crosby (1982) for more on her study of relative deprivation, the paradox, and the "denial of personal disadvantage" thesis. Other researchers (Buchanan 2005; Hodson 1989, McDuff 2001; Mueller and Kim 2008; Phelan 1994) have examined the paradox by looking at differences in job satisfaction between men and women in similar jobs. This research has supplied further evidence of the paradox's existence, but there has only been suggestive, but nevertheless inconsistent, empirical support for other explanations (e.g., differential job values, different gender referents) for women and men's similar levels of job satisfaction.

24. It is worth stating that men rarely expressed a call to "pastor" in their description of their calling experience or in my direct question about what they are called to do. They, like many of the women I interviewed, indicate a call to "preach" or a call to "teach." Only when asked to find their calling among the five offices listed in Ephesians 4—apostle, evangelist, prophet, pastor, and teacher—a listing in which "preacher" is notably absent, are men more likely to say "pastor." When asked to find their calling on this list, women are more likely to say "evangelist" or "teacher."

25. In fact, the biggest irony is that the founder of the denomination was separated from his first wife Alice Saxton until her death twelve years later. Their marriage ended because Saxton objected to Mason's entry into the ministry. Upon Saxton's death, Mason remarried.

26. Bishops have been known to joke about this process, stating that "we don't make them, but we will take them."

27. This critique is similar to those lodged by women in Wiggins (2005).

28. Wiggins 2005.

29. This number (eight) and the numbers that follow do not include Aspiring Ministers and Missionaries.

30. Wiggins 2005:119.

31. As I discussed in chapter 5, men don't tell me that, at the point of their call to ministry, God said "pastor." Like those of their female counterparts, men's calls—whether received in a small voice or in a vision—draw them into preaching, speaking, teaching, and service ministries. Recall that the description of the "call to ministry" says nothing about pastoring. Even the narrow call listed there is to "preach the gospel." The call to pastor is a different animal altogether. I'm uncertain as to where its origins lie for most of these men, , but in some ways it seems more a sociological than a theological construction.

32. Christiano, Swatos, and Kivisto 2002:195.

33. See Baer 1993; Barnes 2006; Butler 2007; Collier-Thomas 1998; Dodson 2002; Frederick 2003; Gilkes 2001; Higginbotham 1993; Hoover 1979; Nelson 1997; and Wiggins 2005 for examples.

34. Zikmund, Lummis, and Chang 1998:130.

35. Ibid., 131.

NOTES TO CHAPTER 7

1. Christopherson 1994:222.

2. Larson 1977:x.

3. A textbook (Brooks and Hawthorne 2002) was created to instruct ordination candidates in "the fundamental truths of the Bible." In many jurisdictions, questions for the written ordination exam are now drawn directly from the training catechism. The catechism asks such questions as "How does one become a member of the Church" (Answer: "You can't join it, you must be born in it.[Jn. 35]) and "What are some of the symbols of the Holy Ghost" (Answers: Dove, Water, Fire, Wind, Wine, and Oil).

4. Weber 1922b:425.

5. Durkheim 1912:55.

6. John Calvin rejected the idea of a special priesthood of the ordained, never mentioning the word "priest" when referring to ministers. See Power 2003 for more on this.

7. Smith-Lovin 2007.

8. Lois 2006.

9. *Lawrence v. Commissioner 1968.*

10. *Knight v. Commissioner 1989.* The petitioner, John G. Knight, was a candidate for ministry who, as a licentiate, was not yet ordained and therefore did not administer the sacraments or have full access to congregational leadership.

11. The U.S. Tax Court approved this test in *Wingo v. Commissioner 1987.*

12. The legal requirement of "licensing, ordination, or commissioning" is intended to exclude self-appointed ministers. The courts defer to the definitions adopted by the religious community the minister claims a relationship to. To date, there have been no serious IRS/legal challenges by COGIC women because the church recognizes the Evangelist license as analogous, in most ways, to the ordained Elder's license. As such, Evangelists can make claims to clerical status for tax purposes with respect to services they perform in the exercise of ministry.

13. Bruner 2001:30.

14. Alice Cullinan (1999) warns aspirants about mistaking coincidences for callings. She compares receiving the call to ministry to that sensation of romance that one feels when they hear a song played at a senior prom or wedding. There are socially orchestrated (and not uncommon) experiences that might trigger one's sense that they're called. For example, it is not uncommon for a combination of songs and sermons to lead one to think God is speaking to them.

17. Cornell and Hartmann (1998:73) use the terms "thick" and "thin" to describe ethnic/racial identities in terms of the comprehensiveness of their relationship with social life and action.

16. This tendency was evident even in Aspiring Missionaries who did not hold the local Deaconess license. They believed that they had a "right" to do the ministry they felt called to and this transcended credentialing stages.

References

Abbott, Andrew. 1988. *The System of Professions*. Chicago: University of Chicago Press.

Adams, Jimi. 2007. "Stained Glass Makes the Ceiling Visible: Organizational Opposition to Women in Congregational Leadership." *Gender and Society* 21:80–105.

Alston, Joshua. 2010. "Land of Inopportunity." *Newsweek*, February 16.

Ammerman, Nancy. 1997. *Congregation and Community*. New Brunswick: Rutgers University Press.

Anderson, Jane. 2005. *Priests in Love: Roman Catholic Clergy and Their Intimate Relationships*. New York: Continuum.

Baer, Hans. 1992. "The Socio-Religious Development of the Church of God in Christ." In *African-Americans in the South: Issues of Race, Class, and Gender*, edited by H. Baer and Y. Jones, 111–22. Athens: University of Georgia Press.

———. 1993. "The Limited Empowerment of Women in Black Spiritual Churches: An Alternative Vehicle to Religious Leadership." *Sociology of Religion* 54:65–82.

Baer, Hans, and Merrill Singer. 2000. "The Historical Development of Black Spiritual Churches." In *Down by the Riverside: Readings in African American Religion*, edited by L. G. Murphy, 232–42. New York: New York University Press.

Barfoot, Charles H., and Gerald T. Sheppard. 1980. "Prophetic vs. Priestly Religion: The Changing Role of Women Clergy in Classical Pentecostal Churches." *Review of Religious Research* 22:2–17.

Barnes, Sandra L. 2006. "Whosoever Will Let Her Come: Social Activism and Gender Inclusivity in the Black Church." *Journal for the Scientific Study of Religion* 45:371–87.

Bartkowski, John P. 2001. *Remaking the Godly Marriage: Gender Negotiation in Evangelical Families*. New Brunswick: Rutgers University Press.

Bassett, Ronald E., Ann Q. Staton-Spicer, and Jack L. Whitehead. 1979. "Effects of Source Attire on Judgments of Credibility." *Communication Studies* 30:282–85.

Baum, William, and Daniel Pilarczyk. 1989. "Seminaries and Vocations." In *Evangelization in the Culture and Society of the United States*, edited by Joseph Cardinal Bernardin and Pope John Paul II, 111–18. Washington, DC: United States Catholic Conference.

Becker, Howard, and James Carper. 1956. "The Elements of Identification with an Occupation." *American Sociological Review* 21:341–48.

Bellah, Robert N., Richard Madsen, William M. Sullivan, Ann Swidler, and Steven M. Tipton. 1985. *Habits of the Heart: Individualism and Commitment in American Life*. Berkeley: University of California Press.

Bender, Lawrence, and Quentin Tarentino. 2004. *Kill Bill: Vol. 2*. [Motion Picture] United States: Miramax Films

Beraud, Celine. 2007. "Permanent Deacons, in between the Altar and the World: A Legitimacy and an Activity on the Borderline." *Social Compass* 54:175–85.

Berger, Peter. 1963. "Charisma and Religious Innovation: The Social Location of Israelite Prophecy." *American Sociological Review* 28:940–50.

———. 1980. *The Heretical Imperative*. Garden City, NY: Doubleday Anchor Books.

Boggs, Beverly. 1977. "Some Aspects of Worship in a Holiness Church." *New York Folklore* 3:29–44.

Bonifield, W. C., and E.W. Mills. 1980. "The Clergy Labor Markets and Wage Determination." *Journal for the Scientific Study of Religion* 19:146–58.

Bradford, James (General Secretary). 2009. "Minutes of the 53rd Session of the General Council of the Assemblies of God." Springfield, MO: Assemblies of God.

Brissett, Dennis and Charles Edgeley. 1990. *Life as Theater: A Dramaturgical Sourcebook*. New York: Aldine de Gruyter.

Broholm, Richard R. 1984. "How Can You Believe You're a Minister When the Church Keeps Telling You You're Not." *American Baptist Quarterly* 3:175–83.

Brooks, P. A., and Charles Hawthorne. 2002. *Understanding Bible Doctrine as Taught in the Church of God in Christ*. Detroit: Church of God in Christ Publishing House.

Brubacher, John S. and Willis Rudy. 1997. *Higher Education in Transition: A History of American Colleges and Universities*. New Brunswick, NJ: Transaction Books.

Bruner, Jerome S. 1990. *Acts of Meaning*. Cambridge, MA: Harvard University Press.

———. 2001. "Self-Making and World-Making." In *Narrative and Identity: Studies in Autobiography, Self and Culture*, edited by J. Brockmeier and D. Carbaugh, 25–37. Philadelphia: John Benjamins.

———. 2004. "Life as Narrative." *Social Research* 71:691–710.

Brushwyler, L. Ronald. 1992. *Bi-Vocational Pastors: A Research Report*. Westchester, IL: Midwest Ministry Development Service.

Bryant, James Arthur. 2002. "Journeys Along Damascus Road: Black Ministers, the Call, and the Modernization of Tradition." PhD diss., Brown University.

Bryman, Alan. 1992. *Charisma and Leadership in Organizations*. Thousand Oaks, CA: Sage.

Buchanan, Tom. 2005. "The Paradox of the Contented Female Worker in a Traditionally Female Industry." *Sociological Spectrum* 25:677–713.

Burns, Thomas A., and J. Stephen Smith. 1978. "The Symbolism of Becoming in the Sunday Service of an Urban Black Holiness Church." *Anthropological Quarterly* 51:185–204.

Butler, Anthea. 2004. "Church Mothers and Migration in the Church of God in Christ." In *Religion in the American South: Protestants and Others in History and Culture*, edited by B. B. Schweiser and D. G. Mathews, 195–218. Chapel Hill: University of North Carolina Press.

Butler, Anthea D. 2007. *Women in the Church of God in Christ: Making a Sanctified World*. Chapel Hill: University of North Carolina Press.

Calvin, John. 1843. *Institutes of the Christian Religion*. Vol. 2. Translated by J. Allen. Philadelphia: Presbyterian Board of Publication.

Cannon, Lou. 1978. "Temple Unlikely to Continue." *Washington Post,* November 21.

Carr, David L., Angeline M. Lavin, and Thomas L. Davies. 2009. "The Impact of Business Faculty Attire on Student Perceptions and Engagement." *Journal of College Teaching and Learning* 6:41–49.

Carroll, Jackson W. 2006. *God's Potters: Pastoral Leadership and the Shaping of Congregations*. Grand Rapids, MI: Wm. B. Eerdmans.

Carroll, Jackson, Adair Lummis, and Barbara Hargrove. 1983. *Women of the Cloth: New Opportunity for the Churches*. New York: HarperCollins.

Cast, Alicia D., Jan E. Stets, and Peter J. Burke. 1999. "Does the Self Conform to the Views of Others?" *Social Psychology Quarterly* 62:68–82.

Chang, Patricia M. Y. 1997. "In Search of a Pulpit: Sex Differences in the Transition from Seminary Training to the First Parish Job." *Journal for the Scientific Study of Religion* 36:614–27.

Chaves, Mark. 1991. "Segmentation in a Religious Labor Market." *Sociological Analysis* 52:143–58.

———. 1996. "Ordaining Women: The Diffusion of an Organizational Innovation." *American Journal of Sociology* 101:840–73.

———. 1999. *Ordaining Women: Culture and Conflict in Religious Organizations*. Cambridge, MA: Harvard University Press.

———. 2004. *Congregations in America*. Cambridge, MA: Harvard University Press.

Christiano, Kevin J., William H. Swatos, and Peter Kivisto. 2002. *Sociology of Religion: Contemporary Developments*. Walnut Creek, CA: Altamira Press.

Christopherson, Richard W. 1994. "Calling and Career in Christian Ministry." *Review of Religious Research* 35:219–37.

Church, Leslie F. 1954. "The Call to Preach in Early Methodism." *London Quarterly and Holborn Review* 179:185–91.

Clark, William. 1937. "Sanctification in Negro Religion." *Social Forces* 15:544–51.

Clemmons, Ithiel C. 1996. *Bishop C. H. Mason and the Roots of the Church of God in Christ*. Bakersfield, CA: Pneuma Life.

COGIC, Women's Department. 1989. *Official Handbook for Department of Women*. Memphis: Church of God in Christ Publishing House.

Collier-Thomas, Bettye. 1998. *Daughters of Thunder: Black Women Preachers and Their Sermons, 1850–1979*. San Francisco: Jossey-Bass.

Conger, Jay Alden, and Rabindra Nath Kanungo. 1998. *Charismatic Leadership in Organizations*. Thousand Oaks, CA: Sage.

Conger, Jay Alden, Rabindra Nath Kanungo, and Sanjay T. Menon. 2000. "Charismatic Leadership and Follower Effects." *Journal of Organizational Behavior* 21:747–67.

Conwill, Kinshasha. 1991. "In Search of an Authentic' Vision: Decoding the Appeal of the Self- Taught African-American Artist." *American Art* 5:8.

Cornell, Stephen, and Douglas Hartmann. 1998. *Ethnicity and Race: Making Identities in a Changing World*. Thousand Oaks, CA: Pine Forge Press.

Croft, Steven. 1999. *Ministry in Three Dimensions: Ordination and Leadership in the Local Church*. London: Darton, Longman, and Todd.

Crosby, Faye J. 1982. *Relative Deprivation and Working Women*. New York: Oxford University Press.

Cullinan, Alice R. 1999. *Sorting It Out: Discerning God's Call to Ministry*. Valley Forge, PA: Judson Press.

Daniels, David D. III. 2002. "Charles Harrison Mason: The Interracial Impulse of Early Pentecostalism." In *Portraits of a Generation: Early Pentecostal Leaders*, edited by J. R. Goff, Jr. and G. Wacker, 255–70. Fayetteville: University of Arkansas Press.

———. 2007. "Follow Peace with All:" Future Trajectories of the Church of God in Christ." In *The Future of Pentecostalism in the United States*, edited by E. Patterson and E. Rybarczyk, 177–87. Lanham, MD: Lexington Books.

Davis, Almond H. 1843. *The Female Preacher, or Memoir of Salome Lincoln*. Providence, RI: Elder J. S. Mowry.

Dessauer, Phil 1955. "God Heals–I Don't." *Coronet*, October .

DeVeaux, William P. 2010. "Prophetic Ministry: The Black Church and Theological Education." Retrieved March 12, 2010. (http://www.resourcingchristianity.org/downloads/Essays/DeVeaux.pdf)

Djupe, Paul A., and Christopher P. Gilbert. 2003. *The Prophetic Pulpit: Clergy, Churches, and Communities in American Politics*. New York: Rowman and Littlefield.

Dodson, Jualynne. 2002. *Engendering Church: Women, Power, and the AME Church*. New York: Rowman and Littlefield.

Dokecki, Paul R. 2004. *The Clergy Sexual Abuse Crisis: Reform and Renewal in the Catholic Community*. Washington, DC: Georgetown University Press.

Dorsett, Lyle W. 1997. *A Passion for Souls: The Life of D. L. Moody*. Chicago: Moody Press.

Durkheim, Emile. 1912. *Elementary Forms of the Religious Life*. Translated by Karen E. Fields. Reprint, New York: Free Press, 1995.

Eckhardt, John. 2007. *Prayers That Rout Demons*. Lake Mary, FL: Charisma House.

Ecklund, Elaine Howard. 2006. "Organizational Culture and Women's Leadership: A Study of Six Catholic Parishes." *Sociology of Religion* 67:81–98.

———. 2010. *Science vs. Religion: What Scientists Really Think*. New York: Oxford University Press.

Economist. 2009. "Oral Roberts—Obituary." December 30.

Fine, Gary Alan. 2004. *Everyday Genius: Self-Taught Art and the Culture of Authenticity*. Chicago: University of Chicago Press.

Finke, Roger, and Rodney Stark. 1992. *The Churching of America, 1776–1990: Winners and Losers in Our Religious Economy*. New Brunswick: Rutgers University.

Fox, Zeni. 2002. *New Ecclesial Ministry: Lay Professionals Serving the Church*. Franklin, WI: Sheed and Ward.

Fraser, James W. 1988. *Schooling the Preachers: The Development of Protestant Theological Education in the United States, 1740–1875*. New York: Rowman and Littlefield.

Frederick, Marla. 2003. *Between Sundays: Black Women and Everyday Struggles of Faith*. Berkeley: University of California Press.

Gannon, Thomas M. 1971. "Priest/Minister: Profession or Non-Profession?" *Review of Religious Research* 12:66–79.

Gardner, William L., and Bruce Avolio. 1998. "The Charismatic Relationship: A Dramaturgical Perspective." *Academy of Management Review* 2:32–58.

Gilkes, Cheryl. 2001. *"If It Wasn't for the Women . . .": Black Women's Experience and Womanist Culture in Church and Community*. Maryknoll, NY: Orbis Books.

Glock, Charles. 1962. "On the Study of Religious Commitment." *Religious Education* 42:98–110.

Goffman, Erving. 1959. *The Presentation of Self in Everyday Life*. Garden City, NY: Anchor Doubleday.

———. 1961. *Encounters: Study Studies in the Sociology of Interaction*. Indianapolis: Bobbs-Merrill.

———. 1983. "The Interaction Order." *American Sociological Review* 48:1–17.

Goldsmith, Peter. 1989. "A Woman's Place Is in the Church: Black Pentecostalism on the Georgia Coast." *Journal of Religious Thought* 46:53–69.

Goldstein, Jan. 1984. "Foucault among the Sociologists: The 'Disciplines' and the History of the Professions." *History and Theory* 23:170–92.

Gorsuch, Richard L., and Craig S. Smith. 1983. "Attributions of Responsibility to God: An Interaction of Religious Beliefs and Outcomes." *Journal for the Scientific Study of Religion* 17:255–68.

Greenwood, E. 1957. "Attributes of a Profession." *Social Work* 2:45–55.

Hall, Timothy D. 1994. *Contested Boundaries: Itinerancy and the Reshaping of the Colonial American Religious World.* Durham, NC: Duke University Press.

Harris, Margaret. 1996. "'An Inner Group of Willing People': Volunteering in a Religious Context." *Social Policy and Administration* 30:54–68.

Harris, Mary, Jocelyn James, Janice Chavez, Mary Lou Fuller, Sally Kent, Carol Massanari, Carolyn Moore, and Frances Walsh. 1983. "Clothing: Communication, Compliance and Choice." *Journal of Applied Social Psychology* 13:88–97.

Hatch, Nathan. 1989. *The Democratization of American Christianity.* New Haven: Yale University Press.

Hatcher, S. Wayne, and Joe R. Underwood. 1990. "Self-Concept and Stress: A Study of a Group of Southern Baptist Ministers." *Counseling and Values* 34:187–96.

Higginbotham, Evelyn Brooks. 1993. *Righteous Discontent: The Women's Movement in the Black Baptist Church, 1880–1920.* Cambridge, MA: Harvard University Press.

Hinson, Glenn. 2000. *Fire in My Bones: Transcendence and the Holy Spirit in African American Gospel.* Philadelphia: University of Pennsylvania Press.

Hodson, Randy. 1989. "Gender Differences in Job Satisfaction: Why Aren't Women More Dissatisfied?" *Sociological Quarterly* 30:385–99.

Hoge, Dean R., and Jacqueline E. Wenger. 2005. *Pastors in Transition: Why Clergy Leave Local Church Ministry.* Grand Rapids, MI: Wm. B. Eerdmans.

Holifield, E. Brooks. 2007. *God's Ambassadors: A History of the Christian Clergy in America.* Grand Rapids, MI: Wm. B. Eerdmans.

Hollenweger, Walter J. 1997. *Pentecostalism: Origins and Developments Worldwide.* Peabody, MA: Hendrickson.

Hoover, Theresa. 1979. "Black Women and the Churches: Triple Jeopardy." In *Black Theology*, edited by J. H. Cone and G. S. Wilmore, 377–88. Maryknoll, NY: Orbis Books.

Howell, Jane M., and Boas Shamir. 2005. "The Role of Followers in the Charismatic Leadership Process: Relationships and Their Consequences." *Academy of Management Review* 30:96–112.

James, Janet. 1980. *Women in American Religion.* Philadelphia: University of Pennsylvania Press.

Jenkins, Philip. 1999. "Creating a Culture of Clergy Deviance." In *Wolves within the Fold: Religious Leadership and Abuses of Power*, edited by A. Shupe, 118–32. New Brunswick: Rutgers University Press.

Jungkuntz, Richard. 1981. "Theses toward a Lutheran Theology of the Call." *Currents in Theology and Mission* 8:141–45.

Kitay, Jim, and Christopher Wright. 2007. "From Prophets to Profits: The Occupational Rhetoric of Management Consultants." *Human Relations* 60:1613–40.

Knight v. Commissioner, 92 T.C. 199 (1989).

Kroll, Woodrow. 2002. *The Vanishing Ministry in the 21st Century: Calling a New Generation to Lifetime Service*. Grand Rapids: MI: Kregel.

Kroll-Smith, Stephen. 1980. "The Testimony as Performance: The Relationship of an Expressive Event to the Belief System of a Holiness Sect." *Journal for the Scientific Study of Religion* 19:16–25.

Kuhne, Gary W., and Joe F. Donaldson. 1995. "Balancing Ministry and Management: An Exploratory Study of Pastoral Work Activities." *Review of Religious Research* 37:147–63.

Larson, Magali. 1977. *The Rise of Professionalism: A Sociological Analysis*. Berkeley: University of California Press.

Lawrence v. Commissioner, 50 T.C. 494 (1968).

Leathers, Dale. 1992. *Successful Nonverbal Communication*. New York: Macmillan.

Lee, Jarena. 1849. *Religious Experience and Journal of Mrs. Jarena Lee Giving an Account of Her Call to Preach the Gospel*. Philadelphia: Jarena Lee (self-published).

Lee, Shayne, and Phillip L. Sinitiere. 2009. *Holy Mavericks: Evangelical Innovators and the Spiritual Marketplace*. New York: New York University Press.

Lehman, Edward C. 1985. *Women Clergy: Breaking through Gender Barriers*. New Brunswick, NJ: Transaction Books.

Leicht, Kevin, and Mary L. Fennell. 2001. *Professional Work: A Sociological Approach*. Oxford: Blackwell.

Leonard, Bill J. 1983. "Early American Christianity." Nashville, TN: Broadman and Holman .

Lincoln, C. Eric, and Lawrence Mamiya. 1990. *The Black Church in the African-American Experience*. Durham, NC: Duke University Press.

———. 2000. "The Black Denominations and the Ordination of Women." In *Down by the Riverside*, edited by L. G. Murphy 367–79. New York: New York University Press.

Lloyd, Richard. 2006. *Neo-Bohemia: Art and Commerce in the Postindustrial City*. New York: Routledge.

Lois, Jennifer. 2006. "Role Strain, Emotion Management, and Burnout: Homeschooling Mothers' Adjustment to the Teacher Role." *Symbolic Interaction* 29:507–30.

Lord, Lucy T. 1854. *Memoir of Mrs. Lucy T. Lord of the Chinese Baptist Mission*. Philadelphia: American Baptist Publication Society.

Lundsknow, George. 2008. *The Sociology of Religion: A Substantive and Transdisciplinary Approach*. Thousand Oaks, CA: Pine Forge Press.

Lupfer, Michael B., Karla F. Brock, and Stephen J. DePaola. 1992. "The Use of Secular and Religious Attributions to Explain Everyday Behavior." *Journal for the Scientific Study of Religion* 31:486–503.

MacRobert, Iain. 2000. "The Black Roots of Pentecostalism." In *Down by the Riverside*, edited by L. G. Murphy 189–99. New York: New York University Press.

Malony, H. Newton. 1988. "Men and Women in the Clergy: Stresses, Strains, and Resources." *Pastoral Psychology* 36:164–68.

Mamiya, Lawrence. 2006. "River of Struggle, River of Freedom. Trends among Black Churches and Black Pastoral Leadership. ." *Pulpit and Pew Research on Pastoral Leadership Reports*.

Maxwell, Joe. 1996. "Building the Church (of God in Christ)." *Christianity Today* 40:22–28.

McCall, George J., and Jerry L. Simmons. 1966. *Identities and Interaction.* New York: Free Press.

McDaniel, Eric. 2004. "Church of God in Christ." In *Pulpit and Politics: Clergy in American Politics at the Advent of the Millennium,* edited by C. E. Smidt, 259–71. Waco, TX: Baylor University Press.

McDuff, Elaine M. 2001. "The Gender Paradox in Work Satisfaction and the Protestant Clergy." *Sociology of Religion* 62:1–21.

McDuff, Elaine M., and Charles W. Mueller. 2000. "The Ministry as an Occupational Labor Market: Intentions to Leave an Employer (Church) Versus Intentions to Leave a Profession (Ministry)." *Work and Occupations* 27:89–116.

———. 2002. "Gender Differences in the Professional Orientations of Protestant Clergy." *Sociological Forum* 17:465–91.

McRoberts, Omar M. 2003. *Streets of Glory: Church and Community in a Black Urban Neighborhood.* Chicago: University of Chicago Press.

———. 2004. "Beyond *Mysterium Tremendum*: Thoughts toward an Aesthetic Study of Religious Experience." *Annals of the American Academy of Political and Social Science* 595:190–203.

Mellow, Muriel. 2007. *Defining Work: Gender, Professional Work, and the Case of Rural Clergy.* Quebec: McGill-Queen's University Press.

Miller, Arthur. 1949. *Death of a Salesman.* New York: Viking Press.

Miller, Donald. 2003. "Emergent Patterns of Congregational Life and Leadership in the Developing World: Personal Reflections from a Research Odyssey." *Pulpit and Pew Research Projects on Pastoral Leadership Reports.*

Moberg, David O. 1962. *The Church as a Social Institution: The Sociology of American Religion.* Englewood Cliffs, NJ: Prentice-Hall.

Mueller, Charles W., and Sang-Wook Kim. 2008. "The Contented Female Worker: Still a Paradox?" *Advances in Group Processes* 25:117–49.

Mueller, Charles W., and Elaine McDuff. 2004. "Clergy-Congregation Mismatches and Clergy Job Satisfaction." *Journal for the Scientific Study of Religion* 43:261–73.

Myers, William. 1991. *The Irresistible Urge to Preach.* Atlanta, GA: Aaron Press.

———. 1994. *God's Yes Is Louder Than My No.* Trenton, NJ: Africa World Press.

Nelson, Timothy J. 1997. "He Made a Way out of No Way: Religious Experience in an African-American Congregation." *Review of Religious Research* 39:5–26.

———. 2005. *Every Time I Feel the Spirit: Religious Experience and Ritual in an African American Church.* New York: New York University Press.

Nesbitt, Paula D. 1997. "Clergy Feminization: Controlled Labor or Transformative Change?" *Journal for the Scientific Study of Religion* 36:585–98.

———. 1997. *Feminization of the Clergy in America: Occupational and Organizational Perspectives.* New York: Oxford University Press.

———. 1997. "Gender, Tokenism, and the Construction of Elite Clergy Careers." *Review of Religious Research* 38:193–210.

Niebuhr, H. Richard. 1956. *The Purpose of the Church and Its Ministry.* New York: Harper and Row.

Oakes, Len. 1997. *Prophetic Charisma.* Syracuse: Syracuse University Press.

Ochs, Carol. 1986. *An Ascent to Joy: Transforming Deadness of Spirit.* Notre Dame: University of Notre Dame Press.

Orwell, George. 1950. *Shooting an Elephant and Other Essays*. London: Secker and Warburg.

Otto, Rudolf. 1926. *The Idea of the Holy: An Inquiry into the Non-Rational Factor in the Idea of the Divine and Its Relation to the Rational*. Translated by J. W. Harvey. Oxford: Oxford University Press.

Paris, Arthur E. 1982. *Black Pentecostalism: Southern Religion in an Urban World*. Amherst: University of Massachusetts Press.

Parker, T. H. L. 2006. *John Calvin: A Biography*. Oxford: Lion Hudson PLC.

Peterson, Richard. 1997. *Creating Country Music, Fabricating Authenticity* Chicago: University of Chicago Press.

Phelan, Jo. 1994. "The Paradox of the Contented Female Worker: An Assessment of Alternative Explanations." *Social Psychology Quarterly* 57:95–107.

Poloma, Margaret M. 1982. *The Charismatic Movement: Is There a New Pentecost?* Boston: Twayne Publishers.

———. 1989. *The Assemblies of God at the Crossroads: Charisma and Institutional Dilemmas*. Knoxville: University of Tennessee Press.

Poloma, Margaret M., and Brian F. Pendelton. 1989. "Religious Experiences, Evangelism, and Institutional Growth within the Assemblies of God." *Journal for the Scientific Study of Religion* 28:415–31.

Power, David. 2003. "Priesthood Revisited: Mission and Ministries in the Royal Priesthood." In *Ordaining the Baptismal Priesthood*, edited by S. Wood, 87–120. Collegeville, MN: Liturgical Press.

Purvis, Sally. 1995. *The Stained Glass Ceiling: Churches and Their Women Pastors*. Louisville: Westminster John Knox Press.

Range, Charles F. 1973."Official Manual with the Doctrines and Discipline of the Church of God in Christ." Memphis: Church of God in Christ Publishing House.

Rasor, Stephen C., and Christine D. Chapman. 2007. *Black Power from the Pew: Laity Connecting Congregations and Communities*. Cleveland: Pilgrim Press.

Reich, Robert. 1992. *The Work of Nations: Preparing Ourselves for 21st Century Capitalism*. New York: Vintage Books.

Roberts, Philetus. 1858. *Memoir of Mrs. Abigail Roberts*. Irvington, NJ: Christian Messenger.

Roof, Wade Clark, and William McKinney. 1987. *American Mainline Religion: Its Changing Shape and Future*. New Brunswick: Rutgers University Press.

Rosenwald, George C., and Richard L. Ochberg. 1992. *Storied Lives: The Cultural Politics of Self-Understanding*. New Haven: Yale University Press.

Rothman, Ellen L. 1999. *White Coat*. New York: HarperCollins.

Rotté, Joanna. 2000. *Acting with Adler*. New York: Proscenium Publishers.

Russell, Charles. 2001. *Self-Taught Art: The Culture and Aesthetics of American Vernacular Art*. Jackson: University Press of Mississippi.

Sawyer, Mary R. 2000."Sources of Black Denominationalism." In *Down by the Riverside*, edited by L. G. Murphy 59–67. New York: New York University Press.

Scanzoni, Letha and Susan Setta. 1986. "Women in Evangelical, Holiness, and Pentecostal Traditions." In *Women and Religion in America*. Vol. 3: *1900–1968*, edited by R. Ruether and R. Keller, 223–65. San Francisco: Harper and Row.

Schmidt, Alvin. 2005. *How Christianity Changed the World*. Grand Rapids, MI: Zondervan.

Schmidt, Frederick. 1996. *A Still Small Voice: Women, Ordination, and the Church.* Syracuse: Syracuse University Press.

Schmidt, Leigh E. 2000. *Hearing Things: Religion, Illusion, and the American Enlightenment.* Cambridge, MA: Harvard University Press.

Searle, Judith. 2001. *Getting the Part: Thirty-Three Professional Casting Directors Tell You How to Get Work in Theater, Films, Commercials, and TV.* New York: Simon and Schuster.

Serow, Robert C. 1994. "Called to Teach: A Study of Highly Motivated Preservice Teachers." *Journal of Research and Development in Education* 27:65–72.

Shupe, Anson. 1998. "Wolves within the Fold: Religious Leadership and Abuses of Power." New Brunswick: Rutgers University Press.

———. 2007. *Spoils of the Kingdom: Clergy Misconduct and Religious Community.* Chicago: University of Illinois Press.

Smallman, Stephen E. 2007. *Forty Days on the Mountain: Meditation on Knowing God.* Wheaton, IL: Crossway Books.

Smilde, David A. 1998. "'Letting God Govern': Supernatural Agency in the Venezuelan Pentecostal Approach to Social Change." *Sociology of Religion* 59:287–303.

Smiley, Tavis. 2003. *State of the Black Union: The Black Church.* [Conference Video] United States: Tavis Smiley Presents.

Smith, Amanda. 1893. *The Story of the Lord's Dealing with Mrs. Amanda Smith, the Coloured Evangelist.* Chicago: Meyer and Brother Publishers.

Smith, Elwyn A. 1962. *The Presbyterian Ministry in American Culture: A Study in Changing Concepts, 1700–1990.* Louisville, KY: Westminster John Knox Press.

Smith, R. Drew, and Fredrick C. Harris. 2005. *Black Churches and Local Politics: Clergy Influence, Organizational Partnerships, and Civic Empowerment.* New York: Rowman and Littlefield.

Smith-Lovin, Lynn. 2007. "The Strength of Weak Identities: Social Structural Sources of Self, Situation, and Emotional Experience." *Social Psychology Quarterly* 70:106–24.

Spilka, Bernard, and Greg Schmidt. 1983. "General Attribution Theory for the Psychology of Religion: The Influence of Event Character on Attributions to God." *Journal for the Scientific Study of Religion* 22:326–39.

Spilka, Bernard, Phillip Shaver, and Lee A. Kirkpatrick. 1985. "A General Attribution Theory for the Psychology of Religion." *Journal for the Scientific Study of Religion* 24:1–20.

Stanley, Susie C. 1996. "The Promise Fulfilled: Women's Ministries in the Wesleyan/Holiness Movement." In *Religious Institutions and Women's Leadership: New Roles inside the Mainstream,* edited by C. Wessinger, 139–57. Columbia: University of South Carolina Press.

———. 2001. *Holy Boldness: Women Preachers' Autobiographies and the Sanctified Self.* Knoxville: University of Tennessee Press.

Stark, Rodney. 2003. *For the Glory of God: How Monotheism Led to Reformations, Science, Witch-Hunts, and the End of Slavery.* Princeton, NJ: Princeton University Press.

Steyrer, Johannes. 1998. "Charisma and the Archetypes of Leadership." *Organization Studies* 19:807–28.

Stillwell, Virginia. 2001. *Priestless Parishes: The Baptized Leading the Baptized.* Notre Dame, IN: Ave Maria Press.

Stone, Perry. 2008. *The Meal That Heals: Enjoying Intimate Daily Communion with God*. Lake Mary, FL: Charisma House.

Strauss, George. 1963. "Professionalism and Occupational Associations." *Industrial Relations* 2:7–31.

Stryker, Sheldon. 1980. *Symbolic Interactionism: A Social Structural Version*. Menlo Park, CA: Benjamin Cummings.

Stryker, Sheldon, and Richard Serpe. 1994. "Identity Salience and Psychological Centrality: Equivalent, Overlapping, or Complementary Concepts." *Social Psychology Quarterly* 57:16–35.

Stuart, Arabella. 1872. *Lives of the Three Mrs. Judsons: Mrs. Ann H. Judson, Mrs. Sarah B. Judson, Mrs. Emily C. Judson, Missionaries to Burmah*. Boston: Lee and Shepard Publishing..

Sugden, Howard F., and Warren W. Wiersbe. 1973. *When Pastors Wonder How*. Chicago: Moody Press.

Sullins, Paul. 2000. "The Stained Glass Ceiling: Career Attainment for Women Clergy." *Sociology of Religion* 61:243–66.

Synan, Vinson. 1997. *The Holiness-Pentecostal Tradition: Charismatic Movements in the Twentieth Century*. Grand Rapids, MI: Wm. B. Eerdmans.

Thumma, Scott, and Dave Travis. 2007. *Beyond Megachurch Myths: What We Can Learn from America's Largest Churches*. San Francisco: Jossey-Bass.

Tucker, David. 1975. *Black Pastors and Leaders: Memphis 1819–1972*. Memphis: Memphis State University Press.

Tucker-Worgs, Tamelyn. 2002. "Get on Board, Little Children, There's Room for Many More: The Black Megachurch Phenomenon." *Journal of the Interdenominational Theological Center* 23:177–203.

United States Census Bureau. 2010. *Statistical Abstract of the United State: 2011* (130th Edition). Washington, DC.

Van Biema, David. 2001. "Spirit Raiser." *Time*, September 17.

Wacker, Grant. 2001. *Heaven Below: Early Pentecostals and American Culture*. Cambridge, MA: Harvard University Press.

Wallace, Ruth A. 2003. *They Call Him Pastor: Married Men in Charge of Catholic Parishes*. Mahwah, NJ: Paulist Press.

Walters, Thomas. 1983. *National Profile of Professional Religious Education Coordinators/ Directors*. Washington, DC: National Conference of Diocesan Directors of Religious Education.

Washington, Booker T. 1901. *Up from Slavery: An Autobiography*. Reprint, New York: Doubleday, Page, 1919.

Weber, Max. 1919.*Ancient Judaism*. Translated by D. Martindale. Reprint, New York: Simon and Schuster, 1967.

———. 1922a.*Economy and Society*, vol. 1. Edited by G. Roth and C. Wittich. Reprint, Berkeley: University of California Press, 1978.

———. 1922b.*The Sociology of Religion*. Translated by T. Parsons. Reprint, Boston: Beacon Press, 1993.

———. 1930.*The Protestant Ethic and the Spirit of Capitalism*. Translated by T. Parsons. Reprint, New York: Routledge, 1996.

Weems, Lovett H., and Ann Michel. 2008. *The Crisis of Younger Clergy*. Nashville, TN: Abingdon Press.

Wessinger, Catherine. 2000. *How the Millennium Comes Violently: From Jonestown to Heaven's Gate*. New York: Seven Bridges Press.

West, Brian P. 1984. *Professionalism and Accounting Rules*. New York, NY: Routledge.

White, Joseph L., and James H. Cones. 1999. *Black Man Emerging: Facing the Past and Seizing a Future in America*. New York: Routledge.

Wiggins, Daphne C. 2005. *Righteous Content: Black Women's Perspectives of Church and Faith*. New York: New York University Press.

Wildhagen, Tina, Charles Mueller, and Minglu Wang. 2005. "Factors Leading to Clergy Job Search in Two Protestant Denominations." *Review of Religious Research* 46:380–403.

Williams, Melvin D. 1974. *Community in a Black Pentecostal Church: An Anthropological Study*. Pittsburgh: University of Pittsburgh Press.

Wingo v. Commissioner, 89 T.C. 922 (1987).

Witham, Larry A. 2005. *Who Shall Lead Them? The Future of Ministry in America*. New York: Oxford University Press.

Woodward, Kenneth. 1977. "Temple Trouble." *Newsweek*, August 15.

———. 1978. "How They Bend Minds." *Newsweek*, December 4.

Woolever, Cynthia, and Deborah Bruce. 2004. *Beyond the Ordinary: Ten Strengths of U.S. Congregations*. Louisville, KY: Westminster John Knox Press.

Zikmund, Barbara, Adair T. Lummis, and Patricia M. Y. Chang. 1998. *Clergy Women: An Uphill Calling*. Louisville, KY: Westminster John Knox Press.

Index

African Methodist Episcopal Church, 17,
27, 112, 240n37, 243n8
African ritual, 25–26
African-American churches, 19, 21–22,
27, 37, 209; characteristics, 17, 50, 153;
and educational credentialing, 112–118;
denominations, 17, 19–20, 22, 27, 112–114,
16–157, 186, 208, 240n37, 243n8
Age Of clergy, 118
Alter egos, 166, 168, 177
Ambiguity, 6, 38, 193, 213; contradictions,
192; task ambiguity, 167–168; zones of,
16, 207–208, 222, 226
Anointing, 115, 125–148, 202, 207, 216, 227;
defined, 126–129, 236n19; anointing
failure, 137–138, 147–148, 198, 241n63;
anointing falling, 135–136, 141; audience's role in, 132–134, 147–148; carriers,
129–131; infusion, 129–131, 141, 169
Anti-intellectualism, 114, 142–143, 157
Apprenticeships, 82, 85, 109–110, 113
Aspiring Minister, 31, 82, 118, 120, 171, 175, 224
Aspiring Missionary, 32, 118, 224, 245n16
Assemblies of God Church, 21, 34–36, 37,
45; denominational structure, 35–36;
and education, 36; and gender, 36, 183,
237n43; origins, 34–36; and race, 35
Audience, role of, 10–11, 74–75, 78, 83,
92–96, 132–135, 147
Authority: autonomy, 107, 111; biblical,
COGIC official manual appeals to, 82,
128; charismatic, 123, 124–126, 136, 209;
and men, 184, 205–207; pastoral leniency, 201–204; pastoral, limits of, 29,
99–103, 224; professional, 7, 86, 83, 107,
121, 123–124, 215; religious/spiritual, 125,

133, 154, 184–185, 209, 215–216; subordi-
nation, 195–198; and women, 158, 182,
184, 195–198, 201–204, 221
Azusa, 19–20, 25–26, 34

Baptism, 131, 167, 187, 196–197, 220–221
Baptism of the Holy Spirit, 18–20, 23, 25, 35
Baptists, 17, 19, 20–22, 27, 45, 110–111,
113–114, 157, 183, 186, 207, 208, 240n37
Bible Personalities: Aaron, 46, 97, 184;
Adam and Eve, 205; daughters of Philip,
185, 196; daughters of Zelophehad, 202;
David, 138, 175; Deborah, 199; Eunice
and Lois, 185, 199; Ezekiel, 241n53;
Gideon, 79; Jeremiah, 241n53; Jesus,
24, 30, 112, 114, 132–133, 147, 148–150,
169–171, 184, 202, 217, 227; Mary Magda-
lene, 199; Moses, 46, 72, 97, 107, 175, 222;
Paul, 18, 47, 61, 145, 153, 160, 176–177, 184,
189–202, 205–207; Philip, 196; Priscilla,
185, 199; Samson, 137; Samuel, 41, 97;
Saul, 137, 206; sons of Sceva, 98–99; sons
of Zebedee, 65; Zephaniah, 60
Biblical inerrancy, 184–185
Bishop Mason, 19–21, 26–28, 34–35, 116, 190
Bivocationalism, 113, 153–155, 176, 213
Blake, Charles Bishop, 21, 27, 116, 164
Blitzkrieg callings, 47–49, 53–54, 62, 159,
178, 192, 208, 223
Boundary markers, 10, 99, 190, 225–226, 228
Bruner, Jerome, 77, 22

C. H. Mason Theological Seminary
(Mason Institute), 117, 240n37
Called identity, 44, 80, 83–84, 95, 141, 168,
224–227

Callings, types/dreams/visions, 57–59, 68, 76, 78, 149, 158, 179–180, 192, 222–223, 244n30; drifting into ministry, 50–51, 52, 61, 66, 192; signs and wonders, 59–61; urges and feelings, 51–54, 56, 60, 223; voices, 54–57, 59, 62, 103, 173, 174, 179, 192–193, 197, 223, 244n30

Canonical, 30, 222–225

Carroll, Jackson, 115, 118, 153

Chaplaincies, 33, 150, 155, 157–158, 171, 191, 237n35

Character, 31, 49, 78, 90–91, 99, 101, 198, 214

Charisma, 122–125, 133, 147–148, 216

Chaves, Mark, 116, 151, 186, 191

Christopherson, Richard, 43, 213

Church Mothers, 28–29, 32, 51

Church polity: charismatic, 26–27, 125, 151; congregational, 12, 26–27, 29, 33, 35–36, 45, 110, 151–152, 156, 238; Episcopal, 12, 26–27, 35, 45, 110, 151, 155, 201; Presbyterian, 12, 26–27, 26, 45, 110, 151

Church planting, 20, 29, 152, 156

Clergy: compared to other workers, 5, 7, 77, 115, 135, 143, 146–147, 167, 177–178; prestige, 8, 45, 70, 81, 98, 108, 110–111, 216; public/private spheres, 62, 160–164, 167, 178–179, 218

Clergy shortages, 6, 73, 111, 151, 183

Clerical credentials: Aspiring Minister (aspirant), 31, 82, 118, 120, 171, 175, 224; Aspiring Missionary, 32, 118, 224, 245n16; Chaplain, 33, 157–158, 191, 237n35; Deaconess-Missionary/Deaconess, 32, 51, 68, 82, 146, 187, 195; Elders, 32, 67, 85, 146, 156, 175, 198; Evangelist-Missionary/Evangelist, 32, 51, 67, 68, 82, 85, 146, 158, 187–188, 191, 200, 202, 208, 221; Licensed Minister, 31, 67, 82, 84, 120, 146, 175, 221; Missionaries, 32, 208, 243n19

COGIC polity: Church Mother, 28–29, 32, 51; District Missionary, 28–29; District Superintendent, 28; General Assembly, 26–29, 33; General Board, 27; General Council of Pastors and Elders, 29; General Supervisor (of Women) 28; Jurisdictional Bishop, 28–29, 32, 119–120, 156, 158, 188, 201–202, 205, 235n15; Jurisdictional Supervisor (of Women) 28–29, 158, 202; Pastor, 29, 32, 187, 188, 189, 200, 221, 222; Pastors' Council, 29; Presiding Bishop, 27–28, 116

Commitment: to an identity, 80, 83, 84, 226; to ministry, 31, 41, 44, 49, 70–71, 84, 90, 99–101, 223

Communion (the Eucharist), 85, 96, 122, 167, 187, 191, 220–221

Compensation for ministry, 44, 152, 154, 156, 161–162, 165, 176, 187; compared to musicians, 164–166; desires for adequate remuneration, 163–166

Competence, 31, 99, 101, 110, 215–216, 223; professional, 7, 108, 120, 214

Confused callings, 98–100

Congregationalist polity, 27, 152, 156, 238n4

Congregationalists, 109–112, 185, 240n19

Congregation-of-origin, 74, 95, 152, 225

Constraints, 102–103, 150, 155–157, 170–171, 183, 189–190, 219, 226

Convocation, 27–28

Counterfeit callings, 95–100

Credentials, Educational, 116–118, 125, 190, 215

Credentials, Religious, 30–36, 43, 56, 86, 90, 119, 165, 221–222

Culture, 49, 199, 222–228

Day Of Pentecost, 20–21, 24

Deaconess-Missionary/Deaconness, 32, 51, 68, 82, 146, 187, 195

Deacons, 30, 41, 68, 165, 198, 221

Denominations: African Methodist Episcopal, 17, 27, 112, 240n37, 243n8; Assemblies of God, 34–37, 45, 183, 237m43; Baptists, 17, 19, 20–22, 27, 45, 110–111, 113–114, 157, 183, 186, 207, 208, 240n37; Calvary Chapel Network, 112; Church of God, 186; Congregationalists 109, 112, 185, 240n37; Episcopalians, 45, 183, 186; Latter-Day Saints, 110; Lutherans, 186, 140; Methodists, 17, 45, 110, 111–114, 151, 183, 186, 240; Presbyterians, 152, 183, 186, 240n37; Quakers, 20; Salvation Army, 186

Discernment, 10, 100, 125, 126, 129, 168, 224
District Missionary, 28–29
District Superintendent, 28
Doctrine, 18–26, 34, 82, 119, 128, 193, 195, 197, 207
Doves, 59, 222, 223, 245n3
Dramaturgy, 74–95; casting, 77–88; costuming, 81–84; learning lines, 86–90; performance, 90–95; rehearsals, 84–86; resume, 75–77; staging, 84
Dress/vestments, 58, 81–84
Durkheim, Emile, 42, 137, 216

Elders, 32, 67, 85, 146, 156, 175, 198
Entrepreneurship: founder-led congregations 26–27, 29, 152, 156, 176, 186; founding of COGIC, 19–22; intrepreneurship and para-church ministries, 70, 152, 159, 179; risks, 156, 163, 179; role of faith, 160, 162–163
Episcopalians, 45, 183, 186
Evangelicalism, 19, 22–24, 35, 37, 114, 145, 184
Evangelist-Missionary, 32, 51, 67, 68, 82, 85, 146, 158, 187–88, 191, 200, 202, 208, 221
Examinations, 111, 119, 188, 215, 245n3
Exorcism, 83, 87, 99, 128, 138–139, 143

Faith, 100, 133, 148, 160, 162, 163
Family: as barrier to full-time ministry, 160–161, 164, 179; church succession, 29, 33, 156, 200; clergy couples, 29, 160, 185, 193, 204–206; as first or primary ministry, 160–161, 179, 218; role in call, 12, 45–46, 61, 64, 78, 144, 198, 218, 223, 237n35; support of ministry, 59, 62, 78, 94, 173
Fine, Gary Alan, 143
Fire, role of in calling, 70
Five-fold ministry, 3, 30, 66, 215, 244n23
Flesh, and the body, 130, 134, 137, 241n63
"Full-ministry," 151
Fundamentalism, 22, 63
Funerals, 33, 36, 191, 194

"Gender complementarity," 209
General Assembly, 26–29, 33
General Supervisor (of Women), 28

Gift Of healing, 25, 34, 52, 128, 129, 133, 138, 139, 143, 168–169
Gift Of prophecy, 54, 138, 143, 168, 190
Glossolalia/tongues, 19, 21–25, 35, 48, 130, 156, 157
Goffman, Erving, 10–11, 74, 75, 81, 93; dramaturgy, 74–95; expressions, 10–11; fronts, 10, 82; identity kits, 81; normative consensus, 10; systems of enabling conventions, 10
Gospel commission/Great Commission, 24, 30–31, 67, 69, 150, 158, 171, 195–198

Health, role of, in calling, 57, 60
Holiness movement, 18, 23, 186
Homeschooling, 218
Horizontal call, 25, 42, 73–74, 78, 94, 103

Identity theory: boundary markers, 10, 99, 190, 225–226, 228; comparisons, 89; feedback loops, 75; identity kits and fronts, 10, 81–82; life-making, 77; master identity, 224–225; role-identity, 80; role strain/role conflict, 180; salience and commitment, 80, 83, 86, 96, 226; self-appraisal, 87–90; self-efficacy, 88; social identity, 73; thick/thin identities, 245n17; tolerance of other, 93; virtual selves, 75
Itinerant preaching, 110, 151, 155, 159–161, 163, 185

Jakes, Thomas "T.D.," 98, 108, 125, 145
Jesus, 24, 30, 112, 114, 132–133, 147, 148–150, 169–171, 184, 202, 217, 227
Job market: appointment systems, 151–152, 154–155, 226; bivocationalism, 153–154, 173–177, 227; difficulties, 5, 150, 155–157, 163, 186–187; itinerancy, 19, 110, 151, 155, 159, 161, 163, 185
Judicatory officers, perspectives of, 69, 76, 96, 101, 120, 179, 215
Jurisdictional Bishops, 28–29, 32, 119–120, 156, 158, 188, 201–202, 205, 235n15
Jurisdictional Institutes, 87, 89, 117, 140, 142
Jurisdictional leadership, 27–29, 32–33, 119, 156, 163, 188, 200–201, 208, 215

Jurisdictional Supervisor of Women's Work, 28–29, 158, 202

Jurisdictions, 12, 27–29, 158, 188, 200–201, 214

Kroll, Woodrow, 47–48

Laity, as ministry co-laborers, 50, 66, 119, 128, 146, 153, 208; attitudes toward clergy, 115, 157, 184, 186; differences between clergy and laity, 31, 42, 46, 65, 69–70, 72–73, 84, 110, 121–122, 146, 165, 188; lay-pastors and lay-ministers, 154–155

Lay-pastorates, 154–155

Legitimization, 9–12, 43, 80, 87, 90, 113, 121, 141, 142, 143–144, 171, 186, 219, 227

Licensed Minister, 31, 67, 82, 84, 120, 146, 175, 221

Literal sacramentalism, 184–185

Lloyd, Richard, 177–178

Men ministers/Aspiring-Minister (aspirant), 31, 82, 118, 120, 171, 175, 224; District Superintendent, 28; Elders, 32, 67, 85, 146, 156, 175, 198; gender specificity in official manual 30; Jurisdictional Bishop, 28–29, 32, 119–120, 156, 158, 188, 201–202, 205, 235n15; less qualified than women, 89–90, 188–189, 198–199; Licensed Minister, 31, 67, 82, 84, 120, 146, 175, 221; obstacles to pastorates 155–157, 179–180; opposition to female clergy, 184–185, 189, 205–207; Pastor, 29, 32, 187, 188, 189, 200, 221, 222 Presiding Bishop, 27–28, 116; primary calls to preach, 68; support of female clergy, 204–206, 209–210. *See also* Women ministers

Metaphor, 56, 58–59, 74–75, 77–78, 103, 133, 149, 166, 222

Methodists, 17, 45, 110, 111–114, 151, 183, 186, 240n37

Methods and sample, 9, 12–14, 235n15, 241n45

Missionary, Credential, 32, 208, 243n19

Missionary, Labor, 52–53, 149, 158–159, 185

Moses, 46, 72, 97, 107, 175, 222

Music as ministry, 127–128, 131, 154, 178, 191, 201, 221; church musicians, 164–165

Narrative, 13, 45, 75–77, 172, 222; calling narrative 10, 42, 49, 76, 79, 222–224

Neo-Pentecostalism, 21

"New paradigm" congregations, 112–113

New Testament, 3, 18, 23–26, 48–49, 62–63, 68, 70, 72, 93, 99–101, 109, 115, 130, 134–135, 147, 149–152, 162, 178–179, 184, 186, 191, 197–198, 200–201, 204, 207–208, 218

Normative callings, 10, 45, 47, 223, 238n28

The Official Manual of the Church of God in Christ/official manual, 30, 32, 49, 76, 82, 128, 187, 207, 219

Old Testament, 17, 43, 48, 53, 57, 62, 74, 81, 99, 166, 191–192, 204, 208

Parham, Charles, 19, 25–26

Pastor: call to, 69, 85, 149, 155–156, 167, 174, 175–176, 180–181, 182, 193, 195, 208, 244n23; COGIC office of, 29, 32, 187, 188, 189, 200, 221, 222; lay-pastorate, 154–155; response to call, 30–32, 53, 76, 78, 80, 89, 99–103, 120, 159, 203, 214, 224

Paul, 18, 47, 61, 145, 153, 160, 176–177, 184, 189–202, 205–207

Pentecostalism, 17, 24, 26, 120, 139, 186, 223

Pneumatology: baptism of the holy spirit, 18–20, 23, 25, 35; the holy spirit's role in doctrine, 19, 22–26, 157; the holy spirit's role in one's calling, 48–49, 111, 112, 114, 126, 130, 138, 187, 189–190; spirit-centered denominations, 45, 120;

Prayer, 42, 47, 91, 93, 102, 162, 203

Presbyterians, 152, 183, 186, 240n37

Presiding Bishop, 27–28, 116

"Priesthood of all believers" principle, 121, 216

Priests and priestly tasks, 36, 58, 66, 73, 121, 124–126, 136, 144, 183–184, 206, 215–216, 227, 241n53

Profane, 23, 69, 137, 216

Professions: characteristics of, 7, 107–108, 118, 152, 214, 228; deprofessionalization of clergy, 146–148; gatekeeping in, 49, 77, 108–110, 121–122; para-professionalism 7, 107, 146, 178, 190; relevant, of respondents, 44, 71, 126, 127, 159, 163, 166, 169–171, 172, 175, 176; secular, similar to clergy, 109–110, 116, 136, 146–147, 162–163, 189; secular, call to, 43–44, 165, 167

Prophet, 122, 123, 124–126, 136, 144, 147–148, 215, 242n21

Protestantism, 18, 23

Pulpit ministry, 58, 68, 188, 191, 195

Qualifications, 30, 122, 126, 188–189, 198–199, 215, 216

Recommendation, 32, 36, 119, 214

Rhetoric, 177–180, 192, 194, 219

Roberts, Oral, 35, 54, 56, 125

Role models, 175–177, 200, 242

Sacralization, 177, 179, 217–219

Sacramentalism, 182, 216

Sacred, 23–24, 69, 137, 172, 177, 216–217, 227

Salience, and commitment, 80, 83, 86, 96, 226

Sanctification, 18–20, 23–24, 66, 69, 156

Satan, as supernatural actor, 58, 95

Satisfaction/dissatisfaction with roles, 53, 86–87, 172, 180–181, 243; satisfaction, 68, 173, 178, 180, 194–195, 244n22

Schema, 22

Scripture references: New Testament, 3, 18, 23–26, 48–49, 62–63, 68, 70, 72, 93, 99–101, 109, 115, 130, 134–135, 147, 149–152, 162, 178–179, 184, 186, 191, 197–198, 200–201, 204, 207–208, 218; Old Testament, 17, 43, 48, 53, 57, 62, 74, 81, 99, 166, 191–192, 204, 208;

Second-career and later-career ministry, 118, 153

Sects, 112, 187

Secular jobs And tasks, 18, 33, 37, 43, 45, 76, 126, 129, 139, 150, 153, 159–181, 217, 227

Self-appraisal, 88

Seminarian, 113, 117, 138–141, 144, 146, 157, 180–181, 193, 213, 215, 226

Servant-ministry, 50–51, 57, 67–68, 189

Sexism, 30, 38, 189, 192, 199–200, 205, 209, 219

Seymour, William, 19, 25

Shadow occupations, 166–168, 170, 177, 217, 227

Shepherdess Sans Portfolio, 33, 191, 194, 200, 222

Skills, 49, 126, 127, 137–138, 141–143

Smiley, Tavis, 114–116, 122

Specialized ministry: chaplaincy, 33, 158, 237; hospital, 31, 50–51, 52, 69, 81, 84, 85, 188, 191, 214, 215, 221; prison, 31, 51, 63, 68, 85, 130, 160, 166, 172, 178–179, 203, 217, 221; street evangelism, 51, 52, 53, 57, 67, 68, 85, 96, 136, 152, 162, 172, 178, 191, 197, 208, 217

Spider-Man, 70, 166

Spirit-centered denominations, 45, 120

Stained-glass ceiling, 187

Struggling with the call, 61–65

Supernatural abilities, 19, 20, 32, 127–129, 139, 217; charisma as, 122–126; discernment, 10, 100, 125, 126, 129, 168, 224; exorcism, 83, 87, 99, 128, 138–139, 143; healing, 25, 34, 52, 128, 129, 133, 138, 139, 143, 168–169; prophecy, 54, 138, 143, 168, 190; tongues, 19, 21–25, 35, 48, 130, 156, 157

Symbols, 81–82, 222–223, 225–226; doves, 59, 222, 223, 245n3; fish, 58, 149–150, 222; harvests, 150, 208; sheep, 69, 203

Talents and gifts, 25, 32, 71, 124, 127–128, 137, 138, 144, 164, 217

Teaching: vs. preaching, 32, 67, 199, 203; as primary ministry, 57, 68, 71, 90, 126, 195, 203; as secular occupation, 44, 126, 169–171, 172

Televangelists: Bakker, James, 35; Coy, Bob, 108; Hinn, Benny, 108; Humbard, Rex, 35; Jakes, T. D., 98, 108, 125, 145; Jones, Jim, 97–98; Osteen, Joel, 108, 145; Roberts, Oral, 35, 54, 56, 125; Swaggart, Jimmy, 35; White, Paula, 108, 145

Tentmaking, 153, 173–177, 227
Timing and seasons, 62, 79–80, 103, 174–175
Traditionalism, 38, 121–122, 190, 209

Unfolding ministry, 173–177

Vertical call, 42–43, 51, 73–75, 78, 102–103, 124, 224

Weber, Max, 18, 43, 120–126, 216
Weddings, 33, 36, 85, 146, 188, 191–192, 194
Wingo and Knight factors, 220–221, 245n10
Women ministers: Aspiring Missionary, 32, 118, 224, 245n16; better qualified than men, 89–90, 188–189, 198–199; as category polluters 226; Chaplain, 33, 157–158, 191, 237n35; Church Mother, 28–29, 32, 51; conventional calls, 51, 208; Deaconess-Missionary, 32, 51, 68, 82, 146, 187, 195; discrimination as an obstacle, 183–210; District Missionary, 28–29; dress code, 58, 82–84; Evangelist-Missionary, 32, 51, 67, 68, 82, 85, 146, 158, 187–88, 191, 200, 202, 208, 221; female gatekeepers, 80, 99, 119, 159, 188; General Supervisor (of Women), 28; Jurisdictional Supervisor (of Women) 28–29, 158, 202; loose coupling of labels, 32, 67, 190–192, 195, 199, 203, 219–220, 222; Missionary, 32, 208, 243n19; opportunities in ministry, 68, 85, 157–159, 187, 209; opposition by men, 184–185, 189, 205–207; opposition by women, 30, 200–201; in other denominations, 36, 183, 185–187; pastoral leniency towards, 194–195, 201–204; personal beliefs as an obstacle, 192–193; power envy, 209; resources as an obstacle, 161–163; responses to doctrinal limitations, 195–198; responses to scriptural limitations, 198–201; and sacraments, 33, 36, 85, 96, 122, 131, 167, 187–188, 191–192, 194, 169–197, 220–221; Shepherdess Sans Portfolio, 33, 191, 194, 200, 222; support by men 204–206, 209–210; timing as an obstacle, 62, 80, 175; and zones of ambiguity, 16, 207–208, 222, 226

Youth ministry, 52, 57, 64, 68, 71, 185, 203, 221; Purity Classes, 82; Sunday School, 49, 144, 184, 208, 209; Young People Willing Workers, 82, 209

Zikmund, Barbara, 45–46, 65, 112, 182, 187, 209

About the Author

RICHARD N. PITT is Assistant Professor of Sociology at Vanderbilt University.